Preface

This guide is one of the new generation of Baedeker guides. These guides, illustrated throughout in colour, are designed to meet the needs of the modern traveller. They are quick and easy to consult, with the principal places of interest described in alphabetical order, and the information is presented in a format that is both attractive and easy to follow.

The subject of this guide is the Lagoon City of Venice. The guide is in three parts. The first part gives a general account of the city and its lagoons, its economy, transport, history, famous people, art and culture. A selection of quotations leads on to the second part, in which, after some suggestions for sightseeing, the principal places of interest are described. The third part contains a variety of practical information designed to help visitors to find their way about and make the most of their stay. Both the Sights and the Practical Information sections are in alphabetical order.

Illustrious symbol of the Laguna City: black lacquered gondolas in the magnificent Canal Grande

Baedeker guides are noted for their concentration on essentials and their convenience of use. They contain numerous colour illustrations and specially drawn plans, and at the end of the book is a fold-out map, making it easy to locate the various places described in the Sights from A to Z section with the help of the coordinates given at the head of each entry.

Contents

Nature, Culture, History
10–49

Facts and Figures 10
Lagoon City 11
Economy 13
Transport 14

History 17
The Venetian City State under the Doges 21

Sights from A to Z
58–168

Sightseeing 52

Arsenale 58 · Basilica di San Marco 59 ·
Burano 69 · Canal Grande 71 · Ca'
d'Oro 89 · Ca' Pesaro 90 · Ca' Rezzonico 91 ·
Chioggia 92 · Collezione Peggy
Gugenheim 93 · Fondaco dei Tedeschi 94 ·
Fondaco dei Turchi 95 · Gallerie
dell' Accademia 95 · I Gesuiti 105 · Il Ghetto 105 ·
Giardini Pubblici 110 · La Giudecca 111 ·
Islands in the Laguna 113 · Lido 115 · Madonna
dell'Orto 116 · Mercerie 117 · Murano 118 ·
Palazzo Contarini del Bovolo 119 · Palazzo
Ducale 119 · Palazzo Pesaro degli Orfei 134 ·
Palazzo Querini–Stampalia 134 · Piazza San
Marco and Piazzetta 135 · Ponte di Rialto 141 ·
San Bartolomeo 142 · San Francesco della
Vigna 143 · San Giacomo dell'Orio 143 · San
Giobbe 143 · San Giorgio Maggiore 144 · San
Giovanni in Bragora 145 · San Giovanni
Crisostomo 145 · San Moisè 146 · San
Nicolò 146 · San Nicolò da Tolentino 146 · San
Pietro di Castello 146 · San Paolo 147 · San
Salvatore 147 · San Sebastiano 147 · San
Silvestro 148 · San Trovaso 148 · San
Zaccaria 148 · Santa Maria della Fava 149 · Santa
Maria Formosa 149 · Santa Maria Gloriosa dei

Practical Information from A to Z
170–210

Airport 172 · Cafés 172 · Camp Sites 173 ·
Chemists 173 · Churches 174 ·
Conversions 174 · Currency 174 ·
Customs Regulations 175 · Disabled
Access 175 · Electricity 175 · Embassies and
Consulates 176 · Emergencies 176 ·
Events 176 · Excursions 178 · Food and

Index 211

Principal Sights 213

Picture Credits 214

Imprint 215

mous People 26   Quotations 48

lture 31
 History 31
rly Printing 41
e Lagoon City in Film 42

ri 150 · Santa Maria dei Miracoli 154 · Santa
ria del Rosario 154 · Santa Maria della
ute 154 · Santa Maria Zobenigo 155 · Santi
ostoli 156 · Santi Giovanni e Paolo 156 ·

Santo Stefano 159 · Scuola Grande dei Carmini
162 · Scuola Grande di San Rocco 162 · Scuola
di San Giorgio degli Schiavoni 164 · Teatro La
Fenice 164 · Torcello 166

ink 179 · Galleries 183 · Getting to
nice 183 · Hotels 184 · Information 188 ·
nguage 188 · Lost Property Offices 191 ·
edical Assistance 191 · Museums 193 ·
usic 193 · Nightlife 194 · Opening
mes 195 · Postal Services 195 · Public
olidays 195 · Public Transport 195 ·

Restaurants 198 · Shopping and
Souvenirs 201 · Sightseeing
Programme 206 · Sport 207 ·
Telephone 207 · Theatres 208 · Time 208 ·
Tipping 208 · Traffic Regulations 209 ·
Travel Documents 209 · When to Go 209 ·
Young People's Information 210

Baedeker Specials

Festival of the Masks 43

Lace and More Lace 70

The Gondola – a Quaint Conveyance 80

The Jewish Ghetto: the Home of
Shylock 106

Biennial Festival of Contemporary Art 111

Cristallo, Aventurin and Millefiori 120

Venetian bacari – an *ombra* with a
cicheti 202

Venezia –

"Venice! Is there a name in human la‍guage which has inspired more drea‍than this? Is there a city more admire‍more celebrated, more hymned by poe‍more beckoning to lovers, more visited, mo‍noble?" Written at the end of the 19th c., the‍words of Guy de Maupassant's, from a record of h‍"wanderings", are no less true today. Even people visiting Veni‍for the very first time cannot avoid seeing the famous city on th‍lagoon through informed eyes, their minds filled with a myriad poetic imag‍of this once great maritime republic.

Approaching Venice by water via the Bacino di San Marco, the former "Bride of the Sea" appears barely touched by the last 500 years. With the buildings of La Serenissima, "the Most Serene Republic", in evidence all around, an enduring history in stone, the visitor crosses the spacious St Mark's Square, described by Napoleon as Europe's most magnificent salon, the sky alone of sufficient grandeur to form its vault. As dusk falls and the five imposing domes of St Mark's Basilica assume a golden sheen in the warm light of evening, this sumptuous church of the doges takes on the quality of a *fata Morgana*. Next to it stands the majestic Doges' Palace, no less impressive a symbol of the city's glorious past.

In the arcades of the venerable Pro-curatie Vecchie opposite, Venetians, and nowadays also visitors, gather to pass

Horses

The horses of San Marco, symbol of Venetian freedom

Canal Grande

Historic Regatta on the magnificent "boulevard" of Venice

Carnival

The Festival of Masks is the hig‍point of the year

La Serenissima

the time of day, drifting between the orchestras of one historic café and another. Walking through the narrow alleyways of the metropolis on the lagoon – "half fairy story, half tourist trap" as Thomas Mann described it in "Death in Venice" – one senses the strangely fascinating morbidity of this slowly submerging amphibian, forever under threat of being overwhelmed: by the sea, by the flood of tourists and by the tide of international high finance. Who, though, has this in mind when cruising along the magnificent Grand Canal or gliding through the narrow side canals by gondola, the crumbling façades of the palazzi magically transformed by the light into a fairy tale composition.

Finding one's way through the labyrinth of alleys, up and down steps and over innumerable bridges, may at first seem bothersome. But before long one succumbs to Venice's special charm, taking a supposed short-cut and finding oneself on some little campo or delightful canal, worlds away from the always crowded major attractions. For a taste of Venice as the Venetians themselves know it, pay a visit to the "bacari", bars named after Bacchus god of wine, where mouthwatering home-made snacks and delicacies can be enjoyed washed down with a glass ("un'ombra") of the local wine. And who, however lightly touched by the romantic spirit, would forgo the experience of a gondola ride by moonlight, to be immersed in the magic of a summer night in Venice accompanied by the strains of the barcarole? Surrender yourself then to this timelessly beautiful city, uniquely fascinating backdrop to reality and dreams.

Romance

promised by a boat party on the canals of the Laguna

Piazza San Marco
The cafés around the square resound to waltz time

Gondolas
decorated with seahorses

Facts and Figures

Coat of arms

General

Venezia Città

Venice (in Italian Venezia) is situated at the northern end of the Adriatic, on an archipelago of little islands in the middle of a lagoon. Lying 4 km off the mainland, and 2 km from the open sea, it is the capital of Venezia province, comprising 43 districts, as well as of the north Italian region of Veneto. Insular Venice, including the islands of San Giorgio and Giudecca, covers little more than 7 sq. km. Greater Venice currently includes the islands of Burano, Murano and Torcello in the lagoon, the Lido and Pellestrina on the coast, and Malcontenta, Dese, Tessera, Mestre and Marghera, Zelarino, Carpenedo, Asseggiano, Trivignano, Favaro and Chirignago on the nearby mainland.

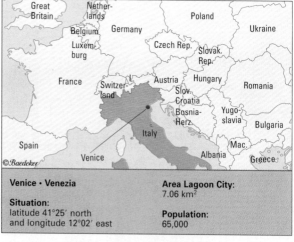

Venice · Venezia	Area Lagoon City: 7.06 km²
Situation: latitude 41°25′ north and longitude 12°02′ east	**Population:** 65,000

Population

The historic island city in the midst of the lagoon measures 4.3 km across at its widest point, and 1.4 km at its narrowest. Of Greater Venice's population of 300,000, Venice proper accounts for just 75,000, only about a third as many as in its heyday in the 15th c. Numbers continue to fall due to an acute shortage of housing and lack of employment, there being an almost complete dearth of affordable space for new enterprises.

◀ *Monumental church in magnificent décor: St Mark's Basilica on Piazza San Marco*

For centuries the city in the lagoon has been divided into six districts or "sestieri": San Marco, Castello, Cannaregio, Santa Croce, San Polo and Dorsoduro, which includes Giudecca and San Giorgio. The houses in each district are numbered consecutively up to 5000 and beyond, a system practically incomprehensible to any but the Venetians themselves.

Sestieri

Constitutional developments in the 11th and 12th c. turned Venice into the first Western republic, the nobility represented by the Great and Small Councils acting as a restraint on the power of the doge. This republic of noblemen was able to preserve its status until the seizure of Venice by Napoleon in 1797, and was the principal factor in the city's becoming a centre of international commerce and trade. Nowadays Greater Venice, like every Italian city, is governed by an elected council (giunta municipale) presided over by a mayor (sindaco). Local government elections are held every five years.

Administration

Venice – Lagoon City

Venice lies in the Laguna Veneta, a salt-water lagoon about 40 km long and up to 15 km wide. Some 55,000 ha in area, and naturally fertile, the landscape was fashioned in prehistoric times from the sand and detritus deposited near the coast by rivers – in particular the Brenta, Sile and Piave – flowing into the Mediterranean. These riverine deposits were moulded into a long line of sand banks, the "litorali", by sea currents some 20 km or so offshore. To arrest further silting, diversion of the largest rivers was begun in the 14th c. Today the lagoon is breached (bocche = breach) in just three places: the 900 m Porto di Lido, the 470 m Porto di Malamocco and the Porto di Chioggia, barely 500 m wide.

Laguna Veneta

Ground rising as islands out of the lagoon provided sites for a number of settlements which gradually over the course of time became Venice. The city remained cut off from the mainland until 1846 when the 3.6 km long causeway was built to carry the railway line. Venice is made up of 118 low-lying, closely grouped islands, originally considered unsuitable for building because of their covering of soft mud. The early settlers overcome this problem by driving oak and larch piles up to 20 m long, packed tightly together, into the solid substrate of heavy clay. More timber was then laid horizontally over these vertical piles, thus providing the foundations for almost all of Venice's 20,000 or so buildings.

Piling

Venice and its lagoons are under threat. Although water has been piped from the mainland since 1884 (until then it was drawn from cisterns supplied by wells in the town), industrial effluent from Mestre and Porto Marghera is rotting the piles on which the city stands. Air-borne pollution is also eating away the fabric of the buildings. Previously Venice was sinking at a rate of 200 mm a century; since the mid 1930s however, the rate of subsidence has been increasing annually by 4–6 mm a year. Land near the coast and the embankment is sinking at a rate of 2–3 mm a year.

Venice in Peril

From 1930, the extraction of ground water to supply the Porto Marghera area led to subsidence in the lagoon, which was only halted by the construction of a water main in 1970. The extraction of methane in southern Polesine also caused subsidence of the bed of the lagoon, continuing until 1961 when production was moved further to the south.

The high tides (acque alte) which occur between September and March have recently been getting higher, and between 1970 and 1990 exceeded the 1.1 m mark on 60 occasions. Since the dredging of the approaches to the Lido and the construction of a ship canal between Malamocco and Marghera, changes in high water levels and in the behaviour of the currents have been detected. The increasing strength of the currents and the salt content of the water have had considerable adverse effects on the brickwork of Venetian buildings. Other reasons for deterioration in buildings are the aggressive effect of chemical waste (including nitrogen and phosphate compounds) in the lagoon, leading to problems caused by the growth of algae in the canals; the harmful emissions in the atmosphere; the deterioration of wooden piles in the foundations of buildings in the city caused by micro-organisms; the growth of mould in the old, permanently damp buildings; and finally the droppings of Venice's innumerable pigeons. International organisations such as UNESCO – Venice is on the list of world cultural heritage sites – are engaged in trying to save the city. Almost every European country, together with the US and Australia, has assumed sponsorship of particularly important buildings.

Since the disastrous floods of 1966, countless conferences have been held examining ways of protecting the city from further flooding. In the mid 1980s it was decided to embark on the ten-year MOSE project (modulo sperimentale elettromeccanico). This envisaged the construction of some 80 floating dykes and barriers made up of cylindrical tanks. Positioned at the three entrances to the lagoon, they were designed to be raised and lowered depending on water levels. Because the heavily polluted lagoon relies entirely on the cleansing effect of the tides however, to avoid endangering the exchange of water in the canals which is essential to life (Venice has no sewage system!), the flood gates could only be operated during storm floods in excess of 1.2 m, thus leaving the lagoon unprotected against less extreme surges. Consequently, in 1990, the MOSE project was abandoned. More recent solutions propose naturalizing (levelling and creating meanders in) the three large shipping channels between the entrances to the lagoon, and dredging the minor canals and rivers to help distribute the volume of water more speedily. Other badly needed measures include a viable sewage system and denying access to large vessels such as cruise liners. Also essential is large-scale support for Venetian industry, some of which is to be relocated in the hinterland.

A much sought after Venetian luxury that has been made on Burano for many generations: embroidered lace

Economy

Some 5000 people commute daily into the city, as compared with about 25,000 who make the journey in reverse to jobs on the mainland. Especially in the industrial suburbs of Mestre and Marghera, as well as agricultural processing plants there are massive refineries and a sustainable metal industry. This mainland industrial zone, incorporated into Venice in 1926, was constructed on land reclaimed from the flood plain with the specific intention of providing employment for the people of Venice.

Industrial zone

The centre of glass and jewellery manufacture is on the island of Murano. The famous Murano glass is exported throughout the world, as well as proving a great tourist attraction (see Baedeker Special, page 120). The people of Murano have been makers of embroidered lace for generations, while along the coast, in Chioggia and Pellestrina, bobbin lace is also produced. In the seventies the manufacture of marbled paper was rediscovered and this is now available in every possible colour. Also most attractive is the cast metalwork, which had its great heyday in Venice during the Renaissance and can still be admired on many old front doors. Finally there are the small-scale craft, jewellery and textile businesses in the historic city, as well as the countless workshops making masks (though most masks on sale in Venice today are, and have been for a long time, imported from countries with low-wage economies).

Crafts catering for the tourist

Tourism is the principal source of employment in Venice. In addition, the city is an important administrative centre with major branches of banks

Service sector

and insurance companies. The service sector thus accounts for more than 80 per cent of all jobs.

Transport

Aeroporto Marco Polo

Marco Polo, Venice's international airport, is situated on the northern shore of the lagoon near Tessera and is reached from Venice by bus or water taxi.

Rail and road

Since 1846 a rail bridge has linked the Santa Lucia railway terminal on the island of Venice with the mainland and the rest of the international rail network. Venice is served by direct express trains from virtually all the main European destinations. Since 1933 Venice has also been joined to the mainland by a 3.6 km road bridge linking it to the Italian road system and, via the Milan–Trieste motorway, the European motorway network.

Car limits

Cars cannot be taken beyond the Tronchetto car park or the multi-storey car park at the Piazzale Roma at the end of the road bridge. Beyond that point all movement in the city is either by boat or on foot.

Shipping

Handling about 30 million tons of freight per annum, the container port of Marghera is one Italy's chief ports. As an oil terminal, however, Marghera is comparatively unimportant. Although the channel through the lagoon has been dredged, the relatively shallow waters of this part of the Mediterranean make it unsuitable for tankers larger than 80,000–90,000 tons.

The port for passenger ships is in the Canale di San Marco, diagonally opposite the Doges' Palace. There are connections with all the main

Canal Grande: the "main street" of Venice

The lively Riva degli Schiavoni, where ships for the other Laguna islands depart

Adriatic ports as well as with Rhodes and Piraeus in Greece. Venice is also popular as an embarkation point for cruises, which usually leave from Zattere and Riva degli Schiavoni.

Since the 118 islands which go to make up Venice are crammed very close together and built-up to their very edges, and at the same time the waterways between them have been kept open, Venice has a network of more than 170 canals, most of them narrow, which serve as the streets of the city. Nowadays the main means of transport is by the various types of motor boat, but the traditional gondolas also continue to fulfill this role (see Baedeker Special, page 80). Craft operating regular passenger services are found only on the Grand Canal, which winds like an inverted "S" though the city from Santa Lucia Station to the Bacino di San Marco, dividing Venice in two. There are also boat services to San Giorgio, Giudecca, to the Lido, Marco Polo Airport and the lagoon islands of Murano, Burano and Torcello. All other journeys have to be made on foot, unless you wish to hire a gondola or motor boat to serve as a taxi.

Besides its canals Venice also has 3000 streets. The main streets, the "salizade", the first to be properly paved, are limited in number. Narrower streets are called "calle", and ones which run along the canals "fondamenta" or "riva". "Ruga" or "rugetta" refer to passages or side alleys, and "ramo" means cul-de-sac. A "lista" was once the site of foreign embassies, "rio terrà" is a filled-in canal, and "mercerie" are shopping streets. There is only one "piazza", namely St Mark's Square; the smaller adjoining squares are called the Piazzetta (in front of the Doges' Palace) and the Piazzetta dei Leoncini (near St Mark's). All Venice's other squares are called "campo", or, if they are very small, "campiello".

The streets and alleys cross the canals by means of almost 400

Streets, squares and bridges

15

bridges, three of them over the Canal Grande: the wooden Ponte dell'Accademia, the famous Ponte di Rialto and the modern Ponte Scalzo from the vicinity of the station to the Piazzale Roma.

History

Folk migrations 4–6th c. AD. Following the final collapse of the Western Roman Empire (AD 476), the turmoil of the great folk migrations soon engulfs the Venice area as elsewhere. In the 5th, 6th and 7th c. large numbers of mainland Veneti, fleeing from the plundering Huns and Germanic tribes, seek refuge on the islands in the lagoon. People from Spina, Aquileja, Adria, Altinum and Padua settle on the islands and a growing lagoon community gradually takes shape. As the whole of northern Italy succumbs first to the Goths and then the Langobards, the little lagoon community puts itself under the protection of Byzantium, heir to the Eastern Roman Imperium.

Beginnings

7th/8th c. In 697 the first Doge (from Latin *dux*, leader), Paoluccio Anafesto, is appointed by the Byzantine exarch of Ravenna and establishes the earliest seat of government on the island of Heraclea. His successor in the second half of the 8th c. resides on the now submerged island of Malamocco, of which the only reminder today is a little village on the Lido. The first century of rule by the doges is characterised by disputes between pro- and anti-Byzantine factions. Scarcely any doge (of which there are nine by the year 804) dies a natural death. Influential aristocratic families with estates on the mainland feud over the rights to the profitable salt industry. Only when the Franks under Charlemagne and his son Pepin lay massive siege to the lagoon in 809, do the islanders realise the strength that lies in unity. Barricades erected on the "Rivus Altus" secure the nucleus of their fast growing town, known at first as "Civitas Venetiarum" and eventually simply as "Venetia".

Political independence

9th–11th c. Increasing in confidence, the Veneti now reach out beyond their territory in the lagoon, half land, half water, in pursuit of military and economic expansion. As accomplished ship builders, skilled ferrymen, brave seafarers (with a tradition inclining towards piracy) and astute merchants, they take over the sea and trade routes between the Adriatic and the East. Slaves and oarsmen are recruited from neighbouring Dalmatia. Distant Byzantium, its position of supremacy in the Mediterranean gradually eroding, grants Venice independence in the form of a free state, as well as generous access to all the Oriental ports and trade routes. The rise of a great new maritime and trading power is becoming apparent.

Rise to supremacy in the Adriatic

In 828 Venetian adventurers carry off the bones of the Apostle Mark from Alexandria to Rialto, securing for the city a vital requisite, a patron saint (it is scarcely possible today to understand the importance in medieval times of the cult of relics and their significance for the standing of a city). The area around the Doges' Palace and new church of St Mark's is becoming the political and religious centre of the city and soon takes on a distinctive character. The population influx from countries near and far leads to rapid development. In contrast to the feudalism common in the period, in Venice numerous influential mercantile families dominate the economic, political and social scene. Most importantly they act as a constraint on the powers of the doges, ensuring a more open, republican style of government and preventing the establishment of a dynasty.

12th/13th c. While self-interest prevents Venice from participating in the first three crusades to the Holy Land, the fourth crusade (1202–04) provides an excuse for the opportunistic betrayal of the city's former ally

Crusades

and protector, Byzantium. Under the leadership of the aged and half blind doge Enrico Dandolo (1192–1205), Venice undertakes the transport by sea of the 30,000 strong crusader army (cost: about 85,000 silver ducats). In his role as commander, the 92-year old doge persuades the crusaders to voyage to Constantinople (Byzantium) instead of Palestine and conquer the old Eastern Roman Empire. This momentous act of aggression is perpetrated on the spurious pretext of restoring the unity of Christendom. Constantinople is destroyed and plundered with unimaginable cruelty. Venice acquires almost half the former Eastern Roman territory.

Proud maritime republic

13th/14th c. The Venetians exploit their newly acquired hegemony to the full in setting up their legendary maritime state (Stato da mar), a network of bases, logistical, diplomatic and economic, encompassing the whole of the eastern Mediterranean. The Venetian Stato da mar comprises most of the Aegean islands, numerous ports in the Peloponnese and some Ionian islands, including Corfu and Crete. Another important island, Cyprus, is added later. Venice is engaged in creating a commercial empire with free passage in the Levant.

Such concentration of power in Venetian hands provokes retaliatory action by Venice's arch rival Genoa. This similarly proud maritime republic, ensconced in its Riviera bay, secures the support of the successors of the dethroned Byzantine emperor and mounts incursions into Venetian waters. The feared Genoese fleet blockades numerous Venetian trading bases and ultimately even occupies the lagoon town of Chioggia. The struggle for ascendancy in the Mediterranean, beginning in 1257 and ending only in 1381, is finally resolved by a settlement under which Genoa acknowledges Venetian supremacy in the Adriatic.

At the end of the 14th c. Venetian dominance in the Mediterranean is again undisputed and the city enjoys the fruits of its enormous economic and mercantile power. The population reaches 200,000 and great ecclesiastical buildings and magnificent palaces are built. In the first half of the 15th c. the numerous shipyards, glass foundries and silk mills together with all the other enterprises, create a balance of trade surplus of some 10 million ducats. There is, furthermore, political stability, the reins of power being firmly in the hands of the wealthy patrician families whom the doge merely represents.

Expansion onto the mainland

In the **15th c.** Venice, ignoring all censure, extends its rule to the mainland – in the first place to defend itself the better against the encroaching Ottoman Empire, in the second to advance its covert aim of political supremacy in Italy. With the aid of armies of well paid mercenaries and the noted "condottieri" (generals), the "Serenissima" conquers huge swathes of territory in Emilia-Romagna, Friuli and on the Dalmatian coast. Under the doge Francesco Foscari (1423–57), Venice achieves its greatest expansion. These new mainland possessions ("Stato da terra") are a constant source of unrest, to counter which governors are appointed, diplomats skilled in preventing the escalation of local disputes. The Papal States and the other major European powers view this Venetian expansionism with extreme mistrust.

The rapacious advance of the Ottoman Empire takes the Venetians by surprise. In 1453 the already weakened Constantinople falls to the Turks, who now seriously threaten the Venetian hold on the eastern Mediterranean. Cyprus, Crete and the Peloponnese are subsequently lost to the Turks. The piratical Ottomans make vigorous incursions into the Adriatic, in 1499 even taking control for a time of Friuli. Venice can no longer avoid military conflict and in time its strength wanes. The Stato da mar experiences gradual decay as Turkish expansionism continues for almost three centuries.

Meanwhile, antagonised by the Venetian Stato da terra, the principal European powers form themselves into the League of Cambrai (1508). This anti-Venetian alliance between Pope Julius II, the Emperor

Maximilian I and the King of France, marches against Venice's merce-
nary army which is defeated at the Battle of Agnadello on the Adda
(1509). So ends the Venetian "excursion" on the mainland. Insular
Venice and its fleet continue to resist however, until the alliance breaks
up. Thus Venice survives, but deprived of its former pre-eminence in
Europe.

16th/17th c. In 1499, with Venice's mercantile empire in the eastern
Mediterranean gradually falling to the Turks, and the Venetians them-
selves driven from the mainland back to their lagoon, the Portuguese
Vasco da Gama discovers the sea route to India – a development with
serious consequences for the Republic's already threatened commerce.
The possibility of safe circumnavigation of Africa shifts the centre of
world trade increasingly to the Atlantic coast, to Lisbon, London and
Antwerp. As Mediterranean trade becomes less and less important,
Venice finds itself the principal loser. The desperate measures to which
the Venetians are forced to resort in the 16th c. in an attempt to defend
their commercial interests, are no better illustrated than by their plan for
a Suez Canal, which however is not yet technically feasible.

Glorious decline

Shift in world
trade

Adversely affected by foreign policy – isolated in Europe and losing territory to Turkish expansionism – mid 16th c. Venice focuses on internal
matters: political consolidation and strengthening its institutional and
social structures. The well organised guilds, the still considerable economic and financial resources, and an effective welfare system, ensure
domestic peace. The Ottoman threat however is far from averted, and
Venice must invest ever larger sums to protect what of its commercial
empire remains. From 1545 the oarsmen aboard Venetian galleys are
armed and the ships carry extra cannon. The Venice arsenals are full to
bursting point.

Internal
consolidation

The naval battle of Lepanto in 1571

History

Battle of Lepanto (1571)

In the mid 16th c. there is outrage across Europe at the cruel havoc wreaked in the Mediterranean by the piratical Turkish fleet. A "Holy League" is formed under Pope Pius V, with half the ships and armaments in its fleet being provided by Venice. In 1571 the "Christian Alliance" embarks on a decisive confrontation with the Turks. In the bloody Battle of Lepanto (1571) the allies are victorious. Though the Venetians impress with their military prowess, their isolation in Europe continues; neither the ambitious Spaniards nor the powerful Papal State will tolerate a revitalised Venice.

Venice and the Church

The Venetians in their turn chart their own course with regard to the papacy. In Venice, Church has always to submit to State – according to the motto: "prima siamo veneziani, poi cristiani" (we are Venetians first, and only then Christians). From the time of the Reformation, Venice sympathises openly with Protestant and Calvinist ideas. The doges are mainly free-thinkers, embracing Renaissance Humanism with enthusiasm. Religion, however, is never allowed to jeopardise trade relations with the Orient or Arab countries. Tension between the Papal State and liberal Serenissima comes to a head under Pope Paul V and the doge Leonardo Donato (1606–12). When two errant churchmen are tried under Venetian law, the pope imposes an interdict on the Venetian priesthood and excommunicates the civic leaders. In 1606, with Paolo Sarpi, an influential Venetian monk, advisor to the doge, as its spokesman, the city rejects these politically motivated measures, causing consternation in the Vatican.

Plague

Following the first great epidemic of plague in 1575, which claims the life of the artistic genius Titian among many others, a second outbreak occurs in 1630 while the Venetians are engaged on the side of France in the Franco-Habsburg War. Quarantine lasts for sixteen months and a third of the population die.

Struggle against the Turks

As Venice slowly recovers from the plague, the Turks again make their presence felt, attacking Crete and drawing Venice into another Mediterranean war (1645). At first the well equipped Venetian fleet is able to recover lost Aegean territory. But decades of fighting in the defence of Crete and the Peloponnese drain the city's resources. Even so, it is only when the new Habsburg super power pushes back the Ottoman Empire and takes the conquered territories for itself, that Venice abandons the last Aegean outposts of its once great Stato da Mar. Thereafter it concentrates on safeguarding its status as a small independent state – in the security of its own lagoon.

End of the Republic

18th c. The Venetian Republic finally comes to an end in the Settecento (18th c.). The "Queen of the Adriatic" has abdicated, and the hitherto stable city state is beset by internal problems. At the beginning of the 18th c. the Venetian patriarchy has shrunk considerably. By 1724 the number of patrician families, who traditionally have exercised power through the Great Council and civil service (in which the route to the top depends upon wealth), has dropped to 216. While this self-indulgent nobility seek to maintain the constitutional framework of the Republic, those less privileged, hitherto kept contented, are demanding change. Ultimately incapable of reform, the city bolsters its coffers by rounding on the Church, from which, after 1750, huge sums are confiscated, partly funding welfare measures to ensure a compliant population. Finance is also required for a dyke to protect the lagoon. The construction of this "murazzi" (14 m wide, 4.5 m high and 15 km long) is the Republic's last great achievement.

Dyke apart, the second half of the 18th c. is marked by political short termism and a sense of helplessness, inducing the kind of mood which bewails the passing of a glorious epoch. The Venetians, haunted by a premonition of decline, abandon themselves to the pursuit of pleasure.

The death-throes of the once great Serenissima are vividly portrayed in the work of contemporary painters (e.g. Tiepolo), writers (e.g. Casanova) and playwrights (e.g. Goldoni).

In 1789 the last doge (Ludovico Manin) is elected. With resigned indifference Venice awaits Napoleon's invasion of the lagoon, which takes place in 1797. In May of that year the Great Council declares the Republic at an end, only 30 voices being raised in opposition. Napoleon dismissively burns the city's Gold Book in which are recorded the names of all the great patrician families. In the same year France cedes the whole of Veneto, including Venice, to Austria.

19th c. Throughout the first half of the 19th c. the old city submits to occupation. Only in 1848, the year of revolutions in various parts of Europe, do the Venetians, led by Daniele Manin, rebel, throwing off the Habsburg yoke for a brief fifteen months. In 1866 however, Austria abandons the Veneto region to the newly formed kingdom of Italy. Venice, by this time, is a mere shadow of its former self. Blighted by misgovernment and political division, the city has more the appearance of a poorhouse than an ambitious metropolis. A third of the population live in poverty.

From Austria to Italy

20th c. The long awaited economic and social revival finally comes during the First World War, bringing with it momentous consequences. A vast heavy industry complex is built in Marghera and the port is expanded accordingly. As the Fascist movement gains momentum, the industrial area of Mestre is enlarged. By the 1930s more Venetians live in miserable industrial suburbs than on the lagoon. Although arms are manufactured in the city, it is largely spared the destruction of the Second World War.

Economic revival

The insidious exodus of inhabitants continues unabated. Apart from tourism and administration, there are virtually no job opportunities in the ageing city. Venice itself faces a host of problems, not least the constant danger of flooding (during the worst such catastrophe, on November 4th 1966, St Mark's Square is under 1.25 m of water), the increase in industrial pollutants in the waters of the lagoon, heavy traffic in the canals and the fact that the city is sinking due to excessive extraction of ground water, not to mention mass tourism with more than 17 million visitors a year. If the population exodus is to be halted and hope – as Venice enters the new millenium – restored, radical and inevitably unpopular measures to protect the heritage city cannot any longer be deferred.

Venice today

The Venetian City State under the Doges

Venice's situation between East and West and the political risks this engendered made it imperative to have a constitution embodying checks and balances on political control. Venice was always a republic which was represented by a doge, underpinned by the aristocracy, and ruled by two forces – the mutual interests of the patrician families, and their fundamental mutual mistrust of one another, of the doge and of the people. The sole aim of the constitution was to neutralise any individual build-up of power and to ensure the two forces remained evenly balanced. The people and the Church were soon eliminated from the political process; and the power of the doges was increasingly curbed. After 1192 the Doge of Venice had to swear to a "Promissio", putting his signature to an agreement in which the electors stipulated the terms for the future government.

Constitution

The Great Council, the Consiglio Maggiore, was the real political power. Its members were the "nobili", the aristocracy, whose interests,

L. Bastiani: Doge Francesco Foscari

G. Bellini: Doge Giovanni Mocenigo

identical with those of the state, lay in trade, which must be pushed, promoted and protected. It was not until late in the 16th and 17th c. when, with the discovery of new routes, trade took a different direction and Venice slowly declined in importance, that the interests of the nobility and the state diverged. If trade went well then all was well with the city, and with it the people and the polity. From the very beginning it was this interdependence of politics and the economy that engendered the community of purpose and action so essential for the survival of the maritime republic.

Office of the Doge

The head of state of the Republic of Venice was the Doge, whose residence was the Doges' Palace. Pauluccio Anafesto, the first Doge (Latin "dux" = Italian Doge, cf. English duke), assumed office in AD 697; Manin, the last Doge, handed back the Doge's cap in 1797 with the words "it will not be needed any more". Over those 1100 years the Republic of Venice had been represented by 120 Doges. Their badge of office, the Doge's cap, was based on a Phrygian fisherman's hat, rising to a point on a stiffened base and set with gold and precious stones to the value of 194,000 ducats.

Originally "primus inter pares" (first among equals), the Doge was elected and endorsed by the populace: "this is your Doge if he pleases you". Once elected his power was virtually limitless: he negotiated in his own right with emperors and popes, decided on war or peace, and personally chose his officials, officers, successor and often his co-regent. His councillors ("pregadi") had an advisory function only. He exercised jurisdiction and possessed the power of pardon.

When in the 10th c. Doge Pietro Candiano IV (959–76) attempted to make the office of Doge hereditary and thus to alter the constitution to rule by dynasty, there was a revolt (in 976). The Doges' Palace and the Basilica went up in flames and the Doge and his young son were murdered. This episode prompted ever more rigorous curbs on the power of the Doge: a law preventing the Doge from appointing his co-regents was followed by another preventing him from nominating his successor (mid 11th c.). The Small Council (Consiglio Minore) was formed to watch over the head of state. Finally the populace was deprived of its voice in the election of the Doge – now it was "this is your Doge" (mid 12th c.) – being replaced by the Great Council (Consiglio Maggiore).

The balloting procedure for electing the Doge from among the members of the Great Council, introduced in 1268, was extremely complicated. Thirty members would first be balloted for, then a ballot held to select nine of them. These nine then nominated 40 provisional electors who in turn chose twelve by lot who then elected 25. These were reduced to nine, who then each nominated five. The 45 so nominated were reduced by casting lots to eleven: nine of the eleven votes were needed to choose the final 41 who, meeting in conclave, would elect the Doge. The future Doge must amass at least 25 of these votes. He was elected for life. This system of election offered every noble the chance to take part without allowing any group or family to exercise undue influence and thus impair the basic principles of the constitution.

Election

In terms of political duties the office of the Doge, from the 13th c. onwards, was more or less the equivalent of a modern head of state; he represented the Republic at home and abroad, had a seat on every body in the government (but only one vote), presided over the Great Council, saw to it that decisions were made and controlled the officers of the state.

Functions

More important however was the list of duties he could not undertake. This being specifically geared to protecting the interests of the Republic and its constitution, was as such unique in the world. A catalogue of those duties not open to him was drawn up in 1600; the Doge was not allowed to appoint his own men nor could he hold external office (this affected, for instance, Doge Enrico Dandalo, conqueror of Byzantium, who was precluded from accepting the imperial crown). No member of the Doge's family was allowed to take part in a business venture; sons and daughters could not marry outside the Republic without the permission of the Great Council. In the Promissio (see Constitution) the Doge must swear not to mount any coup, not to seek to restore the former powers of the office, not to open any letters from outside powers except in the presence of the Councils, not to write any such letters, not to receive envoys, not to accept presents (other than flowers, fragrant herbs or rosewater). His advisers (pregadi) were appointed by the Great Council. He was no longer allowed to erect or improve public buildings, or to have any possessions except those connected with his office.

Finally in the 16th and 17th c. came still further restriction; even in his private apartments he was forbidden to receive foreign envoys or generals. His sons were not permitted to journey abroad; his consort, the Dogeressa, was no longer to be crowned and no longer had an official retinue. Similarly he and his family were forbidden to maintain relations with foreign rulers. After the death of a Doge, his conduct in office was investigated by inquisitors and his heirs made financially responsible for any irregularities in the discharge of his duties. Although in the early years of the office the Doge was commander-in-chief of the army, after the 14th c. this duty was seldom exercised. If he appeared on the battlefield it was to inspire his people, not to lead them.

After 1172 the Great Council, which drew together the great noble families of the Republic, became the supreme legislative body of the state and watched over the Doge. In the early 13th c. the Great Council had 35 members. By 1297 this number had risen sharply to several hundred, and

Great Council

the Council enacted a "serrata" decreeing that henceforth no one whose family was not recorded in the "Libro d'Oro", the register of the aristocracy of the Republic, could become a member of the Council; when the Republic finally ended there were 1218 names in this Gold Book.

The Great Council was only directly consulted on absolutely basic matters, otherwise confining itself to the acceptance of statements of accounts; but its members did determine the membership of the different bodies charged with executing the affairs of state, and it elected the Doge from its own ranks. Each noble held an office in the state organisation, usually as an unpaid servant of the state. He was not allowed to refuse any duty he was called upon to discharge or decline any command. Anyone who failed when in office, whether or not he was at fault, was subject to the harshest penalties.

Their compliance with the strict laws created by the members of the Great Council in the interests of the state was as unquestioning and unconditional as the obedience they expected of other members of the polity.

Silver Book

The middle-class families were recorded in the Silver Book. Although they took no part in the decision-making process, certain administrative offices were open to them. The families recorded in the Gold and Silver Books comprised less than 15 per cent of Venice's population but owned almost 90 per cent of its assets.

Senate

The Senate first developed over a period of time as a body with supervisory powers over the Doges; then around 1255 it became an official assembly with precisely defined duties and the title of "Consiglio dei Pregadi" (its members being requested or "prayed", hence "pregadi", by written invitation, to attend the session). It consisted of 60 members elected from the Great Council, together with the Doge and the "Zonte", the latter made up of six patricians from the Great Council, five representatives of the provinces on the mainland, and five representatives from the religious orders. Other key members of the administration included the Doge's closest advisers, representatives of the judiciary, the Council of Ten, the "avvogadori" (constitutional judges), the "cattaveri" (tax assessors) and the "provveditori (overseers).

In effect the Senate was the state parliament, answerable to the Great Council but empowered to take major decisions: it decided on peace and war and on what edicts should be recommended to the Great Council, and it appointed all the important state officials. It also set up and supervised all the committees charged with bringing the administration into line with political and social developments.

Small Council (Signoria, Collegio)

The Small Council was the Republic's closest approximation to a ruling cabinet. Initially it was composed of the Doge and his six councillors representing the sestieri, the six districts of Venice: Castello, Cannaregio, Dorsoduro, San Marco, San Polo and Sante Croce. In the 13th c. the three heads of the Quarantia Criminal, who presided over the courts of justice, were made *ex officio* members, forming, together with the Doge and his councillors, the Signoria. When later augmented by the Savi (committees of wise men), it became the Collegio, the functions of the Savi Grandi being transmuted to ministerial offices. The Collegio prepared all bills to be submitted to the Senate, decided on what should be witheld from the Senate on grounds of secrecy, received and heard foreign envoys, and served as the supreme judicial court of appeal. The Collegio also represented the Republic in negotiations with the representatives of foreign powers. Its members were drawn from the Great Council and Senate.

Council of Ten

The Council of Ten was intended to act as a liaison body between the legislature, i.e. the Great Council and Senate on the one hand, and the executive, i.e. the Doge and administration including the judiciary on the other. It was called into being when, in 1310, Baiamonte Tiepolo made an unsuccessful attempt to undermine the rule of the nobility by acting as a kind of special court to try enemies of the state.

The Senate decided every year on the ten members of this body. The Doge and his six councillors sat in on the Council, as did a constitutional lawyer (avvocadore) whose job it was to ensure that the decisions of the Council accorded with the Republic's laws and constitution. The names of the members of the Council of Ten were kept secret.

The multifarious tasks and duties of the Council of Ten can be summed up as the guardianship of state security, their principal duty being to deal with acts of high treason, espionage, sabotage, conspiracy, etc. whether planned, attempted or accomplished. The Council was also charged with watching over the morals of the city, preventing duels (strictly forbidden) and punishing participants, preventing acts of violence and anything constituting a disturbance of the peace. Finally the Council was responsible for prosecuting any whose actions endangered the economy.

The three state Inquisitors, an office established in 1539, were initially responsible for the integrity of confidential information. Later they assumed a more general role in affairs of state. Two were drawn from the Council of Ten and one from among the councillors to the Doge.

Three Chief Magistrates (Inquisitori)

Although termed simply "advocates", this triumvirate of lawyers acted as constitutional judges and public prosecutors. It was their job to ensure that decisions of the Great Council, the Senate and the Council of Ten accorded with the Republic's laws and constitution, if necessary exercising a veto. They also monitored the observance of treaties, the collection of fines, and the probity of commercial and private legal procedures.

Three Avvogadori

Hence the institution of the "avvogadori", in existence since the 12th c., was a precursor of the independent administration of justice that exists today in all democratic states. The same can be said of the "Quarantia".

This body, comprising 40 (i.e. "quaranta") members, had existed since 1179. Originally merely a court of appeal of no more than 40 patricians, it quickly evolved into the *de facto* judicial authority of the Republic. In the 14th c. its workload became so great that it had to be split into the Quarantia Civil, dealing with civil cases, and the Quarantia Criminal, responsible for non-political criminal offences such as murder, robbery, etc. Two centuries later, the ever increasing number of civil suits involving, for example, defamation or fraud, caused the Quarantia Civil to be further subdivided into the Quarantia Civil Vecchia and the Quarantia Civil Nuova.

Quarantia

All these various organs of state gradually engendered a network of honorary or paid officials and institutions, who conscientiously carried out the duties assigned to them.

Provveditori, cattaveri, censori

Chief among these were the provveditori, the overseers, nobles who superintended and directed indispensable organisations and projects. Hence the "Provvedori de Mar", a body responsible for fitting out the war fleet, recruiting seamen and rowers, etc.; other provveditori oversaw the welfare institutions or were concerned with the churches, monasteries and religious associations.

Less obtrusive, but much less pleasant, were the cattaveri, the tax assessors. Every Venetian, regardless of person or rank, was obliged to allow them to inspect everything he possessed and then dictate to him how much – and it was always a considerable sum – he had to pay in taxes to the state. And woe betide anyone making a false declaration: they would soon find themselves arraigned before the Council of Ten.

Last but by no means least there were the "censori". Drawn from among the members of the Great Council, their sole duty was to prevent irregularities in the elections for the various bodies and offices.

Famous People

The following prominent historical figures were born, lived, worked or died in Venice.

Jacopo Bellini ca. 1400 to 1470/71

Jacopo Bellini, a pupil of Gentile da Fabriano, spent time in Florence and Rome as well as working at the court in Ferrara and in the university city of Padua. He thus became familiar with the forceful naturalistic style of early Renaissance painting, which he sought to combine with the Gothic elegance still in vogue in Venice. His pictures of the Madonna are characterised by nuance of colour and soft lines. His exquisite drawings, on the other hand, reflect his study of Classical art. His narrative paintings with their blend of realism and rich imagination prepared the way for Venetian historical painting.

His sons Gentile and Giovanni both studied under their father but were also influenced by their brother-in-law Mantegna and went on to become internationally renowned masters.

Gentile Bellini ca. 1420–1507

Gentile, Jacopo's eldest son, was a celebrated portraitist whose work is notable for its sensitivity to character. He spent the years 1479 to 1481 in Constantinople at the court of the Sultan, painting the Ottoman ruler and other prominent figures.

His Venice paintings are notable not only for the realism of his views of the city and acute observation of rich and poor, young and old, but also on account of the scenic richness of works such as the cycle of the Miracles of the Relic of the Holy Cross in the Accademia.

Giovanni Bellini ca. 1430–1516

His younger brother Giovanni is recognised today as the foremost representative of early Renaissance painting. Almost unique among his generation, Giovanni blended a sculptural, graphical style with an unprecedented warmth and luminosity of colour, made possible by the then novel technique of painting in oils which he had learned from Antonello da Messina. His often lyrical paintings, from half-figures of the Madonna to mysterious allegories, are infused with an intimacy of feeling and sense of reverence for nature. The harmony of colour, gradation of light and atmospheric quality of his landscape settings fascinated Albrecht Dürer, who met Giovanni in Venice in 1506 and considered him "the very best of painters". Major works by Giovanni can be seen in the Accademia as well as the Frari and in San Zaccaria.

Canaletto (Antonio Canal) 1697–1768)

Canaletto was one of the last of the great Venetian artists. Born in Venice, he took up painting in the theatre before studying in Rome and turning to nature studies. His first great success in Venice was with "vedute" (views). In 1742, following a second stay in Rome, he began painting imaginary landscapes, before finally adopting the genre he was to make his own – finely detailed townscapes alive with carnivals, festivals and processions.

Canaletto spent two periods in England (1746–50 and 1751–53) and it is there that most of his works are found. Those to be seen in Venice are mainly in the Accademia.

Accomplished lover and dashing philanderer, Giacomo Casanova, self-styled Chevalier de Seingalt, is among the most legendary of Venice's sons. On his travels throughout Europe on a variety of missions, he met many famous contempories from the worlds of politics and literature including Frederick the Great and Voltaire, while also breaking many a maidenly heart. Imprisoned in Venice in 1755 for his atheist beliefs, the following year he contrived a spectacular escape from the "piombi" (lead cells). After a life of restless wandering, in 1785 he finally found a post as librarian to Count Waldstein in Bohemia, where he produced his memoires ("Histoire de ma vie"). Written in French they are among the most important

Giacomo
Girolamo
Casanova
1725–1798

records of the society of his day, revealing great gifts of observation and narrative. He first featured as a figure in literature in the mid 19th c. in early comedies and an opera by Lortzing; later Hofmannsthal and Arthur Schnitzler took up the theme of the celebrated lady-killer. To this day no one better personifies the seducer than Casanova.

Dandolo, scion of an old-established noble Venetian family, was 82 before he was elected Doge. Despite his age he never shrank from any military confrontation which might secure or advance Venetian influence in the eastern Mediterranean, and thus he drove the Pisans out of Istria. As a greybeard of 94, with the lords of the Fourth Crusade, he conquered Constantinople in 1204. On the fall of Dalmatia he secured for Venice a great share of the treasure taken as booty, built stagingposts throughout the eastern Mediterranean and finally made Venice into a world power.

Enrico Dandolo
ca. 1110–1205

The fate of Francesco Foscari is inextricably linked with the policy of extending the Venetian maritime republic to terra firma. Elected Doge in 1423, after 1426 he conducted the four Milanese wars against the other northern Italian city states, securing for Venice its greatest territorial expansion – from Brescia to Ravenna. In 1454, centuries of fighting over sovereignty in northern Italy ended in a compromise enshrined in the Peace of Lodi. The Turkish conquest of Constantinople in 1453, however, considerably weakened the Venetian economy, even resulting in the loss of the century-old trade monopoly. Furthermore, Foscari's expansionist policy on the mainland provoked the displeasure of the emperor and pope, as a consequence of which, in 1509, Venice finally surrendered her status as a great power.

Francesco Foscari
ca. 1373–1457

In 1407 opposition orchestrated by the Loredan family led to Foscari being deposed and his son Jacopo banished. His fate and that of his several times banished son inspired poets such as Lord Byron and composers such as Verdi.

Goldoni, who revived the Italian commedia dell'arte, wrote Rococo comedies in the manner of Molière, reflecting everyday reality. His best-known works include "The Servant of Two Masters", "Women's Gossip" and "Mirandolina". After studying law and philosophy, Goldoni worked from 1744 to 1748 as a lawyer in Pisa, but his youthful involvement with the theatre led him on his return to Venice to begin writing plays, between 1748 and 1753 for the Teatro di Sant'Angelo, and then until 1762 for the Teatro di San Luca. In 1762, competition from rival playwrights caused Goldoni to leave for Paris where he was Director of the Italian theatre until 1764, also mounting productions of his own plays. Impoverished by the Revolution, he died in 1793.

Carlo Goldoni
1707–1793

Famous People

Claudio
Monteverdi
1567–1643

Claudio Monteverdi had an impact on music which extended beyond the 17th c. Born in Cremona, Monteverdi was until 1590 a scholar of composition in his home town, then until 1612 musician and choirmaster at the court of Mantua. From 1613 until his death he was choirmaster of St Mark's in Venice.

In departing from the rigid forms of the 16th c., Monteverdi was the pioneer of greater stylistic freedom in music. He reached the peak of his achievement with the operas "Orfeo" (1607) – which marks the appearance of opera as a genre – "Il ritorno d'Ulisse in patria" (1640) and "L'incoronazione di Poppea" (1642), which exercised a profound influence on European opera from Gluck to Richard Wagner.

Andrea Palladio
1508–1580

This eminent Renaissance architect and architectural theorist lived in Vicenza prior to working in Venice. In 1570 he published his masterly "I Quattro Libri dell'Architettura", in which he gave formulation to the meaning and purpose of his art: "Beauty will result from the form and correspondence of the whole, with respect to the several parts, of the parts with regard to each other, and of these again to the whole; that the structure may appear an entire and compleat body, wherein each member agrees with the other, and all necessary to compose what you intend to form". Bold and ordered, the lightness and clarity of his work, inspired by the architecture of ancient Greece and Rome, influenced European Neo-Classicism into the 19th c. Palladio was exceptionally versatile, designing palaces and country houses for the nobility (among them his famous Villa Rotunda near Vicenza), as well as sublime churches and magnificent public buildings in Venice where his name is associated with three ecclesiastical buildings in particular: the façade of San Francesco della Vigna (an early work); San Giorgio Maggiore, in mature monumental Classical style; and Il Redentore, an important late work. The use of colossal structures with columns and pilasters together with such features of Graeco-Roman temples as entablatures and pediments, were distinctive elements of his work. Palladio's designs for villas of low elevation with open, extended wings, gave crucial impetus to the Baroque and in the 17th and 18th c. Palladianism took England, France and the Netherlands by storm.

Marco Polo
1264–1324

Marco Polo, best known of any medieval traveller to Asia, whose account of his journeys revolutionised the geographical thought of his time and focused the attention of Europeans on the distant Orient, was seventeen when in 1271 he accompanied his father and uncle on their expedition from Venice to trade with China. Their route took them from Palestine to Tabriz, thence to Hormuz on the Persian Gulf, to eastern Persia and Pakistan, through the Pamir and across the Takla Makan desert, past Lop Nur, to Cathay, northern China. They arrived in 1275 at the court of Kublai Khan, where Marco Polo spent the next seventeen years as adviser to the Mongol ruler. In 1292 he was finally given permission to return to Europe. He journeyed back via the South China Sea, along the coasts of Vietnam, Malacca, Sumatra, Ceylon and upper India, to the Strait of Hormuz, then on via Persia, Armenia and Trebizond to Constantinople where, in 1295, he boarded ship for Venice. Marco Polo's account of his travels, "Il Milione", was dictated to his fellow captive Rustichello da Pisa during a ten month sojourn in a Genoese gaol (September 1298 to July 1299). Soon translated into other languages, this "wonder of the world" profoundly influenced geographical ideas in the 14th and 15th c.

The Florentine Sansovino left his mark on the townscape of Venice as no other architect when, after 1527, he was commissioned to redesign the city in the High Renaissance style. He had a hand in or was responsible for the design and erection of no less than fifteen of the city's churches and public buildings, including the Biblioteca Marciana, the Mint (Zecca), the Logetta di San Marco, the church of San Francesco della Vigna and the Palazzo Corner. The statues of Mars and Neptune in the courtyard of the Doges' Palace, the sacristy door of St Mark's, and the tomb of Doge Venier in San Salvatore, testify to his immense talent as a sculptor also.

Sansovino
(Jacopo Tatti)
1486–1570

Inundated with commissions from the families of the Doges and nobility, Giambattista Tiepolo, the outstanding representative of Venetian Rococo painting, produced innumerable altarpieces in addition to wall and ceiling frescoes for churches, palaces and villas in Venice and elsewhere in northern Italy. More distant commissions took him to the Residenz of the prince-bishops in Würzburg and the royal court in Madrid. Examples of his work, distinguished by bold foreshortening and powerful light effects combined with a more relaxed, luminous use of colour, can be seen in Venice in the Accademia, in San Alvise, in the Scuola Grande dei Carmini and in the Palazzo Labia. His son Domenico studied under him, the two often working together as equals on major commissions. Domenico's style is more anecdotal by comparison, the colours more gentle, and his compositions dispense with the complex figural arrangements typical of his father's work. In old age Domenico dedicated himself increasingly to genre painting, seeking inspiration in scenes of the carnival and pulcinellas.

Giovanni Battista
Tiepolo 1696–1770
Giovanni
Domenico Tiepolo
1727–1804

Tintoretto not only occupies a place in the annals of Venetian art as an inspired painter of the Mannerist and Counter-Reformation periods, he also has a niche in history on account of the businesslike approach he adopted towards his work as an artist. Son of a silk-dyer ("tintore": hence his nickname), Tintoretto accepted every commission offered him and attempted to undercut rivals by quoting the lowest prices. Born in Venice he left the city only once in his lifetime (he is known to have journeyed to Mantua in 1580) but was nevertheless influenced by the main artistic movements of his time. His pictures, generally on themes from the Old and New Testaments, achieve a dramatic quality through use of strong contrast of light and shade, bold foreshortening and background views and unusual light effects. In Venice his work can be seen in the Accademia collection in the Doges' Palace, in a large number of churches (Madonna dell'Orto, San Giorgio Maggiore, San Marcuola, Santa Maria della Salute) and in the Scuola Grande di Rocco with its magnificent wall and ceiling paintings.

Tintoretto (Jacobo
Robusti)
1518–1594)

Born in the Cadore valley in the Dolomites, at the beginning of the 16th

Famous People

Titian (Tiziano Vecellio) (1488/90–1576)

c. Titian arrived in Venice where Giovanni Bellini provided the crucial inspiration for his painting. His commissions between 1510 and 1526, which included the Assunta altarpiece and the Pesaro Madonna in the Frari in Venice, established his reputation, and he soon became the most sought-after painter at the princely courts of Europe. The d'Este, Gonzaga and Farnese families kept his order book full, he was held in the highest esteem by François I of France, and in 1533 the Emperor Charles V appointed him court painter. In later life Titian worked almost exclusively for Philip II of Spain. In addition to altarpieces, Titian's great output, which could not have been achieved without the backing of a large studio, includes allegorical and mythological works, nudes and a large number of portraits. Stylistically he stands on the threshold of the Late Renaissance/Early Baroque. Harmony of colour, strong contrasts of light and shade, lively diagonal compositions and atmospheric scenic backgrounds – together with an astute understanding of the requirements of his patrons – characterise Titian's always fascinating work, the technique and range of composition of which pointed the way ahead for following generations.

Veronese (Paolo Caliari) 1528–1588

Veronese, though born, as the name implies, in Verona, is nevertheless without peer when it comes to portraying the Venetian zest for life. He ranks with Tintoretto and Titian as one of the leading artists of Venice in the Late Renaissance.

After working in 1552 on Mantua Cathedral, from 1553 he established himself in Venice where the sensual quality of his painting brought him into conflict with the Inquisition. Always in great demand, his many commissions could not have been completed without the aid of a large studio and numerous assistants. His large-scale, many-figured compositions, such as his banquet scenes and allegorical ceiling paintings, delight with their richness of colour and lively depiction of character.

In Venice works by Veronese can be seen in the church of San Sebastiano (ceiling and wall paintings), in the Accademia ("The Supper in the House of Levi"), and in the Doges' Palace (ceiling and wall paintings; also the supreme example of his late work: "The Triumph of Venezia").

Antonio Vivaldi 1678–1741

Not only was Antonio Vivaldi a brilliant violinist and Venice's most important composer, he also, through his development of the solo concerto, contributed in no small measure to the enrichment of European music.

In 1703 Vivaldi entered the priesthood. In the same year he was appointed "Maestro di violino" at the Ospedale della Pietà, a conservatory for girls in Venice, where he worked almost without interruption, as violin teacher, conductor and composer, until 1740. Vivaldi's style had a distinct influence on many other composers including Johann Sebastian Bach, who transposed several of Vivaldi's violin pieces for the organ. In addition to some 500 concertos, notable for their richly nuanced instrumentation, emotive melodies and lively rhythms, Vivaldi composed more than 90 sonatas, 46 operas, of which 21 are still extant, and three oratorios.

Culture

Art History

Romanesque–Byzantine art

The close relationship with Constantinople had a decisive influence on the development of art in Venice. The five-domed basilica of St Mark's, church of the Republic and the Doges, was modelled on the Church of the Holy Apostles in Constantinople; after 1100 the narthex was embellished with Byzantine mosaics, as was the interior in the 12th c. Byzantine mosaicists worked with Italian assistants to complete the iconographic scheme. While the iconography is strongly reminiscent of its eastern prototype, it is formally different from Byzantine art in its rendering of the surface, figures and stylised folds. This marriage of western stylistic elements with eastern prototypes is an important feature pervading the Romanesque art of Venice.

Another example is the mosaic of the Last Judgement on the west wall of Santa Maria Assunta on Torcello (12th c.). The Byzantine influence on the iconography is again clear, with the Crucifixion, The Descent

"Archangel Michael"
enamel painting on the Pala
d'Oro in the Basilica di San Marco

into Hell, Christ enthroned flanked by Mary and the Evangelist, the Weighing of Souls, Adam and Eve worshipping the Cross, and Christ's empty throne guarded by angels and on which lies an open book, the Word. This Last Judgement is no narrative sequence, but a timeless affirmation. The stylistic influence of eastern art is very evident in the luminous colours, stylised folds and graceful heads.

Architecture

Santa Maria Assunta on Torcello incorporates important features of Romanesque architecture. The triple-naved colonnaded basilica, without transepts and with a wooden roof, is overtopped by a tall campanile; narrow blind arches articulate the walls. In the interior, bare expanses of wall above the slender arcading heighten the two-dimensional effect.

In contrast San Fosca on Torcello (late 11th c.) exemplifies an East Roman architectural scheme. The centrally-planned domed building combines a Greek cross, octagon and circle in an original way, creating a square interior space. Slender arcading borne on tall columns distinguishes the octagonal portico surrounding three sides of the building.

The Basilica di Santa Maria e Donato on Murano is a mixture of Romanesque and Byzantine. Spatially the triple-naved colonnaded church takes on the character of a centrally-planned building by the addition of a massive transept. Furthermore, the exterior of the apse is elaborate and impressive, with two storeys of arcading on paired columns, the lower enclosing niches, the upper a wide gallery. In Venice such arcades, employed for vertical articulation and set forward from the wall, are a typical feature of secular buildings of the pre-Gothic era.

Sculpture

The Eastern Roman Empire also had a strong influence on 11th and 12th c. Venetian sculpture, so much so that it is sometimes impossible to say with certainty whether a work was produced in Venice or imported. The 11th c. iconostasis in Torcello cathedral, with its symmetrically arranged marble panels decorated with tendrils and pairs of peacocks pecking grapes from a bowl, came from Byzantium and symbolises the renewal of life through participation in Christ's death. The relief "The Ascent of Alexander to Heaven" on the north façade of St Mark's, with its simple form and reduced corporeality, dates from the 11th c. and was likewise possibly executed in the Christian East.

Spoils

As well as many imported reliefs and sculptures, in Venice there are also numerous spoils, architectural fragments originating from elsewhere, which here find a new setting. Through its trade links and its bases in major centres in the East, and above all through the conquest of Constantinople in 1204, a vast amount of booty was brought back to Venice. Many of the polychrome marble columns and fine ornamental pilasters in St Mark's were acquired in this way. Among the best-known spoils are the two columns which now adorn the Piazzetta, brought to Venice by ship at the end of the 12th c. The figures on the columns are likewise spoils from the East. The bronze lion – the Lion of St Mark – was originally a chimera until its metamorphosis by the addition of wings and the open book. St Theodore was similarly transformed from a Roman figure into a Christian one.

Gothic art

Architecture

In Venice Gothic refers principally to a decorative style, given special impetus by the redesigning of the Doges' Palace. Here every form is imbued with a particular grace and delight in colour. The ground-level arcades are low, with wide pointed arches, while those of the loggia above are considerably narrower, with quatrefoils cut in the spandrels, creating a see-through effect. The white, red and green, diamond pattern brickwork softens what might otherwise be the massive effect of the wall

The famous Late Gothic palace façade of the Ca' d'Oro

above. Wide lateral windows with pointed arches and oculi embellish the walls, the balconies having elaborate Gothic window frames. Even the flame-shaped merlons are pierced, giving a filigree-like finish to the building.

The exterior of St Mark's likewise underwent important alteration at the end of the 14th c., the upper tier of arches being crowned in Late Gothic splendour by the addition of figured tabernacles, curved canopies and statues on the gables, typical Gothic enhancements.

The most famous Late Gothic palace façade is that of the Ca' d'Oro (1421–1440). The Gothic elements of the once partly gilded main front are clear to see: slender arched arcading with a different design of tracery on each level, balconies, friezes, fine ornamentation and polychrome decoration.

The Dominican church of Santi Giovanni e Paolo and the Franciscan church of Santa Maria Gloriosa dei Frari are the two greatest Late Gothic churches in Venice. Both are constructed in the tradition of the Gothic churches of the mendicant orders: vaulted colonnaded basilicas with a transept and lateral choir chapels.

Venetian sculpture brings together stylistic elements from the most disparate sources. While the Byzantine influence remains by far the strongest, Graeco-Roman elements are adopted and combined with Gothic features. The sculptural decoration above the main door of St Mark's dates from the mid 13th c.; its lively narrative mode and subtle depiction show it to be completely independent of outside influences.

Sculpture

The brothers Jacobello and Pierpaolo dalle Masegne were involved in several important projects in Venice; their sculptures on the rood screen in St Mark's (1394) reveal the immense importance they attached to the sculpting of individual figures, in particular the exact modelling of bodily

Dated 1265: the St Alipus portal of San Marco

form and the lifelike gestures. They even contrived to depict certain apostles in contrapposto.

Nowhere in Venice is the development of monumental sculpture better illustrated than in Santi Giovanni e Paolo, the churches of the mendicant orders being the favoured burial places of the Doges. The construction of the tomb of Doge Michele Morosini on the right wall of the presbytery is typical of the 14th c. It is tabernacular in form, with a pointed arch and canopy over the sarcophagus on which the effigy of the dead Doge lies in state. Consoles either side of the inscription bear his arms. The small sculptures – angels, apostles and an Annunciation – reveal northern influence; the mosaic of the Crucifixion with figures of the donors is reminiscent of Giotto's work.

Painting

Antonello da Messina introduced the technique of oil painting to Venice, his work there having a great influence on Venetian art. The brothers Antonio and Bartolomeo Vivarini shared a studio workshop. Having begun by painting in a somewhat decorative Late Gothic style, with rather stiff figures, from about 1400 onwards Antonio refined his technique. Astonishing realism and sympathetic characterisation infuse his later work. Meanwhile Bartolomeo developed a sculptural style of painting distinguished by a strong use of colour and hard contours. The work of Antonio's son, Alvise, who produced large altar- and devotional pictures, is not dissimilar to that of Giovanni Bellini.

Renaissance

Architecture

Few churches were rebuilt in Venice in the 15th c. One such, and of outstanding importance, was the redesigned church of Santa Maria dei Miracoli, by the sculptor and architect Pietro Lombardo. He had the whole exterior faced with polychrome marble, producing a rhythmic effect by articulating the lower order with pilasters and the upper with blind arcades, all the while adhering to Classical proportions. Marble dominates the interior too, a single barrel-vaulted nave with tall presbytery. The relief-work on the pilasters is especially noteworthy, a series of decorative bands embellished with sculptural, densely worked filigree of animals, vases, heads and masks.

Lombardo, who was also responsible for the façade of the Scuola Grande di San Marco with its trompe l'oil reliefs at the base, did not have a monopoly on major projects. Others were entrusted to Mauro Codussi, including the facing for the façades of San Zaccaria and San Michele in Isola. Both have the semicircular culmination and rounded sections characteristic of his work. San Zaccaria exemplifies his system of articulation in its purest form: successive tiers of vertical elements (pilasters, columns, round-arched windows and blind arcades) horizontally articulated by wide cornices. Round oculi are also a particular feature of his façades. Both Lombardo and Codussi contributed significantly to the evolution of the Venetian palace façade by inserting large windows where previously there had been more or less unbroken wall.

Throughout his time in Venice, Andrea Palladio was involved exclusively with ecclesiastical architecture. He planned three important church façades: San Giorgio Maggiore, Il Redentore and San Francesco della Vigna, distinguished by their plainness and simple proportions. Colossal orders of columns, a pedimented colonnaded portico, and the harmonious relation of wall to column imbue these façades with their special character.

The monument (1476–81) to Doge Pietro Mocenigo in Santi Giovanni e Paolo paved the way for developments in monumental sculpture. In adopting the motif of the triumphal arch, Pietro Lombardo broke emphatically with tradition. Classically-influenced warrior-figures occupy the niches; others, making nine in all, support the sarcophagus, on which the effigy of the Doge is erect, not recumbent. A relief of the Resurrection of Christ appears at the top of the monument.

One of the best known tombs in the church is that of Doge Andrea Vendramin, whose memorial (1493) is the work of Tullio Lombardo, Pietro's son. It too is modelled on a triumphal arch, with a central colonnade flanked by recesses. The iconographic scheme combines Christian motifs with Humanist ideas. The individual figures, in particular of the warriors, suggest a detailed study of Classical sculpture, most evident in the sure proportions, subtle handling of the surface and lively portrayal of physiognomy. The same artist's "Youthful Couple", a marble high relief in the Galleria Franchetti (Ca' d'Oro), is similarly lifelike, the almost fully three-dimensional faces expressing the subtlest of human emotions.

In the latter half of the 15th c. Antonio Rizzo, the second major Renaissance sculptor, executed the marble figures of Adam and Eve which originally embellished the Arco Foscari in the Doges' Palace. In regard to proportion, Eve in particular, with her slight shoulders and wide hips, epitomises the Gothic notion of form; but her posture and withdrawn gestures appear sensuous and introverted. Adam, turning outward and portrayed open-mouthed, his right hand held in front his breast, appears moved. Artists' models posed for both carvings. This pair of figures are certainly not the progeny of Graeco-Roman statuary.

Major contributions were made to the design of St Mark's Square and the Piazzetta by the architect Jacopo Sansovino, who drew up the plans for the Libreria di San Marco and also the Zecca. Although himself a sculptor, he only designed the rich sculptural ornamentation, having no hand in its execution. Venice however is not short of examples of his prodigious talent as a sculptor: the reliefs on the Cantorie and on the doors of the sacristy in St Mark's; the Madonna in the Arsenal; the figure of John the Baptist on the baptismal font in

Sculpture

Vittore Carpaccio: "Two Venecian patrician women"

the Frari; and the niche figures of Pallas Athena, Mercury, Apollo and Pax (personifying the four guiding principles of Venetian politics) on the Logetta at the foot of the campanile in St Mark's Square. It is impossible to ignore the influence of Classical art on these powerful, challenging and realistic bronzes, impressive in their uniformity and the fine treatment of surface structure.

Painting

Venetian painting is distinguished by the strength, vibrancy and splendour of its colouration, reflecting on the one hand the spread and eager reception of Byzantine art, and on the other the city's unique location by the water and the many narrow canals within it, which create unusual conditions of light and shade. In contrast to Florentine painting at this time, with its predilection for the pictorial narrative mode and a heroic style of portrayal, the work of the Venetian masters has a lyrical quality, both in mood and content. There is no better example of this poetic manner than Giorgione's "Tempest" in the Galleria dell'Accademia. This iconographic painting, its defiance of decipherment perhaps an allegory of human life, has a pastoral ambience, tranquil and peaceful, against which the unsettled, almost threatening aspect of the stormy sky creates a stark contrast. Here the mood-bearing qualities of light and colour in a sensual, poetic world are of paramount importance for the artist.

Gentile Bellini, who together with his father and brother Giovanni was employed in the family's studio workshop, had the honour of committing to canvas the likeness of each newly elected Doge. Though few of the original paintings survive, many copies are still extant; all reveal the Bellinis' intense concern with the individuality of their subjects.

In Venice the study of antiquity as revealed in Jacopo Bellini's sketch books, had a significant influence on ideas of form but very little upon content. In this Venice differed from cities such as Florence or Mantua, where as early as the second half of the 15th c., mythological themes were very popular. Those who commissioned works in Venice early in the Renaissance period tended to favour paintings with Christian subjects.

Many of Vittore Carpaccio's commissions came from scuole, for whom he produced substantial picture cycles embellishing their assembly rooms. Fascinating in its delight in anecdotal narrative and love of picturesque detail, his painting is also striking from a formal point of view, with clear spatial relationships and precise representation of the figures.

In creating the Assunta (1516–18), his great altarpiece for the Frari, Titian devised a compositional scheme which was to determine the treatment of this subject for decades. The Assumption of the Virgin takes place in a light-filled, visional space; below, the apostles, profoundly affected, gaze after her, arms up-stretched, as she is wafted away; in the upper part of the picture, God the Father receives Mary. Juxtaposition of light and shade and deployment of colour to capture emotion and emphasise contrasts, are distinctive features of Titian's works.

Whereas Titian was in demand in courts across Europe, Jacopo Tintoretto worked almost exclusively in his native Venice. In addition to a great many commissions for secular buildings, he produced large and important altarpieces. His compositions emphasise the plasticity of moving figures in spatial depths drawn in exact perspective. Especially in his later work light becomes increasingly important in creating atmosphere, drama and artistic vision. This makes him one of the leading masters of Mannerism.

In Paolo Veronese's paintings the main scene unfolds stagelike in the foreground while other, related scenes are played out to the rear. The newly renovated church of San Sebastiano, which he decorated with ceiling and wall paintings, is an excellent place to become familiar with his cheerily narrated stories and his decorative style.

Palazzi

In Venice the term palace originally applied to just one building, the Doges' Palace. The large houses belonging to the wealthy families were modestly called casa (house) or ca' for short, words which still appear in the name of some palaces, e.g. the Ca' d'Oro.

Venetian palace architecture

By contrast with other cities of upper Italy, the builders of Venetian palaces were spared two major problems: first, the city's unusual location on the lagoon meant that no defensive architecture was required, the buildings having the natural protection of the surrounding water; second, because Venice was free of the internecine political feuding which plagued other cities, individual buildings had less need of security and could be constructed with much greater freedom and more openly. Whereas elsewhere palaces tended to be few and far between, Venice's numerous aristocratic and wealthy middle-class families gave rise to an extraordinary number of lavish residences.

The interior of a Venetian palazzo is laid out to a more or less standard plan, which was retained into the 18th c. On the ground floor there is a

The smart palaces on the Canal Grande always have their representative main entrance facing the water

hall extending the full depth of the building and giving access to adjoining rooms. Barely above water level and not very comfortable, from the Renaissance onwards these were seldom used for living purposes, but as utility areas, stores and offices. Frequently mezzanine floors were added to the side of the hall. On the upper floor the staircase opens directly into the "sala", a large room located exactly over the entrance hall below. This provided enough space for large celebrations, festive dinners and theatrical performances, and was appropriately furnished with chairs and tables and with pictures, arms and trophies. The sala is lit by large windows opening onto little balconies. The rooms off it were used for living accommodation.

The Venetian palazzo generally had two entrances: an imposing doorway on the side facing the water, and a plainer one at the opposite end of the hall. Since the Renaissance the status of the entrance area has been enhanced, leading to its being furnished more richly with paintings or sculptural decoration. The staircase, hitherto usually outside – of which the spiral staircase in the courtyard of the Palazzo Contarini del Bovolo is an outstanding example – was also moved into the house. Large inner courtyards were rare on account of the inflated land values.

The main façade always faces the water, rising on a base of dressed stone surmounted by a deep cornice, with a portal of one or more arches, and steps leading up to the entrance. In some cases arcades extend across the whole width of the building at ground level. The windows of the sala are the determining architectural feature on the upper floor. The side rooms generally had two windows, widely spaced, with an expanse of wall between them. The shape of the windows varies depending on when the palace was built: rounded arches, pointed arches, tracery, and squares with triangular pediments are all found. The façade may also be enriched by pilasters, columns and other sometimes exceedingly costly embellishments.

Originally two-storeyed, in the Gothic period palaces were raised by another floor, though care was taken to maintain a uniform height (exceeded only by one or two 16th c. buildings). Until the 13th c. wood was the preferred material for palace building; only after that was it gradually replaced by more durable stone. In due course brickwork gained acceptance and the walls could then be plastered and painted or faced with marble or limestone. The different colour or grain of the stone contributed to the delicate effect of the façade.

Pleasanter surroundings had also to be provided for the less prosperous inhabitants of the city. The numerous terraced houses in Venice are another reflection of the limited amount of space. These houses differ from the palazzi not only in size but also plan. In the scuole and procuratie, apartments, sometimes furnished, were available at a reasonable price or even free of charge.

Scuole

In Venice a "scuola" was a confraternity of burghers of the same profession or nationality with shared charitable or commercial aims. These lay societies or guilds originated in the Middle Ages. By 1500, in addition to numerous little scuole, the Scuole Piccole, the city boasted six large scuole, the Scuole Grandi, with between 500 and 600 members. Each scuola was placed under the protection of a patron saint.

Guilds

At first these fraternities met in churches or sacristies, but soon built their own meeting houses, for which the Scuola Grande della Carità provided the model. The ground floor consists of a low-ceilinged, three-aisled hall, the precise function of which remains obscure. It certainly served as a salon, and possibly as a burial place for members of the fraternity. An altar was placed opposite the entrance, used for fraternal prayers or requiems. On the upper floor was a similarly low-ceilinged hall, the Sala del Capitolo, and next to it a somewhat smaller room, the "Sala dell'Albergo", for the use of the society's officers. An altar was set up in the large hall, and a pulpit could be installed for sermons or readings of documents.

Architecture

The scuole are especially remarkable for their interiors, enriched by often magnificent picture sequences on Christian themes. Among the most impressive is the Scuola Grande di San Rocco. It boasts an extensive Mariological cycle by Tintoretto on the lower floor, and on the upper floor, by the same artist, ceiling paintings on Old Testament themes and a Christological cycle around the walls. In addition there is a most magnificent staircase. Even in the smaller scuole, whose buildings may be less grand, the sumptuousness of the furnishings can be astonishing. The Scuola di San Giorgio degli Schiavoni, for example, has superb imaginative narrative paintings by Vittore Carpaccio.

As inside, so also outside, the scuola is a mixture of secular building and church. Though no specific stereotype evolved, the two-storey interior is generally mirrored on the facade, the design and aspect of which was often influenced by neighbouring churches. The space directly in front of the scuola was sometimes incorporated into the plan. Pietro Lombardo found an unusual solution for the forecourt of the Scuola Grande di San Giovanni, articulating the walls of the small courtyard with chamfered pilasters topped by a wide entablature. The main entrance, the "Porta Magna", is given emphasis by a pediment.

When it came to building, the scuole did not confine themselves to meeting houses. Members frequently provided the altars for churches and chapels. And, depending on their wealth, they owned a considerable number of houses and land.

Giovanni Domenico Tiepolo (1745): Carnival

17th and 18th century

Painting

In contrast to what happened elsewhere in Italy, in Venice painting continued to evolve, drawing strength from an independent tradition and fostered by an affluent middle class. Sebastiano Ricci, Giovanni Battista Tiepolo and the latter's son Domenico Tiepolo, played a leading part in this process. Ricci sought repeated stimulus from Bolognese art, and to expand his repertoire by visits to Florence and Rome. Modelling himself on Ricci, G. B. Tiepolo developed a style in which light was uniformly diffused over the canvas, with subtle but not flat colouring. His compositions have extraordinary spatial depth within which the figures move lightly and effortlessly. Tiepolo received numerous commissions from the Church, as well as many private ones. Before setting off with his sons for Würzburg in 1750, he decorated the Palazzo Labia with frescoes.

Pietro Longhi's pictures, some in very small format, depict popular life in Venice. His paintings are influenced by French art and executed in harmonious colours. In parallel with such portrayals of festive and day-to-day life, a new genre made its appearance: the vedute of Calevaris, Francesco Guardi and Canaletto. Canaletto at first painted his ruins and urban views in starkly contrasting colours, before later changing his style to one of uniform brightness. In the end his topographies, often committed to canvas in the greatest detail, became bland and rigidly formulaic.

Architecture

Baldassare Longhena is considered the leading architect of the Baroque in Venice, and designed the most important Baroque church in the city, Santa Maria della Salute. For this prominent site he devised a centrally planned building with a dome and lantern, ambulatory and side chapels. Forceful architectural decoration and rich sculptural ornament contribute to the effect of the exterior.

The architects of the 18th c. endeavoured to reach back to the tradition of past centuries, to the methods of Sansovino or Palladio. Large-scale, light-filled architecture came into being. With the Palazzo Grassi-Stucky (1749) Giorgio Massari created a simple, sober building with a Classical façade and impressive staircase. For the Chiesa dei Gesuati (1726–43) he chose a façade of extraordinary sculptural effect, incorporating columns, pediments, entablatures and niche figures. A similar Classical colonnaded façade was designed by Andrea Tirali for the church of San Niccolì da Tolentino.

19th and 20th centuries

Lacking space to expand, in the 19th and 20th c. Venice remained largely untouched by the new wave of residential building which transformed other cities and towns. Only a few individual buildings were constructed and the existing architectural fabric was rarely altered.

Conspicuous on La Giudecca is the large, and for Venice untypical, Mulino Stucky. Wishing to build a mill and pasta factory, Giovanni Stucky contracted the architect Ernst Wullekopf to draw up the plans. Work on the building started in 1896. The huge, brick-built, Neo-Gothic "castle" reflects the architect's North German roots.

The pavilions on the Biennale exhibition grounds were constructed at the end of the 19th and in the 20th c. They cover a wide spectrum of architectural development, but since the purpose of the pavilions was to represent the exhibiting countries, the famous architects who designed them drew little on Venetian architecture as such.

Having practised as an architect in Venice since 1927, mainly specialising in interior design, in 1952 Carlo Scarpa was entrusted with the restoration of the Accademia, quickly followed by the Museo Correr (1953–60) and the Galleria Querini Stampalla (1961–63) with the wooden bridge in front. Scarpa's sense of scale and sumptuous decoration can also be appreciated in the Olivetti sales room (1957/58) on the north side of St Mark's Square. By its sensitive use of space around a central pillar and employment of contrasting materials and colour, his scheme cleverly combines old and new.

Early printing

In the 15th c. Venice was an extremely important centre for printing. The first printing press employing the Gutenberg process, i.e. printing with movable type, was set up in Venice in 1469 by the German Johannes de Spira (von Speyer). Quick to seize the moment, Spira purchased a privilege guaranteeing him the sole right to practice the art of printing in the city for a period of five years. Only a year later however, in 1470, Spira died and his privilege expired. This was a great stroke of fortune for his many rivals, who immediately opened print workshops of their own and went into brisk production. As a result printing in Venice evolved quickly from an art into a very important branch of the economy. This surge of activity was helped by the possibility of protecting individual works by copyright and of obtaining privileges from the Collegio or Senate. A blanket privilege such as was granted to Spira was no longer practicable on economic grounds. In these new circumstances, privileges were restricted to the printing and sale of specific titles. Obtaining a privilege secured a patent on any new technique and protected the Venetian printer, publisher or author from unwelcome foreign competition. When a printer, author or dealer was granted a privilege for a particular title, it was printed in full in the book in question, beginning with the words "cum privilegio". As demand for privileges continued to grow, a law was introduced in 1517 regulating book production.

In addition to the many local printers, numerous German printers settled in the city. Wendelin de Spira carried on his brother's business; Johannes von Kíln became very successful as a publisher of legal papers in particular; and Erhard Ratdolt and colleagues produced volumes which excelled on account of their careful layout, beautiful type and illustrations.

The best known Venetian printer at the turn of 16th c. was Aldus Manutius, who ran a flourishing print works in the Campo San Luca (commemorative plaque by the side entrance to the Savings Bank). His home was the Late Gothic palace called the Casa di Aldo Manuzio (Rio Terà Secondo, San Polo 2311). In 1495 Manutius acquired a privilege giving him a monopoly on works in Greek, for which there was a huge demand not only in Venice. He also organised a debating society at whose meetings to discuss Humanist topics Greek was spoken, and he was the publisher of Francesco Colonna's novel "Hypnerotomachia Polphili" (1499), which has exceptional woodcut illustrations.

Another important printing shop was run by Lucantonio Giunta, who evidently put economic interests before scholarly ones. He concentrated on printing liturgical works in Venice while co-operating closely with his brother who had a workshop in Florence specialising in Humanist literature. Between them, and helped by their wide circle of contacts at home and abroad, the Giuntas were guaranteed a market for their publications which brought them great wealth.

As is clear from what has gone before, the output of Venetian printers covered a wide range of topics: in addition to religious works of one sort or another, there were editions of the classics in different languages, also Humanist literature, scientific textbooks, dictionaries and, after 1501, music printing.

An important source of material for the printers was the extremely comprehensive collection of manuscripts on profound subjects bequeathed to the city by Cardinal Bessarion. The Manutius press was particularly indebted to this rich treasury of books for its publications in Greek. Some of the editions had illustrations and woodcuts. Though frequently signed with the letters ia, b, N or F, it is impossible today to ascribe these with certainty to any particular artist. The woodcuts are very simple, usually just outlines, with no attempt at shading to add detail such as depth, shadows or clothing. In rare cases the illustrations were coloured after printing. Venice maintained its prominent position in the world of printing, and also the quality of its output, until the end of the 16th c.

Death in Venice – The Lagoon City in film

Yes, it has already been made! ... that film in which the city on the lagoon is simply the romantic, laughter-filled or exotic backdrop for a pleasant holiday, for falling in love, for a honeymoon, for beautiful costumes and a carnival, for murder and skulduggery of one kind or another, for spies, or for the start of some marvellous adventure – Marco Polo's perhaps. In David Lean's "Summertime" (1955) for instance, Katherine Hepburn plays a no longer quite so young American spinster who goes to Venice on holiday and blossoms there, mainly through meeting Rossano Brazzi who plays the dashing Italian impeccably. In "Venetian Affair" (1967) Elke Sommer acts her way through a spy story, unravelling the mystery of an assassination during a peace conference in Venice. And in "The Venetian Woman" (1986) Sean

Festival of the Masks

It is Sunday, ten days before the beginning of Lent. A dense crowd on St Mark's Square gazes up at the large model of a dove which, in accordance with tradition, is conveyed from the bell-tower to the upper arcades of the Doges' Palace. At noon precisely multi-coloured balloons float up into the sky, confetti rains down from the body of the dove onto the waiting crowd – Venice's Carnival is officially opened. On the city's squares stages and platforms are erected for the giving of concerts and the awarding of prizes for the most imaginative fancy-dress, the international art scene in all its brilliance adorns the theatres and palaces, and magnificent performances staged on the Piazzetta di San Marco bring Venice's past back to life. Thousands of visitors from all over the world throng the 'campi' and 'piazze' to form one vast backcloth to the carnival. Lively and boisterous sounds fill the streets and canals into the early hours, until a giant firework display on Shrove Tuesday finally marks the end of the merry-making.

The first documentary record of the Venetian Carnival is dated 1094 and found in the Chronicle of Vitale Fallero. As with many other civilisations, the original pagan reason for the ceremony was to celebrate the arrival of spring after a long winter and to pray to the gods for the return of sunshine and fruitfulness and for good fortune during the coming year. The name "carnival" (from the Latin "carne vale", "three cheers for the meat") came in with the arrival of Christianity and originally referred to the last meal before fasting began in Lent, but soon stood for all carnival celebrations prior to Ash Wednesday.

In early medieval times these periods of frolicking festivity were the only times when the strict class system was lifted and people could act in an uninhibited and disrespectful way towards the establishment without fear of punishment. Rich and poor all joined as one in the crazy fun and games.

As might be expected, the Venetians reserved their most important performances for St Mark's Square before the doge, high-ranking officials and state visitors from abroad. Bulls were chased through the streets, oxen and pigs slaughtered, there were sword-fights and acrobatic displays; music was played and historical scenes enacted in honour of the Republic, and gambling – normally forbidden – was permitted. The processions on the water with elaborately decorated gondolas were particularly sumptuous. Sixteenth and seventeenth century sources describe the "flight of angels", in which a man dressed as an angel would be pulled up from a float in the harbour to the loft of the campanile, from whence he climbed to the very top of the tower where he would perform some tricks and then walk a tightrope across the Piazzetta di San Marco to the stage in front of the Doge's Palace – a daredevil act which claimed many victims. "Here anything goes!" wrote an eighteenth century traveller about the Venetian Carnival. "If women want to become men and men women, that doesn't bother anybody, and one can dress after the fashion of primeval foreign peoples, even the most remote, unusual and mysterious of them. Absolute freedom to do what you like is the order of the day!"

In 1797, when the last doge, Lodovico Manin, retired and the French entered Venice four days later, Napoleon put an end to the "disreputable carnival". Nearly two hundred years to pass before the legendary "Festival of the Masks" was revived by resourceful promoters and it was again officially celebrated from 1979 onwards. Venice soon developed once again into a carnival stronghold, providing the city with new spheres of interest and activity. The Commedia dell'Arte, for example, gained a new lease of life, costumiers and mask-makers, who had been on the verge of extinction, enjoyed a veritable renaissance of their skills – and today masks made of papier-maché, pottery or leather number among the city's best-known symbols.

Many costumes developed from traditions dating back to Roman times, while an early reference to the wearing of masks in Venice is found in a law dated 1268 under which people wearing masks are prohibited from pelting passers-by with eggs. Two 14th century laws made it illegal to wear masks in the streets of Venice at night, and a decree of 1458 prohibited men from "dressing up as women in order to obtain entry to nunneries and there engaging in dishonourable acts". At the carnival of 1730 a traveller commented "During the whole of the night and until daybreak the masked people indulged in the eternal dream of mankind, they pine for another life and represent the age-old call for fulfilled love and a solitary death". Even if the desire to remain unknown, to live out one's dreams and conceal one's passions is an age-old need, the wearing of masks in Venice emanated mainly from contact with the Orient and Moslem dress and fancy-dress.

Actually the wearing of masks was allowed only during carnival time, but the famous "bautta" were also allowed at special ceremonies, so that it was legal to don masks for almost half the year. One of the first series of pictures of Venetian masks was compiled by the Venetian engraver Francesco Bertelli in 1642. His drawings contained both mystically symbolic work including crude, rustic masks as well as the sensitive work of the commedia dell'arte which mirrors the busy Venetian world of the theatre.

The most common mask was the aforementioned "bautta", a black hood of satin or silk which left the face free, together with a tricorn hat and a long black cloak (tabarro) which was usually decorated with lace. The actual mask was white or black and concealed the upper half of the face; if one wished to remain completely incognito one also wore a lace kerchief on the lower edge of the mask covering the mouth and chin. The bautta was worn by men and women of all classes of society, thus erasing social differences. Originally from Spain was the "domino", a broad cape similar to a monk's robe, which completely covered the wearer. The "moretta", a small, oval satin mask, was worn only by women. Great popularity was enjoyed by the "matticini", colourful jester's costumes with large feather hats. The "medico della peste" came into being as a result of the plague epidemics which frequently affected Venice. The large wrap and a floppy hat pulled well down left only the eyes visible, the long pointed mask completely covered with gauze was supposed to filter the contaminated air, while patients could be examined at a safe distance with the aid of the long stick. Further colour was added to the carnival scene by the figures of the commedia della'arte, the most famous among these being the "arlecchino", a clown known for his pranks and tomfoolery, who was dressed in a brightly-coloured harlequin costume. Arlecchino and his imaginative servant Brighella appear as the two "zanni". The female counterpart is called Columbina, a quick-witted maid with a sound understanding of people, while Pulcinella, from the Neapolitan hinterland, is the show-off. Typically Venetian is the goateed Pantalone, symbolising the sly merchant, in his red knee breeches, red waistcoat and black coat and his precious money purse on his belt. The "dottore", a parody of intellectual vanity, is a learned lawyer dressed in black and with a large, bulbous nose. The "capitano", in his brightly-striped uniform, sword and broad-brimmed hat plays a special role as the symbol of revolt against foreign rule and the personification of the freedom at carnival time to do and say anything one wants.

"This beautiful festival is a coming together of the most boisterous joy and the sweetest melancholy" noted a visitor in 1721. Even if today quite a number of Venetians take refuge away from the city before the carnival starts, there are still many who join in the fun, while others wear expensive gowns to private functions as the professionally-organised masked spectacular so beloved of the media unfolds on St Mark's Square and the smaller squares such as Manin, Santo Stefano or Santa Margherita, and around the Rialto Bridge. Every year a new slogan is devised for the ten-day spectacular which presents both historical costumes and new and imaginative forms of dress. In spite of all the criticism the carnival remains a highlight and a kingpin of Venetian life which is best experienced by actually taking part unrestrained by old inhibitions and by being somebody else if only for a few moments.

Scene from Visconti's magnificent "Death in Venice" (1970), with Silvana Mangano and Bjorn Andresen, after Thomas Mann's novel

Connery Jr experiences the delights of love in an exquisite 16th c. setting, with Laura Antonelli among others.

But these are not the best films about Venice, the ones that really stick in the mind. For that the city has to be more than just a backdrop, it has to be one of the characters, luring people to itself then leading them astray; and not just in a geographical sense either. Something of this "cité fatale" colours Joseph L. Mankiewicz's thriller "The Honey Pot" (1967), a black comedy in which Rex Harrison awaits visits from three former lovers, ostensibly a rich man whose days are numbered, but in reality intent on murder.

That behind the crumbling walls of the city true abysses lurk, that sinking, dying Venice can exert a strange effect on its visitors and its inhabitants, that this labyrinthine topography can give rise to obsession, all this is made much clearer in a film like Luchino Visconti's "Senso" (1954). Taking place during the Italian wars of liberation, Alida Valli's Italian countess becomes completely enslaved, against her political conviction, by Lieutenant Mahler (Farley Granger), an officer in the Austrian army of occupation. Trying to escape him, she wanders at night through the empty alleyways, along the canal sides and over bridges, until, on a square, he catches up with her: and the city takes her in its grasp too. Her obsessive love, which Mahler coldly exploits, eventually leads her into treason.

Visconti, of course, also produced "Death in Venice" (1970), that superlative and stylistically influential film of Thomas Mann's novella, in which the city again plays a leading part. In it an artist called Aschenbach – in the Visconti film a composer, strongly reminiscent of Gustav Mahler whose music Visconti has playing over the action – comes to Venice to convalesce. But this Venice, threatened by cholera, is the wrong place to have come. Aschenbach becomes obsessed by a beautiful young boy, finds his eyes riveted by him; and more and more, in magnificent images, the film exudes an elegiac atmosphere of decay, culminating in a final scene in which the dying Aschenbach lies in a deck chair on the beach, make-up streaming down his face.

Obsession, imbroglio, and finally death are also the themes – so suited to films about Venice – of Nicolas Roeg's morbid, sometimes manneristic, but always gripping thriller "Don't Look Now" (1973). Once again the protagonists enticed to this culture-rich city are cultivated people, a young English couple who, when their child is killed in an accident, come to Venice to work and try to forget. But the city becomes a terrible reminder for the husband (Donald Sutherland) in particular. Again and again he sees something in a red coat flitting through the alleyways, and thinks he recognises his child who was wearing a red coat at the time. Finally this vision – for unknown to him he has second sight – leads him to his death, the black gondolas he once saw being those carrying him to his last resting place.

In a more recent but similarly "authentic" film about Venice, a man lies in wait in his palazzo; lies in wait, that is, for guests, as does the decadent, sinister, impenetrable city itself the film seems to say. In "The Comfort of Strangers" (1991), Paul Schrader's thriller based on a novel by Ian McEwan, a young couple travel to Venice in an attempt to revive their faltering love in the place where it began. These two also go astray, lose their way and end up in the arms of this man (played by Christopher Walken) who extends an invitation to them, then involves them in a game; which we know, in this city, can only lead into the abyss. Yet another film, then, which plays on the morbid atmosphere of the city on the lagoon, and ends with death in Venice.

Quotations

Constitution of the Republic	The State is all; it is for the individual unconditionally to serve the State. No one person may rise above the others, no cult of personality will be tolerated.
Cassiodorus (c. 490–580)	The territory of Venetia is bordered in the South by the eminence of Ravenna and by the Po, in the East by the smiling cities of the Ionian coast. Here the tides suddenly retreat to reveal the changing face of the flooded land then flow back to cover it again. Your dwellings are built, like seabirds' nests, half on sea and half on land, spread, as the Cyclades, over the surface of the waters. Through manmade earthworks you know how to bind your dwellings together. You heap up the sand to break the force of the raging waters and your walls, seemingly fragile, brave the force of the flood.
Marino da Canala 1267	Goods circulate around this splendid city like the streams of water that spring from the fountain.
Francesco Petrarca (1304–74)	Venice is a city rich in gold, but richer still in beauty, mighty in its possessions, but mightier by its virtue; which is founded on solid marble but is yet more secure upon the foundations of the unswerving unity of its population, and which, better than by the sea, is protected and safeguarded by the sagacity and the wisdom of its offspring. Letters, 1364
Philippe de Commynes Ambassador, 1495	It is the finest highway to be found in the whole world, lined by the finest houses, and it passes through the whole of the city. The houses are very lofty and grand and of good stone and the older ones are painted over all, and they have stood there a hundred years. The others that have been built in the last century have façades of white marble that comes from Istria and of porphyry. Inside they all have no less than two chambers with gilded panels, rich chimneypieces of hewn marble and beds with gilded posts and the other chambers are also gilded and painted and furnished very well within. It is the most triumphant street I have ever seen, it is the most joyous city I ever saw.
Albrecht Dürer (1471–1528)	Giambellini, he that had already praised me to diverse gentlemen, he was most desirous to have something of me and is himself come to me and begged me that I should make something for him, vouchsafing that he would make payment for it. On the subject of the painter Bellini following Dürer's stay in Venice
Count Avaux 17th c. ambassador	It seems to me less difficult to have established this city on the face of the bottomless waters than to have united and led so many spirits in the same direction and despite the differing inclinations by which they are moved as individuals to have maintained the corporate body of this Republic, its power intact and unshaken.
Carlo Goldoni 18th c. Venetian	They sing in the squares, on the streets and on the canals. The vendors sing as they cry their wares, the workers sing as they leave their workplaces, the gondoliers sing as they wait for custom.
Emperor Napoleon (1769–1821)	The most beautiful drawing room in Europe, for which it is only fitting that the heavens should serve as a ceiling. (On St Mark's Square)

It was written, then, on my page in the Book of Fate that at five in the afternoon of the twenty-eighth day of September in the year 1786, I should see Venice for the first time as I entered this beautiful island city, this beaver republic ... I have found comfortable lodgings ... not far from the Piazza San Marco. My windows look out on to a narrow canal between high houses; immediately below them is a single-span bridge, and opposite, a narrow crowded passage. This is where I shall live until my parcel for Germany is ready and I have had my fill of sightseeing, which may be some time.
"Italian Journey", 1816

Johann Wolfgang von Goethe (1749–1832)

Underneath Day's azure eyes
Ocean's nursling, Venice lies,
A peopled labyrinth of walls.

Percy Bysshe Shelley (1792–1822)

Once did she hold the gorgeous East in fee,
And was the safeguard of the West: the worth
Of Venice did not fall below her birth,
Venice, the eldest child of liberty.
She was a maiden city, bright and free;
No guile seduced, no force could violate;
And when she took unto herself a mate,
She must espouse the everlasting sea.
And what if she had seen those glories fade,
Those titles vanish, and that strength decay,
Yet shall some tribute of regret be paid
When her long life hath reached its final day:
Men are we, and must grieve when even the shade
Of that which once was great has passed away.

William Wordsworth (1770–1850)

He saw it once more, that most astounding of landing places, that breathtaking composition of fantastic buildings, which the Republic ranged to meet the awed gaze of the approaching seafarer; the airy splendour of the palace and the Bridge of Sighs, the columns of lion and saint on the shore, the glory of the projecting flank of the Basilica of St Mark, the vista of gateway and great clock. Looking, he thought that to come to Venice by the station is like entering a palace by the back door. No one should approach, save by the high seas as he was doing now, this most improbable of cities.
"Death in Venice", 1913

Thomas Mann (1875–1955)

Venice is not only a special city, unlike any other in Italy, but it is also a special region, differing from any other region of Italy, with its own soil, its own sky, its own climate and its own air.

Hippolyte Taine (1828–93)

As I was returning home late one night on the gloomy canal, the moon appeared suddenly and illuminated the marvellous palaces and the tall figure of my gondolier towering above the stern of the gondola, slowly moving his huge sweep. At that moment he uttered a cry like a wild creature, a kind of deep groan that rose in crescendo to a prolonged 'Oh!' and ended with the simple exclamation 'Venezia!' This was followed by other sounds of which I have no distinct recollection, so much moved was I at the time. Such were the impressions that to me appeared the most characteristic of Venice during my stay there, and they remained with me until the completion of the second act of "Tristan", and possibly even suggested to me the prolonged tones of the shepherd's horn at the beginning of the third act.
"Mein Leben", 1911

Richard Wagner (1813–83)

**Sights
from A to Z**

Sightseeing

These suggestions for sightseeing are intended to help those visiting Venice for the first time to make the most of a short stay. Places which appear under a main heading in the A to Z section of this guide are printed in 'bold' type.

Brief visits

For visitors spending only a few hours in Venice who nevertheless want to see the major sights, there is no substitute for a boat trip on the delightful **Grand Canal**. At its southern end lies the spacious **St Marks Square**, fascinating heart of the city, surrounded by majestic buildings: the Procuratie Vecchie and Nuove, the *Campanile* with its panoramic view, the magnificent basilica of **St Marks**, always thronged with visitors, and the huge **Doges Palace**, from which for centuries Venice was ruled. Afterwards there will be a chance to sample the delights, gastronomic and musical, at Quadris, Florians or Lavenas, not so much coffee houses as historic institutions located around the square. And if there is still some time left, it can be spent wandering through the **Mercerie**, Venices shopping mecca between St Marks Square, the Accademia and the *Ponte di Rialto*.

Walks

Grand Canal

Every visit to Venice should include a boat trip on the **Grand Canal**: see town plan pages 54–57, description pages 71–89.

Walk 1
See plan on
pages 54–55

This first walk, round the SAN MARCO district, starts on the ever busy **St Marks Square**, with the monumental **St Marks Basilica**, the majestic **Doges Palace**, the *Campanile* and the two *Procuratie*. Also in buildings around the square are the *Museo Correr*, the *Museo Archeologico* and the *Libreria Vecchia*, the latter containing the Biblioteca Marciana. Leaving the square, proceed westwards through elegant shopping streets such as the Via XXII Marzo, to the Campo San Maurizio, where an antiques market is held in summer. Beyond it is the Campo *Santo Stefano*, surrounded by handsome patrician houses. Here a detour can be made southwards to the **Galleria dell'Accademia** with its important and comprehensive collection of Venetian art from the Gothic to the Renaissance. Returning to the Campo Santo Stefano, now head north via the pretty *Campo Sant'Angelo* to the *Palazzo Pesaro degli Orfei*, housing a museum devoted to the Spanish dress and textile designer Mario Fortuny, he of the accordian pleats and sensuous colours. On the Campo Manin, a short distance east, there is a memorial to the patriot and lawyer Daniele Manin. The inner courtyard of the nearby *Palazzo Contarini del Bovolo* is graced by an enchanting spiral staircase dating from about 1500. Continuing in a northerly direction, go up the busy Calle dei Fabbri to the **Grand Canal** and pretty *Ponte di Rialto*. Until the 19th c., this was the only bridge across the canal. The route back is along the magical **Mercerie**, a shoppers and window shoppers

◀ *Historical gondola regatta on the Canal Grande*

dream, with everything from carnival masks and costumes in all shapes
and sizes to the finest Burano lace and elaborate Murano glass. Finally,
how better to end the walk than by relaxing in a café on ★★ **St Marks
Square**, enjoying a cappuccino, listening to the romantic strains emanating from nearby private chapels, and luxuriating in Venices incom-
parable atmosphere. And later, what better end to the day than a meal
in the pleasing surroundings of one of the many gourmet restaurants
around the square.

The second walk is through the SAN POLO and SANTA CROCE districts, starting at the ★ **Ponte di Rialto**, a footbridge about halfway along
the ★★ **Grand Canal** between the **Fondaco dei Tedeschi** and the handsome ★ **Palazzo dei Camerlenghi**. One of the nicest experiences Venice
has to offer is a visit to the ★ **Rialto market** (every morning except
Sundays) with its variety of fish, fruit and vegetable and souvenir stalls.
Next stop is the ★ Palazzo **Corner della Regina**, a large Baroque building housing the municipal pawnshop, and then on to the imposing
★ **Ca' Pesaro** with the ★ **Galleria d'Arte Moderna** (ground floor) and
★ **Museo d'Arte Orientale** (third floor). Only a few steps further on in
the ★ **Palazzo Mocenigo** there is a fine collection of textiles and cos-
tumes. Anyone interested in the maritime history of Venice and in
seeing the proud, splendid galleys of the doges, should leave time for
a detour to the Museo Storico Navale in the ★ **Fondaco dei Turchi**.
Afterwards turn south along the narrow canals to the spacious Campo
and Church of **San Polo**. The Late Gothic church boasts a "Last
Supper" by Tintoretto. Equally compelling for art lovers is a visit to
★★ **Santa Maria Gloriosa dei Frari** which has masterpieces by Titian,
Bellini and Donatello, and to the neighbouring ★★ **Scuola Grande di
San Rocco**, famous for the sensitive cycles of paintings by Tintoretto in
the great hall. On the way back to the ★ **Ponte di Rialto**, call in at the
★ **Casa Goldoni** where there is a collection documenting the life and
work of the celebrated comic playwright. A ★★ gondola ride through
the narrow side canals will make a captivating, romantic finale to the
walk. But no less charming is a quiet stroll through the little twisting
alleyways, over countless bridges and delightful squares. Here, far
removed from the main bustle of the city, Venice casts its particular
spell.

Walk 2
See plan on
pages 56–57

Suggestions for a longer stay

Anyone staying in Venice for more than a couple of days should include
some longish museum visits in their itinerary, priority being given to the
★★ **Ca' d'Oro**, which houses the Galleria Franchetto, the ★★ **Ca'
Rezzonico**, with the Museo del Settecento Veneziano, and the
★★ **Collezione Peggy Guggenheim**. Another "must" is a boat trip to
★★ **Burano**, celebrated for its superlative embroidered lace, to
★★ **Murano**, the island where the glass is made, and to ★ **Torcello**, where
the colonnaded basilica contains lovely Venetian-Byzantine mosaics.
The history of the Venetian Jewish community unfolds on a tour of the
Cannaregio ★★ **Ghetto**, where five synagogues testify to the rich tra-
dition of Jewish culture in the area. Also well worth seeing are the
Franciscan church on ★ **La Giudecca**, and the island of ★ **San Giorgio
Maggiore** where the campanile of the church of that name affords a
splendid panoramic view of the city and lagoon. Finally, an excursion
could be made to the lively little town of ★ **Chioggia** at the southern end
of the lagoon. Another possibility, especially tempting after hours spent
in the galleries, might be some sunbathing on the large ★ sandy beaches
of the **Lido**, where every year at the beginning of August the Palazzo del
Cinema is the venue for the "Golden Lion" awards (for actors and films)
at Venices international film festival.

Venedig · Venezia
Sestiere di San Marco

— Route 1

150 m

© Baedeker

Campo di San Polo

Calle d. Cavalli

C. Bianca

Campo S. Aponal

SAN POLO

Cam di S Silves

Corte Barzizza

Pal. Barzi

Pal. Papadopoli Coccina

Pal. Businello

S. Si

Pal. Giustinian Grimani

Pal. Bernardo

Palazzi Donà

Canal Grande

*Pal. Grimani

Pal. Pisani Moretta

Pal. Tron

Pal. Corner Contarini d. Cav.

S.

C. d. Scale

Fondaco dei Turchi

Campo San Tomà

**Pal.

*Pal. Corner Spinelli

S. Angelo

Campo S. Benedetto

S. Andr

Pal. Balbi

S. Tomà

Pal. Corner Gheltoff

*Pal. Pesaro d. O.

Palazzi Mocenigo

Pal. Contarini d. Figure

*Ca' Foscari

Calle Mocenigo

Calle Lezze

Salizada S. Samuele

Cpl. Nuovo

Campo

S. Angelo

Pal. Giustinian

Ca' Lin C.

*Pal. Grassi

Calle Crosera

S. Samuele

**Ca' Rezzonico

S. Samuele

Campo San Samuele

Pal. Malipiero

Santo Stefano

Pal. Stern

Ca' Rezzonico

Corte d. Vida

Campo Santo Stefano

Teatro Fenice

San Maurizio

Cpl. d. Caleghert

dietro la Fenice

Pal. Loredan

Pal. Loredan d. A.

*Ca' d. Duca

Pal. Morosini

Campo S. Maurizio

Santa Maria d. Giglio

Pal. Falier

San Vidal

Campo S. Vidal

Pal. Bellavite

Campo S. Maria Zobenigo

Pal. Contarini Scrigni

Pal. Giustinian Lolin

Pal. Pisani

Pal. Corner (Ca' Grande)

P Pi G

Pal. Mocenigo Gambara

Accademia

Pal. Cavalli Franchetti

Pal. Barbaro

Ponte dell' Accademia

Casina d. Rose

S. M. d G

**Gallerie dell' Accademia

Pal. Contarini d. Zaffo

Pal. Barbarigo

Canal Grande

**Collezione Guggenheim

*Pal. Barbaro

Pal. Dario

C. Maggiore

DORSODURO

LA GIU

54

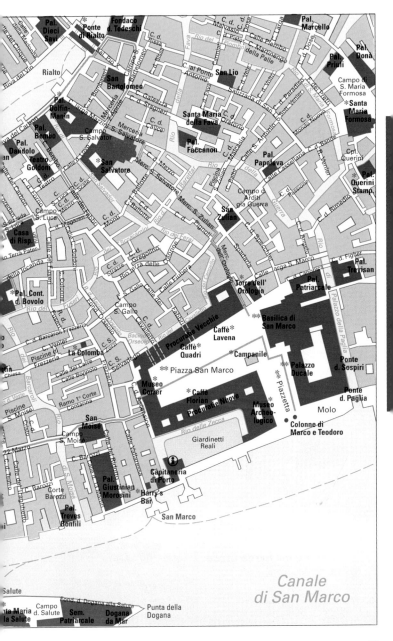

CANNAREGIO

Campo
Santa Geremia

Pal.
Labia

Cpl. d.
Remer

Pal.
Correr

Co
Mo

Contarini

Santa
Geremia

Pal.
Flangini

R. d. Biasio

Grande

Priuli- delle dei Cavalletti

Calle della Misericordia

Calle Ghibellina

Cpl.
Flangini

Calle L. Spiritel

Rio Terra lista di Spagna

Fond.
Croce

Fond. Terra dei
Sabbioni

** Canal

di

Biasio

Pal.
Marcello

Riva
di

Calle Bemba

Campo
S. Giova

decolla

Calle dei Pistor

S. Campo Agnesina
Calle dei Prensi

Cpl.
Zen

Campo
Riello

SANTA

Calle Corte
della Cazza 2a

Cpl.
dell'Isola

Chiesa
degli Scalzi

Fond. dei Scalzi

Ponte
Scalzi

Sottop. Fond. Pistor

S. Campo
Simeone
Profeta

Isla dei Bari

Galileon

Calle dei Savie

Stazione
Santa Lucia

Rio Marin

San Simeone
Profeta

Campo
S. Simeone
Profeta

Calle Lunga

Calle Orseti

C. di
Ruga Vecchia

Cpl. de
Chiesa di
dall'Oro

Ferrovia

Fondamenta di San Simeon

Piccolo

Campiello

Calle Nuova di

Piccolo del Comare

Calle Tintoretto

San Simeone

C. della
Fornace

Pal.
Gradenigo

Fondamenta Rio Marin

C. dei
Croce

Campo S.
Nazario Sauro

Ruga Bella

Corte
dell'
Anatomia

Campo di
S. Giacomo
dall'Orio

San
Simeone
Piccolo

Calle delle Lanca

Calle dei Bergamaschi

Calle della Chiovanetta

Pal.
Chiovarette

Pal.
Sorenzo-
Cappello

Calle Gradisca

Zentarol

Cpl. d.
Strope

Rio di S. Giacomo dell'Orio

Calle della

Corte Canal

Calle Visciga

Fondamenta dei Tolentini

Scontra a conte di Case Nuove

Campo della Lana

Calle larga
Salicineo

Rio di S. Giovanni Evangelista

Calle Maz.

Calle d. Lacca

Stp. d. Lacca

Calle dietro
l'Archivio

*Scuola di
S. Giovanni
Evangelista

Cpl. de
Forner

Calle Zane

Cpl. San
Giovanni

Calle della Vida

SAN

Rio d. Tolentini

Calle dei Croce

Corte Amai

Sottop.
e Corte Amai

Calle dei Cafeti

C. d. Fonderia

Calle delle Chiovere

San G.
Evangelista

Campo
San Stin

Rio Terra San Toma

Fdm.
Contarini

Rio di San

*San Nicolò
d. Tolentini

San Nicolò
da Tolentino

Archivio
di Stato

Calle di Galfaro

*San
Rocco

** I Frari

Campo
dei Frari

Campo
San Rocco

** Scuola Grande
di San Rocca

Salizzada
S. Rocco

Sottoportico S. Rocco

Rio della

Calle Campoli

C. d.
Scale

Campo
San Toma

Venedig · Venezia
Sestiere di
San Polo e Santa Croce

—— Route 2

150 m

© Baedeker

Calle Pratataman

Calle del Pistor d. Pister Coseral

Fond. dei Forner

P
Marce
d. Leo

56

Sights from A to Z

Location
Rio del Arsenale

Quay
Arsenale

From the very beginning Venice's power has been based on the skills of its seafarers and shipbuilders. The Arsenale – the Venetian word which gave the English language "arsenal" – was the city's shipyard, and until the late 18th c. was one of the largest and most productive shipyards in the world. Founded in 1104, it was continuously expanded and in its heyday employed as many as 16,000 workers. These "Arsenalotti" were highly respected and enjoyed such privileges as a pension and free housing. They also provided the guard of honour for the Doges' Palace during his election, and manned the "Bucintoro", the Doges' magnificent gilded barge, the famous symbol of the "Serenissima". Early in the 14th c. the area of the Arsenale was quadrupled by adding the "Arsenale Nove" and in 1473 the Senate decided to extend it by the "Arsenale Novissima" which was to last into the 16th c., building light galleys for the navy and large galleys for the mercantile fleet. The Arsenal was a prohibited area and accessible only by one land and one sea approach. Every worker was privy to its secrets and therefore subject to security checks. Up until the late 16th c. the galleys were the core of the Venetian navy in the Mediterranean; English-type galleons were developed in the 17th c., then in 1724 Venice began delivering the first frigates. About half the vessels from the victorious Christian fleet at the Battle of Lepanto in 1571, including the much-feared "galeazze", the first galleys with port and starboard cannon, came from these Venetian shipyards, as commemorated in the inscription about the lion of St Mark.

Nowadays the Arsenal is the property of the Italian navy and as such is closed to the public, although vaporetti (5/52) regularly pass through the old Arsenal basin. This is where, when the great sheds of the Remiera Francescana are open, the ceremonial barges which emerge on the first Sunday in September every year to take part in the "Regata Storica" can be seen.

Showpieces of the yearly 'Regata Storica'

Ingresso di Terra The landside entrance to the Arsenale is a triumphal arch in the Renaissance style. The white lions on each side of the arch are from ancient Greece, booty brought back by Francesco Morosoni in the 17th c. after the reconquest of the Peloponnese. The crouching lion originally stood guard over the port of Piraeus, while its recumbent fellow is thought to have come from Delos and to have stood at one time on the sacred way from Athens to Eleusis.

★★Basilica di San Marco   K/L 5

The Basilica of St Mark, the church of the Doges and the Republic, dedicated to Venice's patron saint, owes its amazing architecture and magnificent decor to a fascinating blend of different building phases and influences. Initially in 1075 Doge Domenico Silvio sought to involve everyone in the city with the work on their church of St Mark by passing a law decreeing that every traveller returning to Venice must bring some precious object to embellish St Mark's. This accounts for the wealth of ornament and the many rich architectural features from the East – columns, reliefs, sculpture, beaten gold, etc. – in all kinds of rare and costly materials. The interior is covered with over 4000 sq. m of gold mosaics, mostly dating from the 12th and 13th c., but some are from designs between 1500 and 1750 by artists such as Titian, Tintoretto, Veronese and Tiepolo for mosaics to replace a few of the older sections.

History The first church was built to house the remains of St Mark, stolen from Alexandria and brought by two seafarers to Venice, with Mark thus completely supplanting Theodore as the city's patron saint. All that remains of the first two buildings are a few fragments in the

Location
Piazza
San Marco

Quays
San Marco,
San Zaccaria

Opening times:
Church: Mon.–Sat.
9.30am–4.30pm,
Sun. 2–4.30pm;
Galleries: daily
9am–4.30pm

San Marco, church of the Doges, with its extraordinary architecture, featuring decorations in porphyry, granite and marble in every possible shade

From the gallery you will not only have a stunning view on the Mark's Square, but you can also have a closer look at the decorative detail

crypt under the crossing. The present, third building dates from 1063 and was begun by Doge Domenico Contarini on the lines of the Church of the Apostles in Constantinople but deriving something from the Romanesque architecture of northern Italy. The ground plan consists of a Greek cross with two side-aisles.The main dome is over the crossing and there are another four huge domes, one over each arm of the cross, with colonnades linking the massive pillars that support the domes. The basilica was consecrated in the presence of the Emperor Henry IV in 1094, and elevated to the status of official state church. The supervision of its building and maintenance was entrusted to three Procurators (see Piazza di St Mark's, Procuratie). Following the conquest of Byzantium in 1204 alterations to the Contarini building included raising the domes, adding the northern porch and constructing the portico on the western façade. Many of the spoils of the Crusades and other forays were incorporated in the building or used as decoration. The plain brick was clad with marble and mosaics were added to the vaulting. The mosaic over the northern portal of the west façade, the Porta Sant'Alippio, the basilica as it appeared at that time in the 13th c.

The second building phase, which began in the 14th c. and lasted until the 16th century, saw such major changes to the exterior as the addition of Gothic decoration, tabernacles, and sculpture.

Exterior

★★ West façade

The main façade on the Piazza is divided into five great doorways, each lined with two rows of marble pillars, one above the other, and some with finely worked classic capitals. The larger central portal cuts into the balustrade of the gallery holding replicas of St Mark's's four famous bronze horses (see below, Gallery). The gallery backs onto five blind arches holding mosaics and topped by Gothic ornamentation and the Evangelists in gilded tabernacle towers. The early 15th c. angels ascending the central arch, the largest of the five, lead up to the towering figure of St Mark.

The mosaic over the central portal shows Christ at the Last Judgment (1836), while the 17th c. mosaics on the upper storey concentrate on Christ's Passion culminating in the Ascension.

The mosaics (17th and 18th c.) over the other four doorways tells the story of St Mark's remains, starting on the far right with them being smuggled out of Alexandria, their veneration and then their arrival in Venice. The mosaic over the left-hand entrance, the Porta Sant'Alippio, shows the saint's body being brought to Venice against the backdrop of St Mark's as it was in the 13th c.; this is the only depiction of the church that has been retained from the 13th c.

Carvings particularly worth noting on the west façade include the mid-13th c. outer frieze of the central arch depicting the Labours of the Month. The classical-style relief (ca. 1225/50) in the spandrels of the outer arcades recounts the story of Hercules.

Flagpoles Three huge cedar flagpoles in front of the west façade were erected here in 1376 and their rich bronze bases were cast by Alessandro Leopardi in 1505. The base of the middle flagpole has reliefs depicting Justice between an elephant (for Strength and Wisdom) and Pallas (symbol of Plenty). The southern flagpole base has sea-nymphs and tritons, and the northern one has Neptune being offered the fruits of the earth by a satyr – thus demonstrating Venice's mastery over both land and sea.

★**Gallery** It is well worth climbing up to the gallery (above the entrance to the Museo Marciano) not just for the superb view of St Mark's Square

On the parapet over the main portal stand replicas of the famous horses of St Mark's

and the Piazzetta but also because of the chance to get a closer view of the mosaics and carvings.

Nowadays the gallery holds replicas of the four famous horses of St Mark's (the originals can be seen inside the church in the Museo Marciano). This gilded bronze quadriga that originally crowned a Roman triumphal arch was taken to Constantinople in the 4th c. and placed in the hippodrome. It was brought to Venice as spoils of war in 1204 after the fall of Byzantium and set up on the gallery. In 1797 Napoleon carried the horses off to Paris but they were returned and reinstalled here in 1815.

South façade

The format of the south façade shows that it was intended to be an imposing ceremonial entrance facing the lagoon and, with its two-storey design crowned with Gothic tabernacles, represents a continuation of the west façade. Until the Zen Chapel was built the largest arcade had an entrance into the west porch. The portal layout has been retained in the interior and the St Mark mosaics testify to what must probably also have been at one time a wealth of carving. Adjoining the right-hand entrance leading into the antechamber of the Baptistery is the smooth marble-clad outer wall of the Tesoro. The second storey is laid out like the west façade but with more window openings and marble-inlaid tympani. Features worth noting include the two griffins on the first arch, that may well originally have been part of the portal, and the 13th c. Byzantine mosaic of the Virgin, before which two lamps are lit every evening.

Pilastri acritani The south front served as a backdrop for the display of the spoils of war, as was the case with the two marble pillars, the "Pilasters of Acre", draped with carved grapevines, and long thought to have been Venetian booty from the victory over the Genoese at the port of Acre. According to the latest research, however, they came from Constantinople and date from the early 6th c.

★**Tetrarchs** The wall in the south-west corner of the Tesoro holds the Tetrarchs, four porphyry male figures with their arms on one another's shoulders. This 4th c. group, probably from Egypt, was also a trophy and could possibly represent Diocletian, Maximilian, Valerian and Constantius who collectively ruled the Roman Empire. The local theory, though, is that they were four thieves who tried to rob the Treasury of St Mark's and were turned to stone.

North façade

The lower part of the north façade overlooking the Piazzetta dei Leoncini is made up of arcades while above the gallery there are lunettes, tabernacles and similar features to those on the other façades. There are two reliefs that are worth noting: the Byzantine representation of Alexander the Great whose chariot is being drawn aloft by two griffins, and the Etoimasia depicting the empty throne of God surrounded by 12 sheep, symbolising the 12 Apostles, and two palm-trees – probably a medieval work modelled on pre-Christian imagery.

The tympanon of the 13th c. Porta dei Fiori depicts the Nativity framed by foliage and angels in the archivolt; the arch of the porch is carved with busts of Mary and the Prophets on the inside and Christ and the Apostles on the outside.

★★**Narthex** The porches or vestibules of St Mark's, the narthex, date from different building periods. The western porch with the main entrance is from the Contarini building, while the northern portal was added in the 13th c. The oustanding feature of the narthex is the 13th c. ceiling mosaics. These are mainly of themes from the Old Testament, starting chronologically in the southern bay of the west porch with images from Genesis and continuing in the subsequent bays with stories of Noah, Abraham, Joseph and Moses. The account steadily unfolds in great detail, played out by small figures against a sweeping, mainly golden background, enriched by saints and angels. There are

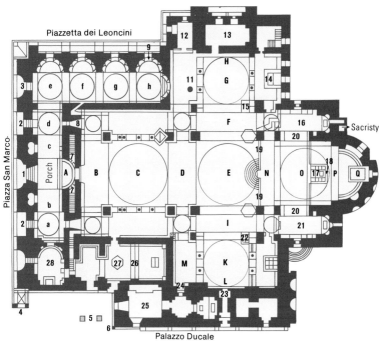

Basilica di San Marco

Piazzetta dei Leoncini

Piazza San Marco

Porch

Sacristy

Palazzo Ducale

25 m

© Baedeker

Basilica di San Marco

1. Main portal
2. Metal grille by the Venetian mastercraftsman Bertuccius (ca. 1300)
3. Porta di S. Alippio
4. Pietra del Bando
5. Pilastri Acritani
6. Sculpture of the Tetrarchs
7. Stairs up to the Museo Marciano
8. Porta di San Pietro
9. Porta dei Fiori
10. Altar of the Annunciation
11. Romanesque stoup with angels (12th c.)
12. Cappella della Madonna dei Mascoli
13. Cappella di Sant' Isidoro
14. Cappella della Madonna Nicopeia
15. Altare di San Paolo
16. Cappella di San Pietro

17. High Altar
18. Pala d'Oro
19. Iconostasis
20. Reliquary
21. Cappella di San Clemente
22. Altare di San Giacomo
23. Passage to the Doges' Palace
24. Entrance to the Treasury
25. Tesoro (Treasury), with goldsmiths' work, etc.
26. Battistero (Baptisery)
27. Font dating from 1546
28. Cappella Zen, named after Cardinal G.B. Zen (d. 1501)

MOSAICS

a. Depiction of Genesis
b. Story of Noah
c. Story of Noah and the Tower of Babel
d. Life of Abraham

e–g. Story of Joseph
h. Story of Moses

A. Arch of Paradise
B. Arch of the Apocalypse
C. Scenes of Pentecost
D. Scenes from the Passion
E. The Ascension
F. St Michael with sword
G. St John
H. Mary's family tree
I. The Washing of the Feet, Temptation in the Wilderness
K. St Leonard
L. Four Miracles of Jesus
M. Legend of St Mark
N. St Peter, the Resurrection etc.
O. Choir mosaics
P. Lamb of God
Q. Christ in Majesty

Rich mosaics create an overwhelming impression of space

discernible traces of Byzantine art but the joyously animated narrative, the sense of motion in the figures and their painstakingly lifelike representation speak of their being more closely related to western late-Romanesque art, of which there are important examples in illustrated manuscripts and paleological Byzantine art.

The marble mosaic pavement, like the rest of the porch, dates from the Contarini church in the west section and the 13th c. in the north section, while the themes and patterns are of eastern origin.

Some of the niches hold the tombs of 12th c. doges. Three portals lead from the narthex into the main body of the church. Porta San Clemente, in the south, is notable for its bronze doors from Byzantium, brought to Venice in the 11th c. These were copied in the 12th c. and those copies used for the middle portal.

Interior

★★Mosaics

The layout of the interior, with its nave and two aisles, is determined by the five domes, supported by huge pillars linked together by broad barrel vaulting. The grand spatial impact that all this makes is further enhanced by the sumptuous mosaics covering almost every surface, for St Mark's is like no other church in the western world when it comes to richness of mosaics. These date not from the first building phase but when the lower parts of the walls were inlaid with marble from the mid-12th c. and onwards into the 14th c., while others were still being added in the 16th, 17th and 18th c.

Despite the central orientation of the architecture, the narrative of the pictures runs lengthwise, with the main themes developing from the apse to the entrance and starting with Christ in Majesty in the east and finishing up with the Apocalypse in the west. Between these panels come the events of the Passion up until the Ascension. The walls of the transept recount the histories of the saints and of Jesus' parents.

The best view of the mosaics is from the galleries, especially the western gallery (entrance from the inner main portal); the view is even better with opera glasses or binoculars.

Choir dome The dome over the choir, the Emanuel dome, has Christ between the Virgin and the Prophets. The mosaic dates from the 12th c. but parts had to be renewed after the fire of 1231, as can be seen from the way the old sections of golden ground stand out from the new.

★Domes

Ascension dome In the mosaics from ca.1200 in the middle dome Christ ascends heavenward encircled by stars borne by angels, with the Virgin and angels at a lower level. The Apostles are ranged around the edge of the dome, separated by olive trees, while the four Evangelists appear in the pendentives.

Pentecost dome The mosaics in the Pentecost dome date from the late 12th c. and have the Holy Ghost in the centre radiating tongues of fire to the twelve Apostles enthroned around the edge, and clad in elaborately pleated flowing drapery.

St John's dome The scenes from the life of St John in the northern transept also date from the 12th c. and show stylistic similarities with the mosaics in the Pentecost dome.

St Leonard's dome The composition in the dome over the southern transept is the odd one out, depicting as it does four saints – Leonard, Clement, Blaise and Nicholas – who had altars dedicated to them in the church.

Legend of St Mark Because of St Mark's importance for Venice the mosaics of his legend, west of the St Leonard dome, are particularly prominent. These show the rediscovery of his bones which had been missing since the church fire of 976. The miracle of their reappearance only occurred after the Doge and the people of Venice had prayed long and hard, whereupon the relics emerged from the opposite wall.

The Zeno Chapel (entrance through the Baptistery) was originally an imposing portal representing the main entrance to the church from the south. Early in the 16th c. the south side was walled up and the space was converted into a chapel. This held the tomb of Cardinal Giambattista Zeno with his recumbent figure and six allegories of the Virtues. Unlike other Venetian tombs, which were usually mounted in walls, this one is free-standing.

Cappella Zeno

A feature worth noting is the "Madonna della scarpa" (the Madonna of the shoe), the early 16th c. bronze Virgin by Antonio Lombardo, seated between St Mark and John the Baptist. Legend has it that a poor man presented the Madonna with his left shoe which as a sign of divine gratitude then turned to gold.

The two 12th c. red marble lions acting as pillar supports were possibly part of the former portal.

The 14th c. mosaics in the Baptistery focus on its baptismal function, namely Christ sending the Apostles "forth into the world to baptise all nations", as well as showing Christ surrounded by angels and Christ on the Cross. The walls have scenes from the life of John the Baptist.

Battistero

The font, with a mid-16th c. basin thought to be by Jacopo Sansovino, also has reliefs of John the Baptist but this time interspersed with the Evangelists.

The Baptistery holds the tombs of two doges: that of Giovanni Soranzo in the antechamber and, opposite the entrance, the more ornate

tomb of Andrea Dandolo, the donor of the mosaics and, in 1354, the last doge to be interred in St Mark's.

The Treasury has its entrance next to the passage to the Palazzo Ducale; it is open Mon.–Sat. 9.45am–5.15pm, Sun. 2–5pm. The ground floor is packed with the booty that the Venetians carried back to their city after the sack of Constantinople in 1204: gold and silver reliquaries studded with precious stones, goblets, glassware, liturgical pieces, ivories, icons, tapestries and small objets d'art. This church treasury, which was also the State treasury, was enriched by gifts and purchases, and, despite considerable depradation through theft and allowing items to be melted down, is nowadays one of the richest in the world. Among its most significant exhibits are the throne of St Mark, a marble reliquary in the form of a seat that is said to have been presented to the Patriarch of Grado in Byzantium by the Emperor in 630. ★Tesoro

The **sacramental altar** on the east wall of the southern aisle dates from 1617. It was where important relics were venerated up until 1810 when the altars were re-organized. The retable on the mensa is Baroque, the baldachin is contemporary. The wall behind this altar is said to have disgorged the lost bones of St Mark in 1094 (see Legend of St Mark).

Altare di San Giacomo Doge Cristoforo Moro donated both the St Jacob altar and the similar St Paul altar left of the Presbytery. The wall altar (no baldachin) is ornamented with exceptional early Renaissance carvings by Pietro Lombardo and his workshop.

Cappella di San Clemente Formerly exclusively the chapel of the Doges, the Cappella di San Clemente is lined with subtly hued 12th c. mosaics of St Clement. The wall of columns is 14th c.; the devotional picture over the altar of the standing Madonna and Infant Jesus is an exceptional work from the school of Donatello.

The Presbytery, which is open Mon.–Sat. 9.30am–5pm, Sun. 2–5pm, was where the clergy, the Doge and Venice's leading dignitaries assembled on high feast-days and holidays. Little remains of the original furnishings, and the Doge's seat has been removed. The Presbytery

Choir stalls The fronts of the two banks of choir stalls, directly behind the rood-screen, are beautifully carved by Jacopo Sansovino with scenes from the life of St Mark. The earlier reliefs on the rostrum by the Presbytery entrance date from 1537, while those on the opposite side are from 1541 and more sculptural in form.

The ★High Altar (1834–36), put together from older pieces, nowadays holds the relics of St Mark (previously kept in the crypt) which can be viewed from above through a grating. The ★High Altar

★Baldachin The four alabaster columns supporting the baldachin, the canopy over the high altar, are well worth closer scrutiny. They are carved with reliefs, in the form of nine intertwined bands, featuring themes from the New Testament. The left-hand rear column tells the story of the life of the Virgin from her birth to her marriage to Joseph, while the front left-hand column carries this on up until the childhood of Jesus; the rear right-hand column shows events in the life of Jesus, culminating in the front right-hand column with Christ's Passion and Resurrection. Dating from the early 13th c., the flat reliefs belong stylistically to late Romanesque, but it is considered that they could also originally be 6th c. Byzantine that was subsequently much reworked and

◀ *Christ the Pantocreator in the centre of the Pala d'Oro: this masterpiece of gothic gold work was completed by Boninsegna in 1345*

restored. Since the scenes with their small figures framed in arcades have much in common with carved ivories it is though that the sequence of events could well be modelled on the work of miniaturists.

★★**Pala d'Oro** Venice's great treasure, its wonderful golden altar-piece, is on a pedestal behind the High Altar (open Mon.–Sat. 9.30am–5pm, Sun. 2–5pm). The Pala d'Oro is the bejewelled work of Byzantine and Venetian enamellers, goldsmiths and silversmiths. The individual sections date from between the 10th and the 14th c., and the Pala d'Oro did not assume its present form until 1345 when Andrea Dandolo had goldsmith Gian Paolo Boninsegna bring the different sections together and mount them within a single gold frame.

The oldest pieces are the small round enamels now mounted in the frame. Doge Ordelaffo Falier and Empress Irene were responsible for having the retable enlarged and placed in St Mark's in 1105. The panels of the story of St Mark and the lively scenes from the New Testament in the lower part of the retable also date from Venice of this time. Striking compositions from Byzantium – six large panels of the life of Jesus, the upper part of the retable and many cruciform discs – were added in 1209.

Venetian workmanship appears again in the central panel of Christ in Majesty, the medallions with the Evangelists and the Apostles which were made here in 1345, as was Boninsegna's Gothic frame which serves to unify the many disparate elements.

Tabernacle

A niche in the apse holds a tabernacle for the sacrament; the relief on its bronze doors is by Jacopo Sansovino and shows the risen Christ surrounded by angels displaying the instruments of torture.

★**The Sacristy doors** constitute another major masterpiece by Jacopo Sansovino; the door surrounds are marble and the slightly bowed doors are bronze. They carry two large square reliefs, the lower one depicting the entombment and the upper one the resurrection, with prophets and saints in the surrounding frame.What is striking is the lack of definition in the contours, with the figures seeming to flow into one another in a painterly fashion. The small half-length portraits are said to be fellow artists: Aretino, Palladio, Francesco and Jacopo Sansovino, Titian and Veronese. Sansovino worked on the doors between 1546 and 1570, undoubtedly much influenced by Ghiberti's "Gate of Paradise" for the baptistery in Florence.

Cappella San Pietro

The Presbytery gives directly onto St Peter's chapel, the Cappella San Pietro. The altar was put together in the 19th c., but the figures of Mary and other women saints on top of the rood-screen are late 14th c. from the studio of the dalle Masegne brothers.

★Iconostasis

The iconostasis, the screen between nave and chancel, was also by the dalle Masegne brothers who worked on it between 1394 and 1404. It consists of eight stocky columns supporting the beam on which stands the Cross Triumphant, with the rounded marble statues of the Virgin, St Mark and the Apostles ranged on either side. The pulpits supported by pillars to the right and left of the screen are of a similar construction and were put together in the 14th c. from old materials, columns and marble panels. The pulpit on the left was for preaching the gospel while the one on the right was where the newly elected Doge presented himself to the people.

Altare di San Paolo

The altar of St Paul is in the same style as its counterpart, the altar of St James opposite. The strikingly worked relief shows the conversion of Saul; the sculpture of Paul was added in the 16th c.

★Nicopeia Madonna

The 10th c. Byzantine icon of the Nicopeia Madonna (known as the "bringer of victory" since the Byzantine army carried it into battle) is housed under a canopy in the east wall of the northern transept. Encrusted with jewels, pearls and gemstones, the icon is another looted item brought to Venice in the 13th c. The image is representative of the Nicopeia pose, as a frontal picture of the Virgin with the Infant Jesus on her lap, and is particularly venerated on her feast-days.

The chapel of St Isidore holds the remains of the saint (in a sarcophagus in a niche in the front wall) which were acquired (some say stolen) from Chios in 1125. The saint's statue rests on the sarcophagus while the 14th c. mosaics recount various episodes from his life, some of them highly dramatic.

Cappella Sant'Isidoro

The chapel gets its name from the 17th c. when it functioned as the chapel of the Mascoli (a bachelor confraternity). The main feature of the barrel-vaulted chapel, which was built in the early 15th c., is its altar with sculptures of the Virgin between St Mark and St John. These are important in art-historical terms in that they mark the transition from late Gothic to early Renaissance. Other features worth noting are the early 15th c. mosaics and the 12th c. stoup on the column shaft.

Cappella dei Mascoli

The Altar of the Annunciation is topped by a polygonal marble canopy shaped like a pyramid and supported by columns surrounding the Byzantine crucifix looted from Constantinople in 1205 and the 14th c. figures of the Annunciation.

The Altar of the Annunciation

★Pavimento It is worth paying special attention to the floor of the basilica, a beautiful 12th and 13th c. mosaic pavement ("pavimento") of multi-coloured marble, mostly in square panels filled with geometric patterns or decorative images of birds and beasts. Intriguingly, the floorplan does not seem to mirror the architecture above, nor does the imagery appear to follow any particular iconographic sequence.

The steep stairway to the church museum, the Museo Marciano (opening times: daily 9.45am–5pm), is on the right side of the atrium inside the main entrance. Here, besides its star exhibit – the originals of the famous ★★St Mark's horses (see Gallery, p. 61) – tapestries, sculptures, liturgical robes are on display, and there is a close-up view of fragments of mosaics. Other major exhibits include the former cover of the Pala d'Oro which was used on weekdays. This was made by Paolo Veneziano and his sons in 1345 and depicts Christ, the Virgin, Saints and the life of St Mark. The museum rooms above the porch formerly served as workshops for the mosaic-makers.

★Museo Marciano

★★Burano   R 1

The island of Burano (pop. 5000), a 40-minute boat-trip just 9 km northeast of Venice, is famous for its fine lace. Also a lively little fishing community, it is strikingly attractive with its small brightly painted houses. These usually have one or two stories and the façades, though unadorned, are a riot of colour. The fishing boats moored alongside the quays lining the narrow canals are in the same vibrant hues and present a delightful picture against the backdrop of the rainbow reflections of the houses.

It comes as no surprise that artists have always been very much attracted to the island, among them the so-called Burano School who sought to capture the special light of the lagoon here before the First World War. Some of their works can be seen in Da Romano, the well-known restaurant at 468 Via Galuppi. From the Piazza Galuppi art-lovers should also take a look in San Martino – the island's church with its leaning bell-tower – which holds the 1725 "Calvary" by Giambattista Tieopolo (see Famous People).

And to round off a visit with a meal try one of the excellent fish restaurants along the Via Galuppi and, for dessert, sample a "bussola", Burano's version of a "rum" baba – without the rum but dipped in sweet wine.

Lace and More Lace

According to legend a sea-captain who was madly in love had to leave his betrothed behind on the Island of Burano and soon after sailed past the Island of the Sirens. While his crew, completely entranced by the magical singing of the sirens, all jumped overboard, the captain resisted their beguiling pleas. Thereupon the leader of the sirens caused a crest of foam to rise out from the sea and turn into fine lace in the hands of the mariner – a wedding veil for his beloved waiting for him on Burano.

Actually, Burano lace does have a special link with the sea, as the stitches used are said to be derived from those used in making fishing-nets. Lace was made in Venice and on the little islands as long ago as the 15th century, but the complicated "air stitch" (punta in aria) was not invented until the 16th century. Soon this fine work was in demand throughout Europe as noble personages and rich citizens sought to adorn themselves with the expensive accoutrements from the Venetian island. In France the lace was so highly regarded in the middle of the 17th century that the minister Colhert even recruited lacemakers from Burano to boost France's own lace production to enable it to compete with the Italian variety. The dissolution of the Republic in 1797 resulted in a marked decline in lace production. By the late 19th century the traditional skills had almost been forgotten when, in 1872, Countess Marcello opened a new school of lace-making on Burano, where Francesca Memo, the last of the lace-makers, passed on her skills. By the early 20th century the island could boast seven large lace manufactories employing nearly 5000 embroiderers. Today only a few women still follow the craft, and genuine Burano lace has become a rare luxury item. As a result most of the work on sale in the numerous shops along the Via Galuppi comes from countries where labour is cheap and plentiful.

Those interested in the history of lace-making should pay a visit to the Galleria del Merletto Antico at 215 Via Galuppi. A small museum there displays some exquisite work from the last two hundred years, including valuable fans, veils and dresses owned by the wealthy aristocracy (open: weekdays during business hours). The Scuola dei Merletti on the Piazza Galuppi (open: Mon., Wed.–Sun. lOam–5pm) provides information about the "punta in aria" technique.

Expensive lace from the Scuolo dei Merletti

Burano, with its brightly painted fisherman's houses.

★★Canal Grande   E–J 3–6

The Canal Grande (Grand Canal), about 5m deep and 30–70m wide, snakes its way in an inverted S for 21.5 miles through the heart of the city, from the Piazzale Roma to the St Mark's Square. In the opinion of Philippe de Commynes, Charles VIII of France's ambassador in 1495, it was "the most beautiful street in the world" and right up to the present this main traffic artery continues to rank as one of the most magnificent of main streets. To the Venetians their waterway, with its three bridges and constant flow of gondolas and motorboats, is also known as their "Canalazzo", a mixture of "canal" and "palazzo", referring to the unique waterfront of 210 palaces and 15 churches to which the Grand Canal owes its unique splendour.

The canal is one of the delta tributaries of the River Brenta which flows through the lagoon here and out to sea. The only way to view the Grand Canal is by boat: the No. 1 waterbus (vaporetto) stops at every stage, while the No. 82 service only stops at main stages such as the station, Rialto and St Mark's. Tickets can be bought from the kiosks at each stop; it is a good idea to get a 1, 3 or 5-day season ticket which is valid for all lines.

From St Mark's Square to the Rialto bridge
(l) = left bank, (r) = right bank

See entry

★★Piazza San Marco (r)

In the early 19th c. the royal gardens west of the Piazzetta were the site of the granary. The classical coffee house (1815–1817) at the western end of the gardens is now Venice's tourist information centre.

Giardini Reali, Tourist Information (r)

Canal Grande

Capitaneria del Porto (r)

The former 15th c. grainstore that at one time took up the rear of the Procuratie (see entry) nowadays houses the port authority. Fans of famous cocktails will enjoy visiting Harry's Bar next door, a one-time haunt of Ernest Hemingway and the original Harry's Bar.

Palazzo Giustinian Morosini (r)

Built in the second half of the 15th c. by the nobles of the Giustinian family, this four-storey Gothic building owes its artistic façade to stone-masons from Bergamo. It was substantially altered in the 17th c. when acquired by the Morosini family and is now the headquarters of the Biennale.

Palazzo Treves Bonfili (r)

The early 19th c. ornamentation on the façade of this Classical palace, built in the late 16th/early 17th c. to designs by Bartolomeo Monopola, is the work of Sebastian Santi and Giovanni Demin.

Dogana da Mar (l)

At the end of the Dorsoduro, the spit of land on the opposite side of the canal, stands the Dogana da Mar, the old "customs house of the sea". Here, atop its tower, returning travellers are greeted by the bronze goddess Fortuna. The Dogana was built between 1676 and 1682 by Giovanni Bernoni when the Senate hoped that strict customs regulations would prevent the decline in Venice's trade; this tended to have the opposite effect, however. The gilded weathervane of Fortuna by Bernardo Falcone stands on a golden sphere supported by two kneeling Atlases.

Seminario Patriarcale (l)

Built in 1669, the work of Baldassare Longhena, the old seminary now holds the **Pinacoteca Manfrediniana**, the remarkable art collection of the Florentine Marchese Federico Manfredini. It includes terracotta busts by Alessandro Vittoria (1525–1608), paintings by Antonio Vivarini (15th c.),

Palazzo Giustinian Morosini: this four-storey Gothic building owes its artistic façade to stone-masons from Bergamo

Dogana da Mar: atop the tower of the old customs house of the sea, returning travellers are greeted by the bronze goddess Fortuna

Cima da Conegliano, Konrad Laib and Filippino Lippi, a major work by Antonio Canova (1757–1822, "Portrait bust of Diammatteo Amadei"), and, in the library, a painted ceiling "Fame of the Sciences" (ca. 1720) by Sebastiano Ricci (viewing by appointment only).

See entry

★Santa Maria della Salute (l))

This small late-Gothic palace from ca. 1480 has a richly ornamented façade. The large triple window on the first floor is particularly striking, as are the marble balustrades with their carved wheel motif. The palace is said to owe its name to a scion of the Contarini family who enjoyed pheasant shooting. Legend has it that this was the home of the beauteous Desdemona, the innocent victim of her husband Othello's wrath in Shakespeare's tragedy.

★Palazzo Contarini Fasan (r)

The twin-arched and quadruple-arched windows on the mezzanine and second floor are in Coducci's Renaissance style but the late-Gothic capitals with foliage and the twin pillars in the balustrades are late 14th c.

Palazzo Manolesso Ferro (r)

The originally Gothic palace was remodelled between 1638 and 1640 by architect Pietro Bettinelli for Tommaso Flangini; it was acquired by the Fini family in the late 17th c.

Palazzo Flangini Fini (r)

The 14th c. cloister and the late 15th c. church, with Gothic windows set in marble, are all that remain of the great Benedictine abbey dedicated to St Gregory.

San Gregorio (l)

The abbey was demolished at the end of the 19th c. and the second cloister was replaced with Tricomi Mattei's mock-Gothic Palazzo Genovese around 1892.

Palazzo Genovese (l)

73

Canal Grande

★Palazzo Barbaro (I)
The superb six-arched window on the first floor of the Barbaro Palace – separated only by a small alley from the Palazzo Dario – is pure Gothic, while the quadruple arcaded window on the second floor is Late-Gothic with pointed elongated arches.

★Palazzo Dario (I)
Like the façades on the Rio delle Torreselle and the garden beyond, the Palazzo Dario was originally Gothic before Giovanni Dario ordered Pietro Lombardo to remodel it in Renaissance style in 1479; its striking features include the beautiful use of coloured marble and the grand chimney pots. Acquired by the Bostonian Curtis family in 1885 the Dario's magnificently refurbished reception rooms soon became a popular meeting place for English and American artists and literati, including the poet Robert Browning (1812–1889), writer Henry James (1843–1916) and composer Cole Porter (1891–1964).

Palazzo Venier dei Leoni (I)
See ★★Collezione Peggy Guggenheim

★Palazzo Corner (Ca' Grande) (r)
Early in the 16th c. Giorgio Corner, brother of the Queen of Cyprus, bought the magnificent Gothic/Byzantine palace for 22,000 gold ducats. In 1532 it was ravaged by fire so his son, Jacopo Corner, commissioned the Florentine architect and sculptor Jacopo Sansovino (see Famous People) to build him this magnificent Renaissance-style three-storey palace, its Venetian arcaded windows blending harmoniously with the Tuscan base. Early in the 19th c. the enormous mansion – hence the name, Ca' Grande: big house – was acquired by Austria as the official residence of the Imperial Governor; nowadays it serves as municipal offices.

Casina delle Rose (r)
In spring the red blossom of the pomegranate tree in the front garden of this house, where the sculptor Antonio Canova had his original

Palazzo Manolesso Ferro

Palazzo Contarini Fasan

74

View from the Palazzo Gritti to the Ca' Grande

studio, first catches the eye. Here he created pieces such as "Daedalus and Icarus", commissioned by the Pisani family, which today can be seen in the Museo Correr (see St Mark's Square). During the First World War this was the home of the Italian writer Gabriele d'Annunzio (1863–1938) who reworked his tempestuous affair with the celebrated actress Eleonora Duse as his semi-autobiographical Venetian novel "The Flame of Life".

This large 16th c. palace is built on clearcut lines, with parallel bands linking the different elements of the façade to form geometric units. The mosaics on the front of the palace were added by Giulio Carlini in the 19th c.

Palazzo Barbarigo (l)

The plans for this, the most remarkable early Renaissance building from the end of the 15th c., are attributed to Mauro Coducci, possibly in association with Pietro Lombardo. The interior still holds a few of the 18th c. frescos by Tiepolo (see Famous People).

Palazzo Contarini dal Zaffo (l)

The Gothic palace on the left was built in the early 15th c., probably by Bon. The palace on the right was commissioned around 1694 by Antonio Gaspari, who was also responsible for the grand stucco decor in the interior.

Palazzi Barbaro (r)

The façade of the Palazzo Cavalli Franchetti, next to the Ponte dell'Accademia, is an outstanding example of late-Gothic architecture. The fine tracery, which dates from 1465, was carefully restored in the late 19th c. The richly ornamented window frames are particularly worth noting. Part of the rear of the palace was extended in mock-Gothic style; there is a little garden between the palace and the Accademia bridge.

Palazzo Cavalli Franchetti (r)

Canal Grande

★★Gallerie dell'Accademia (l)	See entry
Palazzo Mocenigo Gambara (l)	Lazzaro Mocenigo, Procurator of St Mark's, was born here in 1624. A famous sea captain who won several victories over the Turks in the war of Candia, he lost his life off the Dardanelles in 1657. Illustrious members of the Gambara family included four cardinals and Correggio's Veronica, who was famous for her lively verses and a friend of such notable contemporaries as Ariosto and Pietro Aretino.
Palazzi Contarini degli Scrigni (l)	These two adjoining palaces of the influential Contarini family stand at the mouth of the Rio San Trovaso. The first one is Gothic and is distinguished by its façade of lovely arcaded windows. The extension of the adjoining Baroque palace was the work of Vincenzo Scamozzi who kept the floors at the same height.
Palazzo Giustinian Lolin (r)	On the opposite side of the canal, this is one of Venice's first Baroque palazzi. An early work of Baldassare Longhena with Gothic antecedents, it was begun in 1623. Giovanni Giustinian was advanced a considerable sum by his father-in-law Giovanni Lolin for the conversion, hence the double name for the palace. Nowadays it houses the Levi Foundation's Centro Musicale.
Palazzo Falier (r)	The little early 15th c.Gothic building has two covered Renaissance terraces. The Falier family came to live in this quarter in 1084, the year that San Vidal was built by Vitale Falier who was Doge until 1096.
Ca' del Duca (r)	Bartolomeo Bon was commissioned to build a palace here in 1453 but it was never finished. The simple brick building later put up in its place served at times as a studio for Titian (see Famous People).

Palazzo Balbi, in Mannerism style

Palazzo Loredan dell'Ambasciatore

76

Palazzo Malipiero stands on the south side of the Campo San Samuele

The façade of this late Gothic palace (1470) is distinguished by the eye-catching feature of the two shield-bearers (Lombardy school) on the wall of the first floor. The name "dell'Ambasciatore" dates from when the palace became the official residence of the Imperial Envoy in 1752, with the proviso that the Court in Vienna had to pay for 29 years of rent and maintenance costs in advance.

★**Palazzo Loredan dell'Ambasciatore** (l)

The little palazzo, named after an earlier owner, Madame Stern, was built to a mock-Gothic/Byzantine design by the architect Berti early in the 20th c.

Palazzo Stern (l)

Originally Gothic, the palazzo assumed its present appearance in 1622. It stands on the south side of the Campo San Samuele fronting the church of the same name. This was dedicated around 1000 but completely remodelled in 1683, while retaining the 12th c. church tower.

Palazzo Malipiero and San Samuele (r)

The relatively restrained ornamentation on the façade of this three-storey building• strikes a happy medium between Classicism and Baroque. It was built in the mid-18th c. and designed by architect Giorgio Massari who was also responsible for the Ca' Rezzonico (see entry). The wall opposite the magnificent staircase has frescos by Alessandro Longhi depicting a group of noble ladies and their gallants, wearing masks and leaning on a trompe-l'oeil balustrade. Rooms in the upper floor also have frescos, this time in Rococo style by Jacopo Guarana and Fabio Canal. The building was commissioned by the powerful Grassi family who paid out 60,000 gold ducats in 1718 to be allowed to join the Venetian patriciate and who lived in the palace until the mid-19th c when it was bought by the Counts of Tornielli. Subsequently the home of the opera tenor Poggi, in the 19th c. it became the renowned Degli Antoni baths. After its acquisition by Fiat in 1984 it was comprehensively reno-

★**Palazzo Grassi** (r)

Palazzo Grassi houses exhibitions of modern art

vated under the direction of Gae Aulenti and Antonio Foscari with a view to largely restoring the old structure of the patrician palace. The cultural centre for interdisciplinary exhibitions opened here in 1986 with the much-acclaimed Futurism show, and every year since then has staged major retrospectives and other contemporary art events.

★★Ca' Rezzonico (I)   See entry

★Palazzo
Giustinian (I)

This imposing four-storey late Gothic double-fronted palace is another Bon building and dates from the mid-15th c. Richard Wagner lived here for seven months between 1858 and 1859 and during that time composed the second act of "Tristan and Isolde".

★Ca' Foscari (I)

At the broad opening into the Rio Foscari, this major example of 15th c. Venetian Gothic is nowadays part of the University. The site was acquired in 1452 by Francesco Foscari (see Famous People) who had the two Giustinian towers that stood here transformed into a magnificent palace. The outstanding feature of the richly decorated façade is the wonderful array of arcaded windows, with their elegant tracery of pointed ogee arches. In 1574 the young King of France, Henry III, spent a week in this historic palace en route from Poland to Paris where he was to receive the crown of France.

Palazzo Balbi (I)

The palace on the opposite side of the Rio Foscari was the work of Alessandro Vittorio and was built for Nicolò Balbi between 1582 and 1590. The façade demonstrates the characteristic features of Mannerism – the transitional style between late Renaissance and early Baroque – such as twin pillar supports in the arcading, open-ended pediments and oval window apertures. Since 1973 it has been the seat of the regional government.

This imposing palazzo gets its name from the decorative heraldic features between the windows in the marble-clad Renaissance façade. The building was begun in 1504 by Giorgio Spavento and completed in 1546 under Scarpagnino. It became the home of Jacopo Contarini, a great patron of the arts, and famous for his library and picture gallery, which today belong to the collections of the Biblioteca Nationale Marciana and the Doge's Palace.

Palazzo Contarini delle Figure (r)

The first Palazzo Mocenigo-Nero, built in the 17th c., was one of a group of palaces that at one time had all belonged to the patrician Mocenigo family. Between 1414 and 1778 seven members of this family held the office of Doge and thus ruled the destiny of Venice. The adjoining elongated 18th c. palace was where Lord Byron lived in 1818–1819 and wrote works such as his "Don Juan" and "Vision of Judgement". The oldest Mocenigo palace, the next one along, is the Casa Vecchia (1570) in Venetian late Renaissance style.

Palazzi Mocenigo (r)

The palace was begun at the end of the 16th c. and completed early in the 17th in the tradition of Andrea Palladio.

Palazzo Corner Gheltoff (r)

The absolutely symmetrically conceived façade of this late Gothic palace from the second half of the 15th c. is embellished with wonderful tracery. The arches over the two watergates and the lovely windows on the first and second floors are especially worth seeing. Tiepolo and Piazzetta were commissioned to carry out the interior decoration of the palace in 1742. Veronese's work "The Family of Darius at the Feet of Alexander" (now in London's National Gallery) graced the salon up until 1857.

★Palazzo Pisani Moretta (l)

This Renaissance palace, with its balanced proportions and brightly coloured marble medallions, dates from the early 16th c. and belonged to one of the many branches of the Giustinian family.

Palazzo Giustinian Grimani (l)

The late Gothic Palazzo Pisani Moretta, with its absolutely symmetrically conceived façade

The Gondola – a Quaint Conveyance

Owee! owee! echoes the warning cry of the gondolier from afar before his odd craft with its pointed iron decoration on its bow turns the corner of the Palazzo, carefully steered by the boatman in his black trousers, white shirt and straw hat who skilfully manipulates the long oar with its slender blade in its rowlock (forcula) at the stern. "Like a huge, black plumed condor" was Edgar Allan Poe's picture of a gondola, and Thomas Mann described it with the words "This strange vehicle has remained unchanged since the olden days of romantic ballads and is as black as a coffin of all things – it is reminiscent of silent criminal ventures carried out on a wet night, even of death itself; of biers and sombre funerals and the final silent journey". At the same time, how-

ever, in days gone by the gondola was a status symbol and often decorated in magnificent colours with expensive gilding and curtained cabins, until in 1562 the doge Girolamo Pruli imposed a complete ban on such blatant display of wealth and ordered that gondolas must be painted black. At one time over ten thousand gondolas were to be found on Venice's 177 canals which measure over 45 km in length with 400 bridges, but today less than four hundred craft remain. The gondolas stand no chance against motorised craft, even though they are the better ecological alternative, as they have a gentle wake and make few waves. A good, black-painted specimen is expensive, costing between £10,000 and £12,000, or as much as an average car. However, the manufacture of gon-

Magnificent impression of the Canal Grande in the 18th c. by Canaletto: sumptuous gondolas and the Bucintoro, the Venetian Doges' stately galley

The gondola: still a most important way of transport in Venice today

dolas is a specialist art mastered by only a few and carried out at a private boatyard known as a 'squero'. The "axe-master" forms the gondola from eight different woods. The flat floor is made from pine, which expands in water to become watertight, the round planks are of hard oak to withstand jostling. Lime is used for the bow and stern, the cross-members are of pliable elm, light birch is used for the interior floor, the bent parts of the superstructure are of cherrywood and the smart linings are of mahogany and larch. It takes at least two months to construct the 10.87 m boat from 280 parts which have been treated with linseed oil and four full coats of black paint. Weighing empty about 350 kg, the gondola has a life of some fifteen years. It owes its unique shape to the fact that it is asymmetric, the left side being some 24 cm wider than the right. Being always inclined to go to the right, the boat is counterbalanced by the oarsman as he manoeuvres it with the aid of the oar. The manoeuvrability of the gondola depends to a large degree on the 'forcula'. A work of art in itself, this special rowlock cut into the body of the boat permits the oar to be inserted in eight different positions and thus function at varying depths. Decoration on the cradle-like craft, seating six people, is restricted to the iron bowsprit in the shape of a stylised doge's hat with six points, representing the districts of Venice and the metal fitting at the stem, resembling a bishop's crosier, sometimes there is also some highly imaginative decoration on the sides. A trip in a gondola is not cheap, largely because life on the canals is not an easy option. It takes a long while to train to be a self-employed and independent gondolier; maintaining the boats is expensive, moorings and licences also cost money. Many gondoliers earn extra money throughout the year by ferrying both locals and visitors across the Grand Canal for a few hundred lira in a gondola-like boat, somewhat wider and longer than the classic gondola, which will accommodate up to 19 standing passengers. Those of a romantic disposition should take an organised gondola cruise at night with musical accompaniment and then who knows, perhaps as they listen to the barcarolle from "The Tales of Hoffman" they might even see the beautiful Giuletta appear at one of the palace windows.

Canal Grande

★Palazzo Corner Spinelli (r)

Twin-arched windows, curved balustrades and little decorative tondi on the upper floors make a charming contrast with the rustic base. Built between 1490 and 1510 and already showing Renaissance elements this major building by Mauro Coducci served him as a prototype for the massive proportions of his Palazzo Vendramin Calergi (see below); Michele Sanmicheli was responsible for the interior (1542). Before it was acquired by the wealthy Spinelli family the palazzo belonged to Giovanni Corner, a nephew of of Caterina Cornaro, the Queen of Cyprus. Nowadays it is the headquarters of Rubelli, the exclusive textile firm.

Palazzo Bernardo (l)

Built around 1442, this is the epitome of Gothic palazzo architecture with its elegant tracery, beautiful arcaded windows and two side towers.

Palazzi Donà (l)

After passing the Rio della Madonetta the next buildings are the Palazzi Donà which date back to the 12th and 13th c. but were substantially altered over the following centuries.The exceedingly high arches over the middle row of windows and the decorated capitals are particularly striking.

Palazzo Papadopoli Coccina (l)

Construction of the palace was entrusted to Giangiacomo Grigi of Bergamo by the Coccina family in the mid-16th c. The four great canvasses that Veronese painted for the banqueting hall on the main floor – the piano nobile – are now in Dresden. The palazzo was acquired by the Counts of Papadopoli in the late 19th c., and its fabulous coin collection was subsequently bequeathed to the Museo Correr (see Procuratie).

Palazzi Tron (r)

The first Tron palazzo was built in the early 15th c., while the second of the two, in mock-Gothic style, dates from the 19th c.

Dreamlike backdrop for a gondola trip: Palazzi Corner Contarini degli Cavalli, Bembo and Dolfin Manin (from left to right)

This palazzo, begun in 1445, owes its name to the horses in the family coats of arms on either side of the superb six-window arcade on the first floor.

Palazzo Corner Contarini degli Cavalli (r)

According to John Ruskin (1819–1900), in his art-historical treatise "The Stones of Venice", this was the most noble of all the buildings in Venice. The three-storey palace, where the Rio di San Luca meets the Grand Canal, was begun in 1540 by Michele Sanmicheli for the Procurator Girolamo Grimani. The monumental façade, with its great window arches, was finished a year later by Giangiacomo Grigi, who also carried on with the second floor, but it took over thirty years until its final completion by Giovanni Rusconi in 1575. Two Victories by Alessandro Vittoria preside over the portal; nowadays the palace houses Venice's Court of Appeal.

★Palazzo Grimani (r)

Both palaces were constructed in the 17th c. on the walls of older buildings, and have retained parts of these Byzantine predecessors, including the 12th/13th c. capitals.

Palazzo Businello and Palazzo Barzizza (l)

Together the Farsetti and Loredan palazzi make up Venice's City Hall. Both have retained their original 13th c. Veneto-Byzantine basic form on the ground floor but the upper floors were remodelled in the 16th and 19th c. The building that preceded the current Palazzo Dandolo is said to have been the birthplace of Enrico Dandolo who was Doge from 1192 to 1205.

Palazzi Farsetti, Corner Loredan and Dandolo (r) (Municipio)

The outstanding features of this broad-scale late-Gothic palace are the two parallel sets of five-window arcades on the first and second floors; though separated by a central space they are linked together by the balustrade shared by the whole row of ten windows. The Bembo family provided a Cardinal (Pietro) in 1539 and a Doge (Giovanni) in 1615.

Palazzo Bembo (r)

With its impressive Renaissance façade the massive three-storey palazzo – now the Banca d'Italia – was built between 1532 and 1560 by the Florentine Jacopo Sansovino (see Famous People) for Giovanni Dolfin. It was later the residence of Ludovico Manin, the 120th and last Doge, during his period in office. When elected Doge Manin expressed himself as "gripped with such fearfulness that I hardly knew what I did". On May 12th 1797 he it was who had to pronounce the dissolution of the thousand-year-old Republic of San Marco, and, saying "its use is at an end", handed back his Doge's cap. He was also forced to place Campio Formio, his country seat, at the disposal of the French for the negotiations that resulted in Venice being traded to Austria by Napoleon as a "consolation prize".

Palazzo Dolfin Manin (r)

The "Palace of the Ten Wise Men" (the tax collectors of their day) was built by Scarpagnino between 1520 and 1522 to replace an earlier building destroyed by fire in 1513.

Palazzo degli Dieci Savi (l)

See entry

★Ponte di Rialto

From Ponte di Rialto to S. Lucia Station
(l) = left bank, r) = right bank

See entry

Fondaco dei Tedeschi

Diagonally positioned because of the bend in the Grand Canal, this imposing white marble palazzo – now a court building – next to the Rialto Bridge was formerly the offices of the city treasurers, the Camerlenghi. It was built by Guglielmo Grigi, from Bergamo, between 1525 and 1528 on the site of its predecessor, destroyed by fire in 1513. It

★Palazzo dei Camerlenghi (l)

Palazzi Valmarana and Michiel delle Colonne   *Colourful stalls in the Rialto market*

owes its pleasing appearance to such features as its half-relief – interesting evidence of the final stages of Lombardian Renaissance ornamentation – and its balanced proportions.

★Rialto Markets

There were already buildings here in the Middle Ages, around the Rialto Bridge, to store the produce supplied to the many traders here for sale at the Rialto markets. The barges were moored at the various quays for coal (Riva del Carbon), wine (del Vin) and oil (dell'Olio), a few paces away from the busy stalls selling fish, fruit and vegetables, rich textiles, jewellery and costly spices. The old names of the streets and squares in the Rialto Quarter are a reminder of all this activity, and a stroll round the Rialto markets is still one of the best entertainments that Venice has to offer. The long low market building of the Fabbriche Vecchie was designed by Scarpagnino in 1520 while the three-storey galleried Fabbriche Nuove was the work of Sansovino between 1554 and 1556. For refreshment try one of the convivial bars around the Rialto – perhaps the highly traditional Bàcaro Pinto on the Campo della Beccaria – or the elegant Poste Vecchie by the Pescheria.

★Pescheria (l)

The striking mock-Gothic Pescheria, built in 1907 on the Riva dell'Olio by Domenico Rupolo and Cesare Laurenti, stands on the site of the old fish market halls and, with its many stalls, is the unmistakable focus for Venice's bustling trade in fish and seafood (open Tue.–Sat. 5–11am). Using the centuries-old method, it was built on 18,000 oak piles.

Palazzo Civran (r)

The design of the 18th c. palazzo – now the finance offices – is ascribed to Massari who converted an existing building from Gothic to Classicist.

Ca' da Mosto (r)

This dates back to the 12th c. and was built in Veneto-Byzantine style. In

1432 it was the birthplace of Alvise da Mosto, in 1465 the first European to sail round the Canary and Cape Verde Islands. Between the 16th and 18th c. the Ca' da Mosto housed the Albergo Leon Bianco, one of Venice's grandest hotels. Its patrons included, between 1769 and 1775, Joseph II, son of Maria Theresia and Holy Roman Emperor, in whose honour a historic regatta was held on the Grand Canal.

Palazzo Valmarana (r)

The palazzo is principally known as the home of Joseph Smith, the English consul and famed collector and patron of the arts, who was responsible for the English Court and the British Museum acquiring the majority of their Venetian paintings, especially their masterpieces by Canaletto (see Famous People). In the mid-18th c. he had the palace renovated in Classicist style by Antonio Visentini, while Antonio Selva was commissioned to luxuriously refurbish the interior.

Palazzo Michiel delle Colonne (r)

Redesigned by Antiono Gaspari in the closing years of the 17th c., this palace partly owes its name to the unusually tall, slender columns supporting the arcade on the ground floor. The Michiel family acquired it in 1715.

Palazzo Sagredo (r)

The façade of the Palazzo Sagredo has undergone much alteration and is therefore a mixture of Veneto-Byzantine and Gothic styles.Thus the windows on the main floor are still Byzantine and only slightly tapered in the Gothic style, whereas the richly decorated four-window arcade in the floor above is clearly Gothic.

Palazzo Pesaro (r)

The mid-15th c. Gothic palazzo, which dates from about the same time as the neighbouring Ca' d'Oro (see entry), was originally owned by the Giustiniani and only subsequently acquired by the Pesaro family. The top floor was extended in the 19th c.

View from Palazzo Sagredo to Ca' da Mosto

Canal Grande

★★Ca' d'Oro (r)   See entry

★**Palazzo Corner della Regina (l)**   The massive Baroque palace – now the municipal pawn-shop – was built in 1724 to plans by Domenico Rossi. Its predecessor was the birthplace of Caterina Cornaro (1454–1510) who later became Queen of Cyprus, the Mediterranean island that was of great strategic importance to Venice. The patrician Corner family, long-standing members of the Venetian nobility, became so rich and powerful through their sugar-cane plantations on Cyprus that in 1472 eighteen-year-old Caterina married the island's king, Giacomo II di Lusignano. Eight months afterwards he was poisoned, and a year later his son also died. At Venice's insistence Caterina eventually handed her kingdom over to the Republic and in return was allowed to live as befitted her station in Asolo castle and later in her palace on the Grand Canal.

★Ca' Pesaro (l)   See entry

Palazzo Gussoni Grimani (r)   The monumental 16th c. palazzo was probably the work of the Veronese, Michele Sanmicheli; sadly nothing remains of its frescos by Tintoretto.

Palazzo Zulian (r)   Girolamo Zulian, who once owned this 17th c. palace, was a great admirer of the sculptor Antonio Canova.

Palazzo Barbarigo (r)   The fully restored frescos on the façade of this late 16th c. building at the entrance to the Rio della Maddalena are by Camillo Ballini, a pupil of Palma Giovane.

★**San Staè (l) (Sant' Eustachio)**   The church was built by Giovanni Grassi in 1678 on the ground plan of a Greek cross. Thirty years later Domenico Rossi was responsible for the fine Baroque façade on the Grand Canal, a commission by Alvise

Palazzo Zulian was built in the 17th c.

Palazzo Vendramin Calergi, a perfect example of the Venetian Renaissance

Mocenigo II, Doge from 1700 to 1709, whose tomb is in the church. The interior also contains such early 18th c. works as Giovanni Battista Piazzetta's "Martyrdom of St Jacob", Sebastiano Ricci's "Deliverance of St Peter", Pellegrini's "Crucifixion of St Andrew", and "Martyrdom of St Bartholomew" by Tiepolo (see Famous People).

This lovely Baroque palace, topped by its distinctive pinnacles, was designed by Baldassare Longhena in 1647, and conversion of the existing Gothic building lasted until 1663. It was commissioned by Bartolomeo Belloni whose family bought its way into the Venetian patriciate in 1647 for the hefty sum of 150,000 ducats. Typical Baroque features include the open-topped pediments of the extremely ornate windows on the main floor.

★**Palazzo Belloni Battagia (l)**

The old crenellated 15th c. granary was where the Republic kept its emergency store of grain and flour. The relief of the Lion of St Mark on the top floor of the compact brick building is a copy of the original (destroyed in 1797).

Deposito del Megio (l)

A perfect example of the Venetian Renaissance, this palazzo was the work of Mauro Coducci; begun in 1480, after the great architect's death in 1504 it was taken over and completed by Lombardo in 1510. Originally owned by the Loredan family, it was acquired in the early 17th c. by the Calergi, then in 1783 passed to Nicolò Vendramin through marriage. The Grimani wing further back is where Richard Wagner lived from 1882 until his death on February 13th 1883 (the room is now a museum).

★**Palazzo Vendramin Calergi (r) (casino)**

In winter the municipal casino moves into the palace from the Lido (see entry) where it is situated in the summer.

See entry

★**Fondaco dei Turchi (l)**

87

San Marcuola, built by the highly respected architect Giorgio Massari

San Marcuola (Santi Ermagora e Fortunato) (r)

San Marcuola dates from 1728–1736 when it was built by the highly respected architect Giorgio Massari, but the façade on the Grand Canal was never finished. The principal works of art in the church's lofty interior are, on the left-hand wall of the presbytery, Tintoretto's "Last Supper" (1547), his earliest version in the style of the Leonardo da Vinci original in Milan (1495–1497), and on the wall opposite an old copy of "The Washing of Feet" by the same master. Also noteworthy is the fact that the altar is decorated with sculpture rather than a picture.

Palazzi Gritti and Corner Contarini (r)

Both palaces date from the 17th c. The façade on the first floor of the Palazzo Gritti carries the coats of arms of the Gritti and Dandolo families. The Palazzo Contarini is also known as Ca' dei Cuori because of the hearts in the family coat of arms.

Palazzo Marcello (l)

According to legend this was the house of a butcher who, in the early 16th c., used human flesh for his sausages instead of pork – and was beheaded on the Piazza San Marco for his pains.

★Palazzo Labia (r)

Set a little way back from the Grand Canal, on the Canale di Cannaregio, the Palazzo Labia is now the offices of RAI, Italy's state radio. Begun at the end of the 17th c. and completed in the second quarter of the 18th, it is famous for the mid-18th c. frescos by Tiepolo (see Famous People) in the ballroom. These depict "Queen Cleopatras's Banquet in honour of Mark Anthony" (the second figure from the left, in blue, is said to be Tiepolo himself), and "Cleopatra's Embarkation for Rome". The ceiling painting symbolises "Time dismissing Beauty" (viewing by appointment Wed.–Fri. 3–4pm; tel. 5242812).

Santa Geremia (l)

The cruciform domed church was begun in 1753 by Carlo Corbellini and although the first mass was held in 1760 it was not finally completed until 1871. Under the dome, on the right by the choir,there is a painting by Palma Giovane, "The Crowning of Venezia by Saints".

Giuseppe Sardi was the architect from 1664 to 1682 for this Baroque palace, which remained unfinished. It was built for the Flangini family from Cyprus who entered the Venetian patriciate in 1664.

Palazzo Flangini (r)

The late-Baroque "shoeless" church (so-called because of its Carmelite founders) has an ornate two-storey façade dominated by double columns. The interior is partitioned by monumental arcades that resemble triumphal arches. The decoration is highly sculptural, and the high altar, with its spirally twisting pillars, actually takes up the whole width of the choir. Tiepolo's great ceiling painting, lost in 1915, was replaced by Ettore Tito in 1934. Remains of Tiepolo's painting can still be seen in the second chapel on the right.

Chiesa degli Scalzi (Santa Maria di Nazareth) (r)

This Istrian stone bridge dates from 1934 when it replaced the wrought-iron bridge of 1858. It is the starting point each year for the "Regata storica" – the finish is at the Ca' Foscari.

Ponte Scalzi

The church of San Simeone Piccolo, with its green-patinated dome, stands opposite the station. It was built between 1718 and 1738 by Giovanni Scalfurotto on the site of the medieval church Santi Simeone e Giuda. The Late Baroque oval church, based loosely on the Pantheon in Rome, also displays classic Renaissance features. The broad flight of steps leads up to a Palladian pillared portico that fronts the actual church. The interior holds a Pietà by Palma Giovane.

San Simeone Piccolo (l)

Venice's Santa Lucia railway station is right on the Grand Canal. The causeway to the mainland was constructed between 1841 and 1846 and the first station opened in 1860; the present complex dates from 1954.

Station (Ferrovia) (r)

★★Ca' d'Oro with the Galleria Franchetti   J 3

This palace is Venetian Gothic at its most perfect. Commissioned by Marino Contarini it was built between 1421 and 1440 by the great architects of their day, the Bon brothers and Matteo Raverti. Originally richly painted and gilded – hence its name, House of Gold – it has lost its gilding but the tracery fronting the windows with the marble filigree-work of Bartolomeo Bon is still of unrivalled beauty. The interior provides a vivid impression of how Venetian nobles lived in the late Middle Ages. The sumptuous mosaic pavement on the ground floor – modelled on the one in Basilica San Marco – and the red marble wellhead in the courtyard with allegories of Strength, Justice and Mercy, completed by Bartolomeo Bon in just seven months, are both particularly worth seeing.

Location
Canal Grande

Quay
Ca' d'Oro

Opening times:
daily 9am–2pm

The palace now houses, in the Galleria Franchetti, the important art collection assembled by Baron Giorgio Franchetti (died 1922) which he bequeathed to the State in 1915, together with the palazzo. A wealthy patron of the arts, the Baron had bought the palazzo in 1896 and had it carefully restored; during his time here his illustrious guests included the writer Gabriele d'Annunzio.

The collection consists of splendid Gothic and Renaissance furniture, Flemish tapestries and Persian carpets, as well as a great many works of art. Among the finest are Titian's "Venus before the Mirror", Paris Bordone's "Venus and Cupid", views of Venice by Francesco Guardi, Vittore Carpaccio's "Annunciation", van Dyck's "Portrait of a Nobleman" (1622–1627), and the unfinished "Martyrdom of St Sebastian" (ca. 1550) by Andrea Mantegna. Bronzes and terracottas by Bernini, Giambologna, and Andrea Tullio Lombardo complete the collection, together with fragments of frescos (1508) by Giorgione and his pupil Titian which once adorned the façade of the Fondaco dei Tedeschi (see entry).

★Ca' Pesaro with Galleria d'Arte Moderna and Museo d'Arte Orientale J 3

Location
Fondamenta
Mocenigo/Canal
Grande

Quay
San Staè

The palace – one of the largest and most imposing palazzi on the Grand Canal –was built on the site of three Gothic buildings between 1676 and 1710 by the masters of Venetian late-Baroque, Baldassare Longhena and Antonio Gaspari. Building work was held up when Longhena died in 1682 and then resumed at the start of the 18th c. by Gaspari who completed the construction of the second floor according to Longhena's plans then used his own design for the façade on the small canal at the side. Sansovino's Libreria Vecchia on the Piazzetta served as the model for the magnificent main façade. After the death of the last Pesaro in 1830 there was a succession of owners before Ca' Pesaro was bought by the City of Venice in 1902.

★Galleria d'Arte
Moderna
(Currently closed
for remodelling)

The gallery on the ground floor of the lavishly appointed interior houses the Galleria d'Arte Moderna (Gallery of Modern Art) which was founded at the end of the 19th c. after the first biennial in 1897, but which is currently being remodelled under the direction of Boris Podrecca. It has an extensive collection of 19th and 20th c. paintings, drawings and sculpture, including Gustav Klimt's erotic "Salome", Max Klinger's "Bathers", Wassily Kandinsky's "White Zigzag", and Giacomo Favretto's

The late-baroque Ca' Pesaro houses the Galleria d'Arte Moderna: Wassily Kandinsky's "White Zigzag"

Mondo Nuovo scene by Giandomenico Tiepolo in the Museo del Settecento Veneziano

"San Marco's Walk" (1884), plus works by Auguste Rodin and Marc Chagall.

The third floor holds the Museum of Oriental Art, an outstanding collection of Far Eastern objets d'art such as Chinese porcelain and lacquerwork, Japanese paintings from the Edo period (from the collection of Count Enrico de Bourbon), and Indian sculpture. Opening times: Tue.–Sun. 9am–2pm.

★Museo d'Arte Orientale

★★Ca' Rezzonico
with Museo del Settecento Veneziano   G 5

The massive building was begun for Filippo Bon in 1660–1682 by Baldassare Longhena, Venice's greatest Baroque architect, but it was nearly a century later that Giorgio Massari completed it for the Rezzonico family, elevated to the aristocracy in 1687 – one illustrious member of the family even managed to become Pope (Clemens XIII, 1758–1769). The second floor, as designed by Longhena, was finished early in 1752 and the waterfront steps in 1756. The part between the courtyard and back garden was all Massari's own work. In the mid-19th c. the palazzo was acquired by the English poet Robert Browning who lived there until his death in 1889. In the Thirties it was purchased by the city who converted it to a museum and completely restored it in 1995–1997.

Location
Rio di Santa
Barnabà/Canal
Grande

Quay
Ca' Rezzonico

The museum's collection, in keeping with the palazzo's suberb decor, gives a fascinating glimpse of life in Venice in the Rococo period, the "Settecento veneziano" – although "settecento"means 700, this also

★★Museo del
Settecento
Veneziano

(Currently closed
for remodelling)
stands for the 18th c. The 40 or so rooms illustrate every facet of fashionable art in 18th c. Venice: magnificent silk carpets, Flemish tapestries,
ornate furniture such as the superb items by Andrea Brustolon, the chi-
noiserie and laquerwork that was so popular in that period, Venetian
porcelain, ceramics and bronzes.

An elegant flight of stairs leads up to Massari's vast ballroom which
spans the whole of the building. Its ceiling painting by Giovanni Battista
Crosato represents the four quarters of the globe with Phoebus passing
through in his chariot. The beautiful wedding allegory (1758) in the
adjoining room is the work of Tiepolo (see Famous People) and immor-
talises the lavish marriage of Ludovico Rezzonico to Faustina
Savorgnan. The fresco in the throne room, "Merit between Nobility and
Virtue" is also by Tiepolo.

The highlights of the second floor include humorous sketches of
everyday Venetian life by Pietro Longhi (1702–1785), such as "Breakfast
Chocolate", "Pastrycook" and "The Rhinoceros", Canaletto's views of
Venice, Piazzetta's grand historical canvas "Alexander before the Body
of Darius" (1746) and the elegant Green Salon with ornate lacquer furniture from the Palazzo Calbo-Crotta. The frescos (1791–1797) painted by
Tiepolo's son Giandomenico for the Villa Zianigo are particularly interesting – wistful impressions in pastel shades such as "New World
Scene", "The Walk" and "Last Day of Carnival". The third floor has an
apothecary's shop from the Campo Santo Stin and a reconstructed 18th
c. puppet theatre.

★Chioggia   Q2

Location
45km south of
Venice

The lively little fishing port of Chioggia (alt. 2 m; pop. 55,000), on two
long parallel islands near the south end of the lagoon, was formerly the
centre of Venice's salt production. Legend has it that it was founded by
Clodius, and in fact there was a settlement here long before the arrival
of the Romans in the first century BC. In the 9th c. the aspiring trading
base was destroyed by Pippin's troops but it was back to be rebuilt shortly thereafter. Thanks to its salt pans Chioggia's commerce thrived from the 11th
c. onwards and by the end of the 12th c. it was even exporting around
70 salterns abroad. In 1379 the town was taken by the Genoese but it
was back in Venetian hands two years later and – particularly after the
decline of the saltworks – developed into an important fishing port; a
busy fish market still flourishes here every morning except Monday.

Topi and Bragozzi

The fisherfolk of Chioggia evolved special kinds of boats for fishing in
the shallow waters of the lagoon, among them the traditional "topi" –
sailing boats with enough space amidships to serve as holds – and, in
the late 18th c., brightly coloured "bragozzi", with trapezoid sails.

Tour

In the 19th c. many Venetian artists such as Ettore Tito and Italico Brass
sought to capture the special atmosphere of Chioggia in idyllic images,
and its picturesque alleys and charming canals, reminiscent of Venice,
are still the main attraction for the many visitors that come here today.
At the start of the Corso del Popolo, the main street lined with cafés,
restaurants and shops, stands the 12th c. Cathedral of Santa Maria, renovated in the 17th c.by Longhena and containing paintings by Tiepolo,
Palma Giovane and Piazzetta. Also on the Campo del Duomo is the little
brick Gothic Church of San Martino, dating from around 1392. Opposite
San Giacomo is the birthplace of the painter Rosalba Carriera
(1675–1757), famous for her pastel technique, who was much in demand
for her portrait-painting at the royal courts of the 18th c. In his comedy
"Le baruffe Chiozzotte" (1762, Quarrels at Chioggia) the Venetian playwright Carlo Goldoni (see Famous People) amusingly exploited
Chioggian foibles and mores.

★★Collezione Peggy Guggenheim

in Palazzo Venier dei Leoni   H/J 6

The single-storey palazzo, begun in 1749 under the direction of Lorenzo Broschetti, was never completed. Although the story goes that the patrician Venier family kept lions here in large cages, the "dei Leoni" is more likely to relate to the stone lion's heads that decorate the façade at water-level.

The American art collector Peggy Guggenheim (1898–1979) opened a museum of contemporary art in London early in 1938, following it up in October 1942 with the "Art of this Century" gallery in New York in October 1942. This was the basis of her private Venetian collection of Cubist, Abstract and Surrealist art, and in 1948 she showed this for the first time at the Venice Biennale. Shortly afterwards she made her new home in the Palazzo Venier dei Leoni where she opened her collection to the public. Nowadays, with the proviso that it must stay in Venice, it belongs to the Solomon R. Guggenheim Foundation formed by her uncle in New York in 1937.

Entry to the palazzo is through a wrought-iron gate by Claire Falkenstein (1961) and a delightful garden that contains many 20th c. sculptures as well as the Byzantine throne on which Peggy Guggenheim allowed herself to be photographed. The items from the collection on display in the private rooms represent an outstanding selection of classic modern art. Cubism is represented by works by Picasso ("The Poet", 1911), Georges Braques ("Clarinet", 1912), and Fernand Leger ("People in the City", 1919), along with pieces by the leading figures of Dada such as Francis Picabia ("Very Rare Picture of the Earth", 1915) and Marcel Duchamp ("Sad Young Man in Train", 1911/1912). The harmonious and rhythmic

Location
Grand
Canal/Fondament
e Venier

Quays
Salute,
Accademia

Opening times:
from April to Oct.:
Mon., Wed.–Sun.
11am–6pm

★★Art collection
of classic modern
art

Joan Miró: "Moonbird"

Jean Metzinger: "Velodrome"   *Paul Klee: "Portrait of Mrs. P. in the South"*

interplay of form and colour feature in the abstract painting of Wassily Kandinsky ("Landscape with Red Spots", 1913) and Paul Klee ("Portrait of Mrs. P. in the South", 1924, and "Enchanted Garden", 1926). The dynamics of modern life are reflected in the futuristic works of Gino Severini ("Sea = Dancer", 1913/1914) and Jean Metzinger ("Velodrome", ca. 1914), while Marc Chagall's "The Rain" (1911) represents a naive dream vision from Jewish folklore and religious art. Piet Mondrian's "Composition" (1938) uses horizontal and vertical lines and basic colours to achieve maximum expression with minimum means, while De Chirico evokes a feeling of solitude and menace in his "Red Tower" (1913). The Surrealists are represented by, amongst others, Salvador Dali ("The Birth of Liquid Desires", 1931/1932), René Magritte ("Realm of Light", 1953/1954), the Catalan artist Joan Miró ("Dutch Interior II", 1938), and Max Ernst – Peggy Guggenheim's second husband – with "The Kiss" (1927) and "The Antipope" (1941/1942). Peggy Guggenheim was also a patron of Jackson Pollock ("Moon Woman", 1942), and his first one-man show was in her New York Gallery in 1943. The most notable sculptures in this gallery include Constantin Brancusi's "Maiastra" (ca. 1912; polished bronze figure of the kind-hearted bird from a Rumanian fairytale), Alberto Giacometti's appealing "Woman Walking" (1932), Joan Miró's "Moonbird" (1944/1946) and Marino Marini's "Angel of the City" (1948) on the terrace by the Grand Canal.

Fondaco dei Tedeschi   K 4

Location
Ponte di Rialto

The first recorded mention of the Fondaco (from the Arabic "funduk" = commodity exchange) dei Tedeschi, the German commodity exchange – now the main post office – was in 1228. The "Germans" in question also included Poles, Czechs and Hungarians, but whereas the commodity exchanges of most other nations were dispersed throughout the city, the Germans had theirs directly on the Grand Canal. Only the exchanges of the Turks (see Fondaco dei Turchi) and the Persians enjoyed equally favourable locations; however, nothing remains of the Persian exchange, which was immediately next to the Fondaco dei Tedeschi.When the German exchange burned down in 1505 the Republic paid for it to be rebuilt, and the decoration of the façade was entrusted to Giorgione and Titian; what little remains of their frescos can be seen in the Ca' d'Oro (see entry). The prime position on the Rialto and the fact that the Republic financed the rebuilding were testimony to the commercial importance that Venice attached to the Fondaco dei Tedeschi; the Republic levied a hefty commission on every transaction concluded – and these usually involved very considerable sums – and it was not without reason that in the 16th and 17th c. the Fondaco was known as "the golden ark of the Senate". The exchange was the traders' lodgings as well as their place of work, and they were not allowed to act alone or conduct any business outside its walls: Venice was determined to protect its business knowledge. They were subject to strict rules, and had to lead communal lives – on a men only basis – under Venetian supervision, while to the outside world they were presented as a "confraternity", with their own church (see San Bartolomeo).

True to Venetian tradition, the façade on the Grand Canal is in three sections, with a five-arched portico in the middle and the refectories in the corners of the floor above, topped by an ornamental merlon-like moulding. The architecture of the building corresponds exactly to its functional purpose: 160 rooms distributed over four floors surrounding a courtyard. The customs post overlooked the canal, while the shops were in the outer rooms on the ground floor; the other rooms were used for storage, and the upper floors contained the living quarters and the offices.

★Fondaco dei Turchi
with Museo di Storia Naturale   H 3

The building dates from the 9th c., making it one of the oldest in Venice. It owes its present Veneto-Byzantine form to the commission in the mid-13th c. by the wealthy merchant Giovanni Palmieri. In the 14th and 15th c. it was the Venetian residence of the Dukes of Ferrara, and Emperor Friedrich III was their guest here in 1452 and 1469 during his time in Venice. From 1608 the palazzo was the official residence of the imperial envoy Georg Fugger, then in 1621 the Republic allocated it to the Turkish traders to serve as their warehouse and living quarters, hence the name (Fondaco = commodity exchange). In the early 19th c. it was rescued from near total dilapidation by the City who after 1858 had it rebuilt in its original 13th c. style; since 1880 it has functioned as a museum.

Nowadays the Natural History Museum here provides fascinating insights into the underwater world of the Adriatic and the local flora and fauna, as well as showing the fishing techniques traditionally practised in the Venetian lagoon. Also among the main attractions are the dinosaur skeletons from the Sahara and the big game display. The exhibition of Venetian well-heads on the ground floor is also worth seeing.

★★Gallerie dell'Accademia   H 6

The Gallerie dell'Accademia – or Accademia for short – possesses the most important and comprehensive collection of 15th to 18th c.Venetian art in existence. The basis of the collection, ranging from Gothic to Rococo, was the Accademia di Belle Arti, founded by the painter

Quay
Rialto

Location
Fondamento del
Megio/Rio
Fortego dei Turchi

Quay
San Staè

Opening times:
Tue.–Sun.
9am–1pm

Location
Canal
Grande/Porta
dell'Accademia
(entrance)

95

Gallerie dell'Accademia

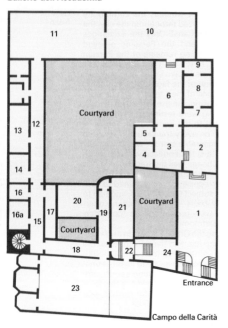

1 14th–15th c. panel painting
2 15th–16th c. Venetian Renaissance altar-pieces
3 16th c. Venetian panel-painting including G. Bellini
4 Mantegna, Piero della Francesca, Hans Memling
5 G. Bellini, Giorgiona
6 16th c. Venetian painting including Veronese, Tintoretto
7 Lorenzo Lotto, Bernardino Licinio
8 Palma the Elder, Romanino
9 School of Titian
10 16th c. Venetian masters including Veronese, Tintoretto, Titian
11 Tintoretto, Strozzi, Tiepolo
12 Corridor: 18th c. landscapes
13 Bassano, Tintoretto, Titian
14 Early 17th c.
15 Corridor: Tiepolo, Pellegrini Solimena
16 Early work of Tiepolo
16a A. Longhi, Piazzetta, Galgario
17 Caneletto, Guardi, Tiepolo P. Longhi, Carriera
18 18th c. paintings
19 Montagna, G.A. da Lodi, Boccaccino
20 "Miracles of the Relic of the True Cross"
21 V. Carpaccio "Legend of St Ursula"
22 Bookstand
23 Former monastery church: G. Bellini, B. and A. Vivarini
24 Former Hall of the Carità Brotherhood: A. Vivarini, Titian, G. d'Alemagna

Quay
Accademia

Opening times
Mon. 9am–2pm,
Thur.–Fri.
9am–9pm, Sat.
9am–11pm, Sun.
9am–8pm

Giovanni Battista Piazzetta in 1750. Since 1807 it has been housed in three former religious buildings, all of which were deconsecrated around 1800, namely, the Church of Santa Maria della Carità (1441–1452), the 15th c. Scuola Grande di Santa Maria della Carità (the living quarters of the lay confraternity founded in 1260), and the adjoining 16th c. monastery buildings of the Lateran Canons. In 1802 private art-lovers set up a makeshift "depot" here for works of art made "homeless" by Napoleon's suppression of churches and monasteries and the clearance of patrician palazzi. This unique gallery, which was also to be steadily enlarged by gifts and purchases, was thus assembled in a very short time. The collection is arranged roughly in chronological order in 24 rooms, and the following sections highlight its most significant works of Venetian art on a room by room basis.

Room 1

The magnificent nine-panel altarpiece of the ★Coronation of the Virgin (★polyptych, ca. 1350) from the Church of Santa Chiara is by **Paolo Veneziano**, active from 1333 to 1358 and effectively Venice's first major artist. The centre panel depicts the Coronation, with the life of Christ on the other panels on either side. The Coronation shows, from left to right, the Whitsuntide miracle, St Mathew the Evangelist, Investiture of St Clara, St John the Evangelist, St Francis receiving his clothes, Stigmatisation of St Francis, St Mark the Evangelist, Death of St Francis, St Luke the Evangelist, and Christ in Majesty. Paolo Veneziano's artistry, particularly in the centre panel, is marked by its delicate coloration and decorative effect but also the icon-like rigidity of the figures, indicative of the strong Byzantine influence, though with a growing tendency towards realism in the scenes from the life of Christ.

The polyptych (1357/58) of the Annunciation with God the Father (a later addition) and Saints by Lorenzo Veneziano (recorded 1356–1372) is

96

still in the Byzantine decorative two-dimensional tradition but with heightened colour configuration and bulkier saints of a statue-like appearance. The "Virgin with Child" (1934) by Nicolò di Pietro (recorded in Venice 1394–1427) shows the new aiming for corporeality combined with tender human features in the depiction of the Virgin, the Christ Child and the Angel. The triptych with Justice between Archangels Michael and Gabriel (1421) by Jacobello del Fiore (recorded 1400–1439) is in the European courtly International Gothic style. The enthroned personification of Justice, with sword and scales, plus two lions as symbols of wisdom, is easily identified with the personification of Venice, as borne out by the banner which reads "I will heed the angel's admonitions and the holy word and be gentle with the godly, hostile to the wicked and proud towards the haughty". The "Coronation of the Virgin in Paradise" with choirs of angels and Saints, the four Fathers of the Church and the four Evangelists (ca. 1448) by Michele Giambono demonstrates the striving for a spatial illusion of depth through the construction of the throne and the semi-circular groups of figures, showing further signs of Gothic style in the naturalistic reproduction of miming and gesticulation by the increasingly individualised figures. Forceful individual personalities dominate another five-panel altarpiece (1450) by Giambono of St Jacob the Elder between St John the Evangelist, the venerable Filippo Benizi and Saints Michael and Louis of Toulouse.

The ★★**Pala di San Giobbe** (pre-1490) clearly illustrates the move from the smaller multi-panelled altarpieces of Late Gothic to treatment as a unified space in the single large square panel of the Renaissance. One of the great masterpieces of Early Renaissance Venetian painting, this work by **Giovanni Bellini** (1430–1516) shows the Virgin and Child flanked by Saints, with, from left to right, St Francis, inviting adoration of the Virgin, John the Baptist, his curly head inclined towards the Child, St Jove,

Room 2

"Coronation of the Virgin Mary" from around 1350, by Paolo Veneziano, effectively Venice's first major artist

patron of San Giobbe e Bernardino, the church for which this altarpiece was destined, St Dominic with a book representing Learning, St Sebastian as the embodiment of ideal classical Christian beauty, and St Louis of Toulouse as a bishop, representing the Church. By directly linking the painted architecture to the real architecture of the frame Bellini succeeds in giving the illusion of a chapel opening out of the church, and realistically rendering the setting as a church interior with marble-clad walls and gold mosaics in the vaulting indicative of San Marco. Seraphim appear in the golden semi-dome with the inscription Ave Gratia Plena (hail to thee, full of grace). By the depiction of saints grouped around the Madonna in a kind of holy conversation (Sacra Conversazione) Bellini created the Venetian prototype of a Renaissance altarpiece, which was much copied as for example by Giambattista Cima da Conegliano (ca. 1459/60–1517/18) with his Virgin and Child with angel musicians (1496–1499), with Saints Anthony Abbot, Sebastian, Lucia, Nicolas, George and Catherine, and Vittore Carpaccio (ca. 1465–1526) with his altarpiece of the Presentation in the Temple with saints and angel musicians (1510).

Other works here by **Giambattista Cima da Conegliano** are the ★**Madonna with the Orange-tree and Saints Louis and Jerome** (1495–1497), remarkable for the balanced composition, delicate choice of colour, naturalistic landscape and contemplative atmosphere, and his "Christ with Doubting Thomas and Bishop Magnus" (ca. 1505), a magnificent composition of light and shade which makes the figures stand out against the clear sky and a distant landscape. The altar paintings "Summoning the Sons of Zebedee" (1510) and "Christ on the Mount of Olives" (1516) are by Marco Basaiti (ca. 1470/75 to after 1530) and owe their appeal not so much to the figures as to the use of light and the romantic landscape.

Room 3

This room holds Venetian Renaissance panel paintings by the circle of Giorgione including Rocco Marconi's "Christ and the Adulteress".

Room 4

Giovanni Bellini was inspired by the perspectival synergy of colour, light and form evolved by the great Umbrian painter **Piero della Francesca** (1416/17–1492). This is embodied in della Francesca's ★**St Jerome with Donor** (ca. 1450) against a landscape in which foreground and background are bound together by the cylindrical shapes of the tree-stump with crucifix on the left and the large tree on the right.

The painting of ★**St George**, in a garlanded portal frame with a view of the hilltop town of Silena, is by **Andrea Mantegna** (1431–1506), who as Bellini's brother-in-law introduced Venice to the sculptural, contoured painting style of Tuscany. The youthful armoured and self-assured St George appears as victor over the dragon in a composition typical of Mantegna's mastery of perspective and taut sense of reality.

The ★**Madonna with sleeping Christ Child** (1459–1463) by **Cosmé Tura** (1430–1495) is also known as Madonna of the Zodiac, since Aquarius, Pisces, Sagittarius and Virgo feature on the left of the picture. His clearcut composition with enamel-sharp colours produces an almost tangible graphic quality. The naturalistically painted goldfinches pecking at the grapes refer to Christ's sacrifice.

The ★**Portrait of a Young Man** (ca. 1478) is by **Hans Memling** (1435/40–1494), the Bruges painter who was popular with the Italians as a portrait artist. It is imbued with the spirit of Humanism, as expressed in the dignified, gentle and thoughtful set of his features.

Late Gothic, on the other hand, still features in "Madonna with Child" (ca. 1448) by Jacopo Bellini (recorded 1424–1470/71), father of Gentile and Giovanni, who was responsible for another, already more markedly Renaissance-like Madonna with the Christ Child and Cherubim.

The ★**Madonna with standing Christ Child** (1475–1480) is again the work of **Giovanni Bellini**, with gentle merging colours underlining the quiet closeness of mother and child against a chiaroscuro hilly landscape. The tender relationship of mother and child, as they gaze at one another, is equally apparent in "Madonna with the Red Cherubim" (after 1488), also set against a seemingly infinitely undulating landscape. Bellini's "Madonna and Child between St Catherine and St Mary Magdalene" (ca. 1500) is outstanding for its impressive use of colour and representation of the softly lit figures silhouetted against the dark background.

As Venice's most important Renaissance painter Giovanni Bellini num- Room 5
bered many Madonna paintings among his great range of expression and this room holds two more, "Madonna of the Little Trees" (1487), highly atmospheric and full of human dignity, and "Madonna and Child with John the Baptist and a Saint" (ca. 1505) against the background of a charming hilly landscape. Bellini's "Pietà" (ca. 1505) is interesting both for the worldliness of its setting and its Late Gothic piety. The mourning figure of Mary with her son's body on her lap is set against a broad backdrop that combines the townscapes of Vicenza (Cathedral, Basilica) and Cividale (Nasone Bridge).

Besides Titian, Bellini's most important pupil was **Giorgione** (1476/77–1510). ★★**The Tempest** (shortly after 1505), Giorgione's most famous painting, was commissioned by Gabriele Vendramin, a member of those cultivated humanistic circles in Venice that took pleasure in wittily coded pictorial subjects, a fact that even today makes the interpretation of this picture more difficult. The inherent tension in the work is striking, ranging from the contrast between the man and the woman as metaphors of inherent strength and maternal security, via the ruins as symbols of the past and the infant embodying new life, to the confrontation of town and country, fire (lightning) and water, rural idyll and wild nature. Even more important is that Giorgione, by means of overlapping and interwoven layers of colour, achieved the innovative synthesis of colour and space that lends this picture its particularly atmospheric intensity. Giorgione's "Portrait of an Old Woman", on the other hand, is stamped with blunt realism, more or less sub-titled "this is what Time has done to me", thus also making the portrait an allegory of ephemerality or "Vanitas". The four small panels by Giovanni Bellini are also allegorical in nature: the depiction of Bacchus offering fruit to a young warrior are about Virtue and Luxury; the woman with putti playing around her in a tiny boat with a big sphere is the allegory of fickle fortune or Melancholy; the female nude with a mirror standing on a pedestal is meant as an allegory of shrewdness or Vanitas, while the man wriggling through a shell – symbol of life and reproduction – is understood as an allegory of wisdom.

The works of Mannerism include the legendary ★**Presentation of the** Room 6
Ring to the Doge (1545–1550) by **Paris Bordone** (1500–1571), from Treviso, who sets the remarkable group portrait of dignitaries, each one highly individualised, in the midst of an imaginative architectural prospect in subtle cool hues. A similar narrative quality is evident in the "Banquet of the Rich Man" (1543–1545) by Bonifacio de' Pitati, comparing the rich spendthrift, in merry company with musicians under the portico of his villa, with the ragged pauper Lazarus, waiting in vain for his alms. The falconry and the lovers in the garden allude to the pleasures of life while the burning buildings in the background probably refer to the fires of Hell.
    Titian's powerful Mannerist figure of ★**St John the Baptist**, on the other hand, is reminiscent of the sculpture of Michelangelo.

The ★**Portrait of a Gentleman** by **Lorenzo Lotto** (1480–1556) is a mas- Room 7
terpiece of Mannerist art, outstanding for its cool colouring and enigmatic melancholy. Saints Anthony Abbot and Paul the Hermit (1520), as portrayed by Girolamo Savoldo (1480– ca.1550), appear powerfully realistic, standing out as though sculpted by the light.

Gallerie dell'Accademia

Room 8

Notable among the 16th c. works in this room are the "Slaughter of the Innocents" by Bonifacio de'Pitati; "The Holy Family with St Catherine and John the Baptist", a late piece by Palma Vecchio (1480–1528; real name Jacopo Negretti) depicting a three-way Sacra Conversazione with diffuse light and superb colour harmonies; and "Lamentation with Saints" (1510), the first known work of the Lombardy artist Girolamo Romani, or Romanino, in a sonorous colour tone.

Room 9

The pictures in this room are mainly by pupils of Titian, including an "Ascension" by Titian's brother Francesco Vecellio.

Room 10

The differing approaches to painting during the Counter-Reformation are clearly demonstrated by a comparison between Paolo Caliari (1528–1588), called Veronese, and Jacopo Robusti (1514–1594), called Tintoretto. The whole of one wall of the room is taken up with **Veronese's** enormous canvas, ★★**Feast in the House of Levi**", which was commissioned for the refectory of the Dominican church Santi Giovanni e Paolo to replace a destroyed Last Supper. Barely three months after its completion, in April 1573, Veronese was ordered to appear before the Inquisition on a charge of heresy. His "Last Supper" had been adjudged much too permissive and breaching canonical tradition with such figures as a dwarf with parrots, drunkards and dogs. Despite Veronese's passionate defence on the grounds of artistic freedom he was ordered to alter the picture within three months at his own expense. His only alteration, though, was to change the name of the picture, probably in consultation with the Dominican scholars who had commissioned it, citing Chapter 5 of St Luke's Gospel: "and Levi set before him a great feast in his house". Thus the Last Supper became a Feast, a theme frequently worked by Veronese as a sumptuous festive setting. Despite the picture's largeness of scale figurative and scenic elements form a magnificently unified whole, thanks to the skilful architectural sub-structure and the harmonious use of colour.

Tintoretto, on the other hand, was a master of the dramatic effect and the unreal. The ★★**Miracle of the Slave**, painted for the the Scuola Grande di San Marco in 1548, shows one of the miracles of St Mark, whereby a pious slave, who had left his master without permission to venerate the Saint's relics, was saved by St Mark from being blinded and having his legs broken. In the composition, marked by sharp colour contrasts and unnatural lighting, the unease is further intensified by having Mark effectively falling from the sky with his face being seen directly from below, a pictorial element that was to be a landmark for the future direction of Venetian ceiling frescos. No less spectacular are the special effects in Tintoretto's version of "Abducting the body of St Mark from Alexandria" (1562) – the unusual spatial alignments, the lightning rending the tempest-torn sky and the scenic tension between those fleeing in panic and the imperturbable Venetians. Tintoretto's "St Mark rescues a Saracen Believer at Sea" is probably from the same year, another example of his exciting painterly craft, with its intensive use of red, blue and yellow.

The deeply moving uncompleted ★**Pietà** by **Titian** (1488/90–1576; proper name Tiziano Vecellio) was his last work and shows, in sober colours and the diagonal arrangement to illustrate sinking from life to death, the group of mourners with the body of Christ in front of niches with statues of Moses and a Sibyl: compared with the invigorating joie de vivre of his earlier work, as in the "Assunta" in the Frari church, in old age Titian confronts the inexorability of death. Giovanni Antonio de'Sacchis, called Pordenone (1483/84–1539), in his altarpiece of the Blessed Lorenzo Giustinian, Venice's first patriarch who died in 1456, appears Mannerist in style but also influenced by Raffael and Michelangelo.

Room 11

The ★**Mystical Marriage of St Catherine** (1575) in the front part of the room is a late work by **Veronese** of almost Baroque pathos in the blend-

Circular ceiling fresco by Giovanni Battista Tiepolo: "The Finding of the True Cross by St Helena, mother of the Emperor Constantine"

ing of the colours, the draping of the garments and hectic party atmosphere. Other works by Veronese, mostly earlier ceiling frescos, are the "Homage of Ceres and Hercules to Venezia" (1575–1577) and "Reception of St Nicholas as Bishop of Myra". Setting the trend for the Baroque altarpiece is Veronese's Madonna and Child with John the Baptist and Saints Joseph, Jerome, Francis and Justina, notable for its earthy broken colouring, emphatic body language and monumental architectural backdrop. Both "Adam and Eve" and "Cain and Abel" are early works (ca. 1550) by Tintoretto, each fully integrated into the landscape, whether as front and back views of nudes harmoniously resting or as locked in combat. The back part of the room holds works by Baroque and Rococo artists among them the non-Venetian masters Pietro da Cortona (1596–1669), from Tuscany, with the Roman-Baroque "Daniel in the Lions' Den", Luca Giordano (1634–1705) from Naples, with a "Descent from the Cross" and "Crucifixion of Peter", with strong chiaroscuro effects, and Bernardo Strozzi (1581–1640) from Genoa, with "Feast at the House of Simon".

Venetian painting achieved a fresh uplift with the luminous colours and busy compositions of the Rococo artist **Giovanni Battista Tiepolo** (1696–1770), represented here by the circular ceiling fresco of ★**The Finding of the True Cross by St Helena, mother of the Emperor Constantine**.

Marco Ricci (1676–1739) was among the most significant contributors to the ★**art of landscape painting** in the 18th c. His compositions featured ranges of hills shimmering on the horizon, sweeping plains with rushing streams, tall stands of trees against clear skies and magnificent light effects, as evidenced here by "Landscape with Stream, Monks and

Room 12

Washerwomen", and "Landscape with Horses" (both ca. 1720). The pictures of Francesco Zuccarelli (1702–1778) demonstrate his delicate Rococo skill with busy pastoral scenes as expressed in, for example, "Hunting the Bull" (ca. 1732), "Rape of Europa and Bacchanal". Giuseppe Zais (1709–1784) painted purely decorative ruins or pictures of sheep.

Room 13

Examples of 16th c. portraiture in this room particularly worth noting include ★**Tintoretto's portrait of the Procurator Jacopo Soranzo**, as both character study and official portrait, and "St Jerome in Meditation" by Jacopo da Ponte, called Bassano (1517–1592).

Room 14

The early 17th c. is represented by a portrait-like version of David by Domenico Fetti (1589–1623), using a fascinating chiaroscuro technique reminiscent of Caravaggio, and by the work of Johann Liss (1595–1629) from Oldenburg, who impressively combines dramatic treatment with lyrical landscape in, for example, "Adam and Eve mourning Abel", and "Sacrifice of Isaac".

Room 15

Besides works by Tiepolo the highlights of this room are the "Allegory of Painting and the Art of Sculpture" by Giovan Antonio Pellegrini (1675–1741), with its delicate colouring and flowing line, and works by Francesco Solimena (1657–1747) with rich colour contrasts and electrifying wealth of movement.

Room 16

The four mythological scenes Rape of Europa, Diana and Actaeon, Diana discovering Calypso, and Contest between Apollo and Marsyas, are early works (1720–1722) by Giambattista Tiepolo from his cool colour period.

Room 16a

The "Fortuneteller" (ca. 1740) by Giambattista Piazzetta (1683–1754) is at the same time a genre piece and an intriguing character study both for its psychology and use of colour. The large group portrait of the family of the Procurator Luigi Pisano and "The Allegory of Art and Fame", his entry for admission to the original Accademia di Belle Arti, are by Alessandro Longhi, son of the artist Pietro Longhi. Also worth noting is a sympathetic portrait of Count Vailetti by Fra Galgario.

Room 17

Picturesque imaginary architecture, Capricci ruins and views with strong contrasts of light and shade, transformed in his later work to radiant pure luminosity, are the hallmarks of **Canaletto** (Antonio Canal; 1697–1768), whose ★**Capriccio** (1765), his entry for admission to the Accademia, and imaginary views with ruins and classical buildings or with the Porta Portello in Padua entertainingly and capriciously combine observed reality with force of imagination.

The work of **Michele Marieschi** (1710–1744) also consists of amusing ★**Capricci** and panoramic views dotted with sketchy staffage figures and flaring lights, as for example in "Capriccio with Gothic building and Obelisk" and "Capriccio with antique Arch and Goats".

Francesco Guardi (1712–1793) is another master of atmospheric views of Venice, with an equally irresistible appeal. His flowing, almost impressionistic style of painting can be seen here in works such as ★**Bacino di San Marco with San Giorgio and the Giudecca** (before 1774). On the other hand, the view of "Rio dei Mendicanti with Scuola di San Marco" (ca. 1740) by Bernardo Bellotto (1720–1780) shows an almost photographic gift for observation.

Rosalba Carriera (1675–1758) acquired great fame with her highly renowned ★**pastel portraits**, which range from the tender study of a child in shimmering pastel shades to the psychologically profound insight of the adult portrait. As a sharp-eyed chronicler of every day life in 18th c. Venice **Pietro Longhi** (1702–1785) was virtually in a class of his own. His **genre scenes** are charming, often gently satirical renditions of contemporary high and low life, whether they be of the Apothecary, the Fortuneteller or the Dancing Lesson.

This room holds less important 18th c. paintings. Room 18

Bartolomeo Cincana, called Montagna (recorded 1459–1523), painted Room 19 "St Peter with Donor" – a harmonious interweaving of human figure, architecture and landscape – early in the 16th c. Giovanni Agostino da Lodi, active at the turn of the 15th/16th c., brought the Renaissance forms of Brabante and Leonardo to Venice in such works as "The Washing of Feet ". Boccaccio Boccaccino (ca. 1465–1524), from Cremona, also painted in the Renaissance manner, as is evident in "Mystic Marriage of St Catherine" (1508/1509).

The cycle of paintings of ★★**the miracles of the relic of the True Cross** by Room 20 **Gentile Bellini, Carpaccio** etc., is unique as a self-portrait on the grand scale of Venice and its people. It was executed by the city's leading artists between 1494 and 1502 for the Sala dell'Albergo in the Scuola di San Giovanni Evangelista where a relic of the True Cross had been kept since 1369. The painting by Gentile Bellini (1429–1507) of the Procession on the Piazza San Marco faithfully reproduces the square in every detail as it was around 1500. The 13th c. mosaics, later replaced, still gleam above the five portals of the Basilica di San Marco. On the left there is the colonnade of the Procuratie Vecchio without the clocktower which was to be added later, while on the right of the church a corner of the Doges' Palace is visible with the coloured façade of the Porta della Carta and behind it the brightly ornamented Late Gothic main façade of the east wing. Next to the Campanile stands the Orseolo hospice instead of the present Libreria and Procuratie Nuove. The pictorial chronicle continues with Gentile's portrayal of the Miracle of the Relic on the Ponte San Lorenzo where, with the press of the crowd during the annual procession, the reliquary fell into the water then placed itself in the hand of the Grand Master of the Scuola who was searching for it, and pulled him ashore. On the left of the picture can be seen, witnessing this event, Catarina Cornaro, Queen of Cyprus, and her retinue, and on the right the members of the Scuola. Gentile sets the miraculous Healing of Pietro de Ludovici inside a church, presumably San Giovanni Evangelista. Vittore Carpaccio (1465–1526) places the miracle of the Healing of the Madman by the holy relic (on the far left of the picture) in front of the Rialto bridge, and precisely reproduces the townscape of the busy merchant quarter. What he shows is the wooden bridge erected in 1458, which could be raised to allow the passage of large boats and which collapsed in 1524 when it was replaced by the present stone bridge. Also present, on the right of the picture, is the Fondaco dei Tedeschi which was burnt down in 1505. The lines of washing, throng of gondolas, packed crowd of onlookers, some deep in conversation, among them smartly gowned Cavaliere, turbaned Mohammedans, and Knights of St John, all contribute to this portrait of cosmopolitan, pulsating life in the Rialto quarter. By contrast the "Gift of the Relic of the True Cross to the Members of the Scuola di San Giovanni Evangelista" by Lazzaro Bastiani (recorded 1449–1512) is a relatively stiffer ceremonial painting set on the square before the church. The painting of the Miracle on the Campo San Lio by Giovanni Mansueti (ca. 1485–1527) depicts how during a funeral procession because of doubt about the authenticity of the relic it became so heavy that it had to be temporarily deposited in the church of San Lio. In his version of the miraculous Healing of the lame Daughter of Benvegnudo da San Polo Mansueti provides a glimpse of the interior of a patrician Venetian palazzo. The inner courtyard of a palazzo is also the setting for the miracle of the Healing of the Grandson of Alvise Finetti after his Fall from the Roof, by Benedetto Rusco, called Diana (ca. 1482–1525).

The cycle of ★★**Scenes from the Legend of St Ursula** is solely the work Room 21 of **Vittore Carpaccio** (ca. 1465–1526). According to the legend, Ursula, the Christian princess of Britain, assented to marriage with the heathen prince Aetherius provided that he was baptised and accompanied her and her train of maidens on a pilgrimage to Rome. On the return journey Ursula and her maidens were slaughtered by Huns, as predicted in a dream, before the gates of Cologne. Using the Renaissance architecture typical of the period and atmospheric landscapes, Carpaccio painted in the style of contemporary historic imagery the arrival of the envoys of the English King, their dismissal, the return of the envoys to the English court, the meeting of Ursula and Aetherius and the departure of the pilgrims, their reception by Pope Cyriacus before the walls of Rome, with the exact reproduction of Castello San Angelo, the dream of Ursula as a charming interior, arrival in Cologne, the martyrdom of Ursula and her virgin train, and the apotheosis of St Ursula.

Room 23

The former church of Santa Maria della Carità contains works from the Venetian Early Renaissance, including such altarpieces from the 1460s as early works by Giovanni Bellini and his workshop, including the triptych of St Sebastian between St Antony Abbot and John the Baptist. The full length portrait of the blessed Lorenzo Giustiani is an early work of Gentile Bellini, elder brother of Giovanni, showing him as a sharply outlined dignified old man. Vivid colours and the sculptural quality of the figures, despite the traditional gold ground, distinguish the polyptych (1477) by Bartolomeo Vivarini (ca. 1430 to after 1491) of Ambrose, Father of the Church, and Donors between Saints Louis, Peter, Paul and Sebastian.

★**Madonna with Saints** (1480) is a sacra conversazione by **Alvise Vivarini** (1442/1453–1504/1505), with the Madonna encircled by Saints Louis of Toulouse, Anthony of Padua, Anna, Joachim, Francis and Bernhardin of Siena.

Room 24

In the Albergo of the Scuola della Carità, the living quarters of the confra-

Santa Maria Assunta was built in the Roman Baroque style for the Jesuits

ternity, which has been preserved in its entirety, the first canvas that meets the eye is the large triptych (1446) by Antonio Vivarini (1415/1420–1476/1484) and his brother-in-law Giovanni d'Alegmana (recorded 1441–1450) of the Madonna Enthroned between the Early Fathers Gregory, Jerome, Ambrose and Augustine, in which Late Gothic exuberant decoration and the decorative Byzantine heritage are combined with naturalistic human portrayal and the exciting perspective of the Early Renaissance to form a magnificent whole. Stylistically part of the High Renaissance, **Titian**'s huge ★★**Presentation of the Virgin** (1534–1538) takes up the whole wall of the room, for which it was originally painted and therefore had to take into account the positioning of the doors on either side. Saturated with differentially lit colour, it creates a carefully calculated tension between architecture and landscape, the group and the individual, foreground and background, movement.and repose.

For centuries the Ponte di Rialto (see entry) was the only bridge over the Grand Canal. A second footbridge was not built until 1854 when the Austrian forces of occupation – Venice had been part of the Hapsburg Kingdom of Lomardo-Venetia since 1815 – constructed the iron Ponte dell'Accademia, subsequently replaced by a wooden bridge in 1932.

Ponte
dell'Accademia

★I Gesuiti · Santa Maria Assunta K/L 3

Santa Maria Assunta was built in the Roman Baroque style for the Jesuits – hence I Gesuiti –by Domenico Rossi between 1714 and 1729 on the site of an earlier 13th c. church. It has a barrel-vaulted single nave, side-chapels, transept and choir but its most striking feature is the magnificence of its sumptuous decor: green and white marble walls, massive pillars and colonnades, gilding, and a High Altar with a baldachin and sculptured retable.

Its outstanding works of art include Tintoretto's "Assumption" in the left transept, Palma Giovane's frescos in the Sacristy, and, above all, **Titian**'s ★★**Martyrdom of St Lawrence** (1558–1560), a sublime nocturne in which a bright shimmering light proclaims to the tortured saint the divine message of the hope of eternal life for the soul.

Location
Campo Gesuiti

Quay
Ca' d'Oro

★Il Ghetto G/H 2

Traces of its ethnic character still linger on in Venice's original Jewish quarter, where the Calle del Ghetto Vecchio, lined by its high-rise façades, leads you over a narrow bridge into the rambling Campo del Ghetto Nuovo. Here, at the heart of the first-ever Jewish enclave to bear the name ghetto, you can buy kosher food in the corner-shop on the right. Nowadays only a few of Venice's 520 or so Jews still live in this quarter, among them the pensioners in the modern buildings of its retirement home, the Casa Israelitica de Riposo. In 1516 Venice's Council of Ten decreed that the Jewish moneylenders, traders, weavers and boilermakers must be confined with their families to the site of a former cannon foundry (or "geto" in Venetian). Originally this islet could only be reached by two bridges and was barred at night by two watergates. Because of the great lack of space the inhabitants of this "ghetto" – which in the 17th c. contained 5000 people – were forced to live in buildings up to eight stories high, often in narrow, low-ceilinged rooms. Faded inscriptions such as "banco rosso" at No. 2912 recall the Jewish banking houses which were called "banco verde" "negro" or "rosso" according to the colour of their credit notes, and which made loans to every strata of Venetian society. Inconspicuous façades also front the three synagogues in the Ghetto Nuovo and the two others in the Ghetto Vecchio. These were simply called Scola, meaning buildings for communal prayer with adjoining Talmud schools.

Location
Ghetto Vecchio
and Ghetto
Nuovo

Quay
San Marcuola

The Jewish Ghetto: the Home of Shylock

Shylock, Venices most famous Jew. was of course only a fictional character invented by William Shakespeare, but he bears all the characteristics of a real man who finally begins to hate as a result of the constant humiliation and insults he has to suffer. His antagonist, the rich Venetian merchant Antonio, who abuses and spits on Shylock in the street simply because he is a Jew but later tries to obtain a large loan from him, portrays the hypocritical moral code of a society which calls itself Christian yet finds nothing reprehensible in despising and humiliating its fellow men. Shakespeare's play "The Merchant of Venice" (1596/7) gives merely a condensed dramatic picture, whereas in truth Venetians and Jews coexisted quite differently.

In Venice Jews were made thoroughly welcome from the 13th century as moneylenders and in fact played an essential role in the economic development of the city, since canonical law prohibited Christian merchants from doing business on credit against payment of interest. Above all, in the 14th century, as a result of the war with Verona and Genoa and the economic problems caused by the plague epidemic, the city needed money and Jewish bankers brought in more and more capital. Interest rates were, however, contractually fixed and controlled by the government. Each short-term contract (condotta) negotiated between the Jewish bankers and the Republic of Venice in 1382, for example, laid down a maximum interest rate of 10 per cent for loans against pledged security amd 20 per cent for promissory note loans, in addition to which the Venetian government could also demand compulsory

loans. After large credit institutions came to the fore there were Jewish banks offering credit to small borrowers from 1389 onwards.

In marked contrast to their indispensability as money-lenders, however, was the way in which the Jews were regarded in a social context, even in such an open climate as that which existed in Venice. Where – as the merchant Antonio found – "profit and trade is dependent upon all the citizens of this city". In order to be allowed to live and carry on business in the city the Jews had to pay a special levy to the community. As they were not allowed to own land or property they were obliged to amass large financial assets which would give them a high level of cash flow and mobility. This also led to ongoing feelings of mistrust between business partners, and the Venetian patriarchy regarded Jewish merchants and traders as troublesome competitors. Furthermore, religiously-motivated anti-Semitism came into play, together with open hostility towards and persecution of Jews accused of heresy, the murder of Christ and of poisoning streams during the plagues.

Towards the end of the 14th century there were once again large numbers of complaints about the behaviour of Jews in Venice who were accused of not giving enough to the poor, with the result that in 1397 the community voted to expel them. They then settled in nearby Mestre from whence they could continue to engage in financial business in Venice. Fresh harassment and decrees further restricted their freedom to trade, however. For example, they were obliged during their permitted two-week stays in the city (which were usually months apart) to wear a yellow star sewed on their clothing and later an even more obvious pointed hat of the same colour.

However, when Venice found itself in financial straits in the early 16th century as a result of costly wars the Venetian government passed a surprising decree on March 29th 1516 which granted the Jews their own cordonned-off district in the city: "The Jews must all live together in the complex of houses in the ghetto near San Girolamo. To prevent them from straying out during the night two gates are to be constructed, one on that side of the Ghetto Vecchio where there is a small bridge and the other on the far side of the said bridge. Each gate must be opened each morning on the ringing of the Marangona bell, and locked at midnight by four Christian guards who will be employed and paid for doing this by their Jews at a rate which our committee shall decide is fitting". Thus the world's first ghetto, covering an area of some 35,000 sq. m, came into being in Venice. The name comes from the original use of this island-like district of Venice by metal foundries (gettare = to found or cast: getio = casting). It was not until later that this name for the Jewish quarter of a town or city became synomous with such sad discrimination and the terror which results from contempt for one's fellow man.

The Jewish quarter of Venice is divided into three areas. The first to develop was the Ghetto Nuevo, inhabited mainly by German and Italian Jews, followed in 1541 by the Ghetto Vecchio for traders from the Levant and refugees from the Spanish Inquisition, and then by the Ghetto Nuovissimo, where from 1633 wealthy Sephardic families could settle. Jews were still not allowed to own land or property but were given wide renting rights. To look after their interests the inhabitants of the ghetto elected the "università", a committee with originally twelve, later six, members with far-reaching social, religious and economic powers. They negotiated with the Venetian government and regulated internally the financial burdens imposed on them in the way of taxes and compul-

Nine-branched candelabra for the Hanukkah festival (Museo Ebraico)

sory loans. In spite of all the oppressive regulations the number of ghetto inhabitants grew: in 1516 there were 700, but this number soon doubled and by 1630 it reached 5000. This meant that in the 17th century the Jews represented betwen 2.5 and 3.3 per cent of the total population of Venice, but in the 18th century this figure fell to 1.2 per cent.

In the overcrowded houses of the ghetto (at times there have been as many as 897 people per hectare, compared with 236/96 in the rest of the city) there was a colourful mix of people and languages from Mediterranean countries, Poland and Germany. Venice's multicultural Jewish community produced some leading rabbis, academics and writers but also attracted entrepreneurs and adventurers. Spiritual leadership came from the rabbis who were also teachers, preachers and judges. These included the famous rabbi Leone da Modena (1571–1648) and his popular Talmud seminary, the learned Simone Lazzatto (1583–1663), whose political history dissertations and analyses of the Venetian economy were of great importance, and Simone Calimani (1699–1784), who tried through his extensive writings to break down the prejudice against Jewish religious life and culture. Also of immense importance in helping to

ברוך הבא מלך המשיח ב"ה

In the Campo di Ghetto Nuovo you can buy kosher food

cement Jewish-Christian relations was the exchange of letters between the writer Sara Coppa Sullam (1590–1641) and the Catholic nobleman, poet and translator Ansaldo Cebà from Genoa. who was almost 30 years her senior. Leading lights in a world of mystic and Messianic thought and ideas were Mosè Zacuto (1625–92) and Mosè Chaim Luzzatto (170–46). Hebrew printing was essential for the dissemination of these ideas, and it had its centre in Venice where works by philosophers, grammarians, religious thinkers and other writers from the whole of Europe were published. Educational aspirations are clearly evidenced by the fact that, between 1517 and 1721, 250 Jewish students obtained their doctorates at the University of Padua which was sponsored by Venice. In spite of all the care needed in associating with Jews many Venetians were quite happy to be treated by highly-trained Jewish doctors. Even noble ladies crept secretly into the ghetto from time to time to have extravagant silk dresses made by the tailors.

Even though the Jewish community in Venice encountered a certain degree of hostility ranging from malicious anti-Jewish preaching on the part of some religious orders to reservations among the rank and file regarding the Jewish way of life, language, religious rites, food and clothing, nevertheless the Jews lived in relative safety and their lives were not threatened. In the records of the senate meetings, side by side with the frequent blackmail demands from the "Serenissima" (Venetian Republic). can be found repeated warnings of the need to exercise tolerance towards the Jews, particularly in times of crisis. However, even the capital supplied by the Jews proved insufficient to avoid the economic slump in Venice in the 18th century. Nevertheless, during the period from 1669 to 1700 the Jewish community paid an immense sum of over 800,000 gold ducats. Compulsory loans increased during the following decades largely because of the Turkish wars, the tax burden became heavier and heavier and the funds available from Jewish moneylenders finally dried up. Lending banks found themselves on the verge of bankruptcy when income from Jewish merchants and businessmen proved insufficient to cover the amount out on credit. By the end of the 18th century there were still 1620 Jews living in the ghetto, about a third of whom were financially sound while the rest lived on the edge of poverty. Finally it needed a show of force from outside to improve their lot. On July 7th 1797 French soldiers of Napoleon's army tore down the gates to the ghetto and planted a "Freedom Tree" in the Campo di Ghetto Nuovo as a symbol of a new epoch, in which all Jews could take their place as equal citizens in Venetian society.

Campo di Ghetto Nuovo – heart of the old jewish quarter, built by decree of Venice's Council of Ten in 1516

The Scuola Grande Tedesca, recognizable by the five large arcaded windows in its façade, was built by German Jews in the Ghetto Nuovo in 1528. The irregular floor plan of the interior is softened by the oval surrounding gallery. The prayer benches are from the Renaissance period while the Baroque gilded walls serve to frame the Aron (the shrine for the Torah), flanked by two windows, and the fine Bima (pulpit) with prayers and commemorative inscriptions.

★★Synagogues

The Scola Ganton, which probably owes its name either to the donor family or its corner position, was founded in 1531 but underwent much alteration. The frequently restored 17th c. Bima stands on five wooden steps under an arch supported by double pillars.

The Scola Italia, built 1571–1575, with an ornamental small dome over its Bima, is distinguished by five broad windows and a cartouche with the inscription "Santa Communità italiana". The Scola Levantina, with its polygonal oriel window, is in the Ghetto Vecchio and contains an impressive richly carved lectern (Tewa) on spiral columns by Andrea Brustolon of Belluno.

Venice's largest synagogue is the late 16th c. Scola Spagnola, which was remodelled in 1635 by the famous Baroque master Baldassare Longhena; its lavishly decorated interior boasts brass candlesticks, gilded wood carvings, polychromatic marble and a sumptuous balustrade.

The small Museum of the Jewish Community is worth a visit. It contains manuscripts and documents on the history of Venetian Jewry and religious artefacts such as parts of the "Magiolere", the Venetian term for the ark containing the Torah, and the protective cover, dating from the 5th c. BC, for the Esther scroll which told how Persia's Jews were saved by Queen Esther.

Museo
Communità
Ebraica

Opening times:
Mon.–Fri., Sun.
10am–5pm

Biennial Festival of Contemporary Art

The oldest international forum of contemporary art, the Venice Biennial Festival, was founded in 1895 on the initiative of the Venetian man of letters, artist and mayor Riccardo Selvatico in order to promote cultural exchanges. It can now look back on over one hundred years of varied history marked by both the presentation of avant-garde painting and sculpture and by the politics of the great powers and of the art market. When, on April 30th 1895, on the site of the Giardini di Castello on the edge of the historic city centre, the gates to the first Biennial Festival were opened under the patronage of the King Umberto I of Italy and his consort Margherita of Savoy, 516 works by 285 artists could be viewed in one, single, classically designed pavilion. It exceeded expectations by attracting nearly 225,000 visitors. In all, 186 works of art were sold, and of the 156 foreign exhibitors the German artist Max Liebermann distinguished himself by winning the Prize of the Province of Venice.

Its success with the public continued at subsequent festivals. In 1909 457,960 art enthusiasts came to Venice, a record which stood until 1976. Initially the exhibitions were arranged by subjects, not by countries, whereby the works were judged after discussion with both Italian and foreign societies and committees. However, these popular exhibitions of art soon awakened a lot of political interest; for instance, in November 1905 Kaiser Wilhelm II visited the festival only to find that his favourite painters Adolph Menzel, Anton von Werner and Hermann Joseph Wilhelm Knackfuss were not represented. The result was that for the first time the festival of 1907 had national exhibition tents; the number of these has since increased to 26 and they are under the charge of superintendents appointed by each country. After the Second World War national representation played an important role.

Critics of this art exhibition continually bemoan the fact that little new is dis-

---

Guided tours of the synagogues leave from the museum every 30 minutes, starting at 10.30.

Memorial

The close on 200 Venetian Jews who died between 1943 and 1944 in the Holocaust are commemorated on a wall in the Ghetto by barbed wire and a bronze relief (deportation, concentration camp, forced labour, execution, mass graves) by the sculptor Arbit Blatas.

Giardini Pubblici · Biennale Pavilions   O–Q 6/7

Location
Riva dei Sette
Martiri

Quay
Giardini

The "Public Gardens" were laid out by Napoleon I at the south-east end of the main island. Nowadays, however, much of the site is covered by the modern pavilions that house the "Biennale", Venice's biennial international exhibition of contemporary art which takes place in odd-number years. These still leave enough room for Rococo and late 19th c. statues and, naturally, walks among the palms, acacias and plane trees. Giuseppe Garibaldi is commemorated by a monument unveiled in 1855 at the north-west end of the park.

played, and that instead the works exhibited are by artists who have made the grade solely on the basis of national prestige. They maintain that consequently the festival serves less to encourage experimentation, international dialogue and changes in cultural awareness and is in fact designed more to support the commercial interests of the art market and to maximise tourism figures. The overall management of the 46th Biennial Festival in 1995 (there having been none in 1916, 1918, 1944 and 1946) was also a non-Italian, namely, the Frenchman Jean Clair, Director of the Picasso Museum in Paris. In addition to contributions by 134 artists from 51 nations, 1995 was highlighted by an exhibition portraying the history of art over the past hundred years, under the title "Being one but being different – Pictures of the Body 1895–1995". As in previous years, with the exception of the period from 1970 to 1984, the four-person international jury awarded numerous prizes. The Golden Lion for Painting went to Ronald B. Kitaj (USA), the Golden Lion for Sculpture to Gary Hill (USA), the National Prize to Egypt. The 48th festival of 1999, under the management of Harald Szeemann, included the APERTO programme for young artists and for the first time the Arsenal was included to house ensemble exhibitions. The German pavilion

Poster of the 'Biennale' 1995

was dominated by the black-and-white eye of the Video Installation by Rosemarie Trockel. In the American pavilion were avalanches of colour by Anne Hamilton, while in the Arsenal the Chinese Cai GuoQuiang created an ambiguous history workshop.

The main entrance is by Antonio Selva (1810). Among the most striking Biennale pavilions, starting immediately to the right of the entrance, is the Venezuelan pavilion (1954–1956) by Carlo Scarpa and the Russian pavilion next door (1914), then, taking the broad walk straight out from the entrance, the classical-style Italian pavilion is reached. Other famous architects who have designed pavilions include Josef Hoffmann (Austrian pavilion, 1934), Gerrit Thomas Rietvals (Dutch complex, 1954) and Alvar Aalto (Finnish pavilion), while the Glaswegian James Stirling was responsible for the glass-walled Book Pavilion.

La Giudecca (Island)   E–L 7/8

Originally known as "Vigano" or "Spina Lunga" (long thorn) because of its elongated shape, the island probably owes its present name to the "Giudicati", people banished from Venice who initially settled here out of necessity. The monastery island, which covers an area of 78 ha is separated from the city by the broad Canale della Giudecca and div-

Quays
Zitelle, Redentore,
Palanca,
Sant'Eufemia,
Sacca Fisola

111

ided into eight adjacent islands by small canals. From the 14th c. onwards wealthy Viennese nobles built their villas and pleasure gardens looking out towards the city centre, whilst the side overlooking the lagoon was the site of seven monasteries and small palazzi belonging to the literary academy. During the 19th and 20th c. several commercial enterprises were established here, amongst them the Stucky noodle factory, a long-abandoned ice plant and Fortuny, manufacturer of high-class goods.

★Il Redentore
(Church of the
Redeemer)

Location
Campo Redentore

Quay
Redentore

The white Franciscan church is one of the principle works of Andrea Palladio (see Famous People). He based his designs on ancient models, in particular on the ten books on architecture written by the Roman architect Vitruvius at the time of the Emperor Augustus. Consequently he based the façade of the Church of the Redeemer on three superimposed temple fronts. The double gable and attic were adopted by Palladio from the Pantheon in Rome. The dominant dome forms the central part of the single-aisled hall church between the nave and the monastic choir. The Festival of the Redeemer and this church date back to a plague epidemic of 1576. At that time the Senate vowed to build the church and hold a Festival of the Redeemer (Redentore). The Franciscans undertook the religious obligations. The building of the church began in 1577 and was completed in 1592. Following the death of Palladio in 1580, the architect Antonio da Ponte took over supervision of the works. On both sides of the nave, the architecture of which is reminiscent of a Roman bath-house, are three elliptical side-chapels. Their altarpieces portray scenes from the life of Christ. Of special interest are the "Baptism of Christ" from the studio of Veronese and the two altar wings, the "Scourging" and "Transfiguration of Christ" from the school of Tintoretto. Although the Late Baroque high altar was not finished until 1680 the bronze Crucifixion group dates from the end of the 16th c. Like

The Italy Pavilion is one of the Biennale pavilions in the Giardini Pubblici, where Venice's biennial international exhibition of contemporary art is held

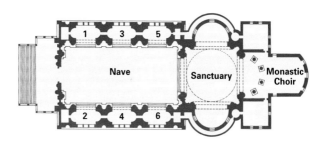

Altarpieces
1 "Transformation of Christ" (school of Tintoretto)   4 "Baptism of Christ", Veronese
2 "Birth of Christ", Francesco Bassano   5 "Interment of Jesus", Palmail Giovane
3 "Resurrection of Christ", Francesco Bassano   6 "Scourging of Christ", school of Tintoretto

the high altar, this is a work of Girolamo Campagna (1550–1623). Also notable is a painting of the Madonna by Alvise Vivarini.

After the dedication of the church the Doge came here every year with the chief officials of the state to a thanksgiving service. The Venetians still make a pilgrimage here on the third Sunday of July to thank the Redeemer for the end of the epidemic. A bridge of boats is constructed from Zattere across the Giudecca Canal, over which the procession makes it way to the Church of the Redeemer. In the evening the festival concludes with a magnificent fireworks display and a procession of illuminated boats.

The Church of the Virgin, some 500 m east of the Church of the Redeemer, also has a façade which is said to date back to Andrea Palladio, albeit much altered by the architect Jacopo Bozzetto. Otherwise the building is essentially a work of the 18th c.
Zitelle
Santa Maria della
Presentazione

Approximately 600 m west of the Church of the Redeemer lies a church founded in the 9th c. and dedicated to the Roman martyr Euphemia (Quay: Sant' Eufemia). This basilica-style church was remodelled by Tommaso Ternanza in the 18th c. and painted by Giambattista Canal, taking Il Gesuiti (see entry) as his model. There is a fine painting of St. Roch (1480) by Bartolomeo Vivarini on the first altar in the south aisle.
Sant' Eufemia

It is worth taking a walk past "Harry's Dolci" which sells all Cipriani products and the Fortuny factory founded in 1919 (No. 804) to the gigantic Mulino Stucky. The wealthy noodle manufacturer Giovanni Stucky had the plant built in neo-Gothic style by the architect Ernst Wullekopf from Hannover in 1895. By the Second World War it was one of the largest noodle factories in Italy, but had to be closed in 1954. The plant was sold to Dutch investors in 1994.
Mulino Stucky

Islands in the Lagoon   Q–R 1/2

Like enchanted oases, more than 30 small islands lie in the shallow waters of the Lagoon of Venice. Emilio Casteler sang about them as "swimming gardens, anchored in this sea of indelible memory and eternal poetry", and Lord Byron, who was a permanent guest here, wrote of Venice: "I saw from out the waves her structures rise, as from the stroke of the enchanter's wand". Apart from the larger islands, Burano, Murano
Venice's
Archipelago

113

Murano, stronghold of the glass blowers, is one of the most visited islands

and Torcello (see entries) which have been densely populated from time immemorial, only a few of the smaller islands are still used nowadays. Anyone looking at these lonely islets, overgrown with vegetation, would never believe that they were the scene of bustling activity in previous centuries. The islands in front of the city were used for the most diverse purposes, for example to accommodate pilgrims, the sick and the banished, as well as dangerous goods and festive events such as that held in 1782, when a great reception was held on San Giorgio in Alga for Pope Pius VI on his return from Vienna. Long abandoned also are the isles with their octagonal forts and semi-circular batteries built since the Middle Ages to defend the Serenissima. An association of state-owned and private firms, known as the "Consorvio Nuova Venetia" are working on a concept for redevelopment of and new uses for this island world for the end of the 1990s. The larger islands are connected to the "Vaporetti" system, but anyone planning a trip to the more remote islands should find out about excursions. It is also possible to hire a boat to explore on one's own.

★★Burano | See entry.

★La Giudecca | See entry.

Lazzaretto Nuovo | The first inhabitants of the island were hermits, and from 1486 the island was used for storage in quarantine of goods which might possibly have been carrying diseases. During the 1576 plague epidemic, people suspected of having the plague were isolated here, whilst those actually sick were taken to Lazzaretto Vecchio. Today nature has largely won back this fortified island.

La Grazia | The many pilgrims who set sail from Venice to the Holy Land in the Middle Ages found their own accommodation on the islands of La

Grazia and Lazzaretto Vecchio. As the name "Lazaret" suggests, hospitals were established here during epidemics. Today the city dog pound is situated here.

Lazzaretto Vecchio

See entry.

★★Murano

According to legend, St. Francis of Assisi rested on this tiny island south of Burano (see entry) after returning from the Holy Land in 1220. The island was inhabited by Franciscan friars from the 13th to the 15th c., and was then abandoned until the 19th c. The little church, dating from 1228, situated amongst proud cypresses, has a delightful atmosphere. After viewing the Franciscan convent, it is customary to make a small donation to the friars (open daily 9am–11am, 3pm–5pm).

★San Francesco del Deserto

See entry

★San Giorgio Maggiore

In the 12th c. monks set up a leprosy hospital on San Lazzaro, and in 1717 the island was taken over by Armenian monks. The cloister museum now holds the largest. most valuable collection of Armenian manuscripts in the west, with more than 150,000 volumes and a late 18th c. print shop. An exhibition room is dedicated to Lord Byron who spent a great deal of time here, and learned the Armenian language.

★San Lazzaro degli Armeni

This cypress-covered "Isle of the Dead" was inhabited by Camaldolites in the Middle Ages, was later used as a prison and since 1870 has been Venice's cemetery island. The famous people whose last resting place this is, include the Russian ballet master Sergei Diaghilev (1829–1929), his compatriot, the great composer Igor Stravinski (1882–1971) and the American poet Ezra Pound (1885–1972). Of the former monastery the 15th c. Gothic cloister and the pretty Renaissance church of San Michele, built by Mauro Coducci from 1469 to 1478, still remain. Also worth seeing is the hexagonal Cappella Emiliana, which was added by Guglielmo Bergamasco in 1530 and is decorated with red and green marble.

★San Michele

For centuries these two islands opposite the Lido harbour have been famous for their vegetables, especially asparagus and artichokes.

Sant' Erasmo and Le Vignole

See entry.

★Torcello

Lido

The Lido, just 12 km long and up to 4 km wide, is a narrow, flat strip of sand, separated by the sea from the Venetian Lagoon. In the 19th c. writers such as Lord Byron, Shelley and Musset discovered the island, which developed into a fashionable seaside resort of the Belle Epoque. Almost half the island is made up of beaches of fine, smooth sand. Apart from the usual bathing (most of the beach is divided into sections, each belonging to one or several hotels), there are various sports facilities, including riding and golf courses, and tennis courts.
    The Lido's architectural character is determined by late 19th c. buildings, Liberty villas and the monumental building of the Summer Casino (in winter the Casino Municipale is situated in the Palazzo Ventramin-Camerlenghi), as well as imposing *fin de siècle* hotel complexes, especially the neo-Moorish Grand Hotel Excelsior and the elegant Hotel des Bains, once a favourite meeting place for European High Society and the illustrious setting for Luchino Visconti's film "Death in Venice", based on Thomas Mann's novella.

Quay
Santa Maria
Elisabetta (off
Riva degli
Schiavoni)

Car ferry from
Venice-Tronchetto

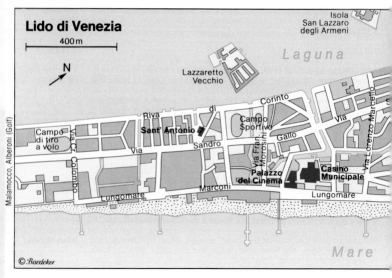

The Golden Lion

Throughout the history of cinema, Venice has been a favourite setting and for over half a century has provided an international forum for this film competition. The first Venetian Film Festival was held in the Excelsior luxury hotel at the beginning of August 1932, and proved a great success. Three years later the Palazzo del Cinema, designed by Luigi Quagliata was opened on the Lido, and the famous "Premio Leone D'Oro di San Marco" is now held here annually at the end of August and beginning of September. This is Italy's answer to the American "Oscar", awarded to the best films and actors (Palazzo del Cinema, Lungomare Marconi, tel. 041 5267887, fax 041 5267898). Great directors including John Ford, Louis Malle, John Cassavetes, De Sica, Fellini and Visconti have celebrated major triumphs at the "Mostra del Cinema", and today the "Golden Lion", abandoned in 1968 but long since been reinstated, is one of the most coveted honours in the art of cinema.

San Nicolò	See entry.
★Cimitero Israelitico	The iron gates of the Jewish cemetery at San Nicolò open onto a delightful park, where, amongst the lush vegetation, gravestones made from shining limestone date back as far as 1389. The plague epidemic of 1630–1631, which claimed almost 2000 Jewish victims, is commemorated by a simple stone plaque over a mass grave.

★Madonna dell'Orto · Santa Maria dell'Orto   J 2

Location
Fondamenta della
Madonna
dell'Orto

A figure of St. Christopher by Bartolomeo Bon, above the portal, testifies to the fact that this church was originally dedicated to that saint. The charming brick façade of the church, completed in 1462, represents a

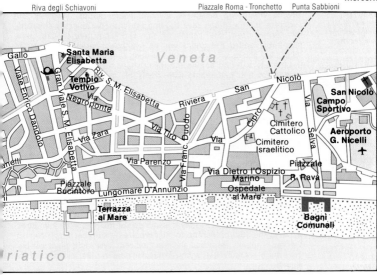

Riva degli Schiavoni   Piazzale Roma - Tronchetto   Punta Sabbioni

blend of Gothic and Renaissance and is adorned by figures of the twelve
apostles, ascribed to Jacobello dalle Masegne and his workshop.

Quay
Madonna
dell'Orto

Inside the colonnaded, flat roofed basilica, in the chapel to the right of
the Presbytery, the painter Tintoretto (see Famous People) was buried in
1594, next to his son Domenico. Whilst still a young man, Tintoretto created for this church the "Last Judgment" (on the right of the choir), the
"Worship of the Golden Calf" (on the left of the choir), "The Raising of
Licinius, son of a Roman Prefect, by St. Agnes" (fourth chapel on the
left) and the "Presentation of Mary in the Temple" (ca. 1552) above the
entrance to the Cappella di San Marco in the right aisle. There are also
noteworthy works by other artists: a "Madonna" (1480) by Giovanni
Bellini (see Famous People) in the last chapel in the left aisle and "John
the Baptist with Saints" (1493) a panel by Cima da Conegliano on the
first alter on the right.

★★Mercerie   K 4

Venice's classic shopping quarter extends between the Ponto di Rialto
(see entry), on the south side of which there is a small square with
the Carlo Goldoni memorial (see Famous People) and St
Mark's Square where the Merceria dell'Orologio, a street
lined with small jewellers' and souvenir shops,
emerges under the clock-tower. In the Calle Fiubera,
which branches off to the west from the Merceria
dell'Orologio, elegant fashions, finely crafted carnival
masks and costumes are on display. The Mercuria San
Zulian and the Mercuria San Salvatore continue north-
wards to the Rialto Bridge, with shops also selling
masks, expensive jewellery, leather and Murano
glass. Venice's most prestigious shopping addresses
are in the Calle Vallaresso, branching west from St.
Mark's Square, and its continuation, the Via Larga XXII
Marzo, an unusually wide street by Venetian standards.

Murano

Location
between Rialto
Bridge and Piazza
San Marco

uay
Rialto/San Marco

This is where top designers, elegant leather shops, jewellers and exquisite antique shops have become established. Generally speaking, the further from the centre of the shopping quarter, the more favourably priced the goods will be – although prices anywhere in Venice are above average. Visitors wishing to take a break from exploring the city will find among the many shops a rich selection of small cake-shops and restaurants with irresistible delicacies and local specialities.

★★Murano   N/O 1 (A/B 7/8)

Quay
Murano
(Lines 12 and 13
from Fondamenta
Nuove)

The famous glass island, with its main canal joined by many small side canals, is reminiscent of Venice city centre. From the quay, the Rio dei Vetrai (Glassblowers' Canal), leads past numerous workshops where the glassblowers can be seen at work – with showrooms where souvenirs of Murano glass can be purchased.

This was already a lively centre of trade in the 10th c., thanks to its saltworks and fishing. At the end of the 13th c. Venetian glass production was moved here, and continued to dominate the European market until the 18th c. Today it is still one of the lagoon's main attractions. In the 16th c. Murano found favour as a summer resort for rich Viennese nobility who had their magnificent villas and pleasure gardens here – finally Italy's first botanical garden was laid out on the island.

★★**Museo d'Arte Vetrario**

Anyone interested in the history of Venetian glass-blowing should not miss the Museum on the Canale Di Donato, housed in the Palazzo Fiustinian which was built for the Bishop of Torcello in the 17th c. There are more than 4000 items on display, dating from Roman times to the

Murano with its canals is reminiscent of Venice city centre

present day, including works by Bohemian and Moorish glassblowers. The most important item is the Barovier Cup, a 15th c. marriage bowl, dark blue and decorated with enamelled medallions with pictures of the bride and groom, and allegorical scenes. This was probably a work of the daughter of Angelo Barovier.

This church was originally dedicated to Mary, but from the 12th c. also to Saint Donato, and is one of the oldest buildings on the lagoon, having been built between the 7th and 12th c. Built in the form of a basilica with a large-scale apse, it combines Veneto-Byzantine and Early Romanesque elements. The nave is separated from the two aisles by columns of Greek marble with Veneto-Byzantine capitals. The magnificent 12th c. mosaic floor resembles an oriental carpet, with vivid animal figures and artistic decorations. The painted relief figure of St Donato above the first altar on the left is dated 1310 and is thus one of the earliest examples of Venetian painting. According to legend Venetian crusaders brought the body of St Donato from Euboea to Venice and gave it to the basilica, together with the remains of a dragon killed by the saint; these relics are kept on the wall behind the high altar. Other splendours of the church include: a Byzantine mosaic "Madonna at Prayer" (ca. 1450), the altarpiece "The Death of the Virgin Mary" (late 14th c.) on the wall of the north aisle, a "Madonna with Saints" at the entrance to the Baptistery, painted in 1484 by Lazzaro Bastiani, and in the Baptistery itself, a sarcophagus from Altinum, formerly used as a font.

★Santa Maria e Donato

This 14th c. church on the Fondamenta Cavour, rebuilt in 1511 after a fire, has several fine paintings in its south aisle. These include Giovanni Bellini's "Madonna in Majesty with St Mark and the Doge Agostino Barbarigo" (1488) and his "Assumption of the Virgin" which he painted between 1505 and 1513. In the north aisle are Paolo Veronese's "St Jerome in the Wilderness" and "St Agnes in Prison".

San Pietro Martire

★Palazzo Contarini del Bovolo   L 5

The Palazzo Contarini del Bovolo is probably the only palace in Venice which has a courtyard that is more interesting than the façade overlooking the Canal, the Rio dei Barcaroli. In the courtyard is the famous Scala di Bovolo, a spiral staircase built about 1500 by the architect Giovanni Candi, which gave the palace its nickname ("Bovolo" = spiral).

Location
Calle della
Vida/Rio dei
Barcaroli

Quay
Rialto

★★Palazzo Ducale   L 5

The Doges' Palace, through the course of its history, has fulfilled various functions, having been used as a government building and as law courts, with many of its rooms belonging to the state prison, besides being the residence of the Doges. The present palace, which was built in three phases, had two predecessors, whose character was that of castle-type fortifications, rather than of an imposing prestige residence. The first building, a gloomy wooden structure with massive defensive towers, was built in 814. It was surrounded by the lagoon on the south side and canals on the other sides, and was entered by a drawbridge on the north side. Large parts of this "moated" fortress were frequently destroyed by fire, and then rebuilt time and again.
   In the 12th c. the palace was rebuilt under the Doge Sebastiano Ziani in the Byzantine style. The external appearance cannot be reconstructed with any certainty; towers and arcades were decisive motifs. When the number of members of the Great Council rose to 900, a new building with a large meeting hall became necessary, so in 1340 work began on

Location
Piazzetta

Quay
Riva degli
Schiavoni

Opening times:
Daily 9am–7pm,
last admission
6pm

Cristallo, Aventurin and Millefiori

Glass was already being produced in Venice at the end of the 10th c. and, after the Fourth Crusade, the city developed its own special glass production, based on oriental techniques. After the great fire of 1291 the Republic moved all the glassblowers' workshops to Murano – officially to counter the risk of fire. Unofficially, and more probably, it was so that espionage could effectively be prevented. The first guild regulations date from this period, and these were written down in special books such as the "Mariegola", a 1441 edition bound in velvet and silver which today can be seen in the Museo Correr. By the mid-14th c. Murano glass had long been established as a coveted luxury article that was exported as far as Russia and China. In the 15th c., besides beads and lenses for spectacles, the main products were ornately framed mirrors. Their pro-

duction goes back to Muzio da Murano who, in the 14th c. was the first to discover that applying a solution of tin and mercury to glass would give it a reflective surface.

In the mid-15th c. Angelo Barovier developed a glass that was free from bubbles and tinges of colour, which was given the name **Cristallo**, as it resembled rock crystal in brilliance and purity. This transparent glass was made from silica from the River Tessin and soda, with Piedmontite manganese oxide as a colouring agent. At about the same time, another master created **Calcedonio**, a multi-coloured glass resembling agate. **Rubino**, whose pink tinge was achieved by mixing in a gold solution, was a 16th c. invention, and the mysteriously shimmering **Aventurin** glass, speckled with particles of copper, was developed by the Venetian Briani in the 17th c. One of Murano's most refined glass-making techniques, dating back to the 16th c., is that used to produce **Filigrana**, which resembles lace, and is used to make reticulated glasses, by applying fine white and coloured threads to the surface of the blown glass. The ancient technique known as murrine or **Millefiori** involves working tiny coloured rods into transparent glass, whilst **Lattimo** is milk-white glass, which in the 15th c. was usually lacquered to resemble porcelain in appearance.

The main raw materials used for Venetian glass are quartz sand (which until the 17th c. was mostly silica from the River Tessin), limestone and soda. Together with other substances these are heated in a furnace to 1400°C to produce a red-hot molten mass. Moulding takes place after cooling to between 1000°C and 500°C, before the objects modelled are slowly allowed to solidify in a cool furnace. The various colours are achieved by adding metal oxides.

Until well into the 17th c. glass produc-

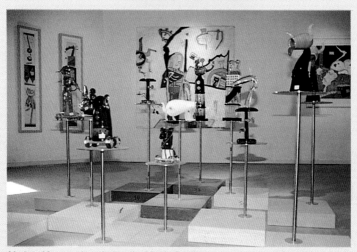

Modern Murano glass designs by Martin Bradley

tion was the Senate's best-kept secret. The glass blowers were paid handsomely and enjoyed enormous privilege, being allowed to bear arms and to marry into Venetian patrician families. However they were forbidden to leave the Lagoon under pain of death, so that their knowledge of this flourishing craft which had long since developed into one of Venice's main commercial sources of income, could under no circumstances be divulged to outsiders. In 1454 the Council of Ten issued a decree stating: "Any glass blower who, to the detriment of the Republic, takes his skill to another country, shall be summoned to come home; should he refuse, his next of kin shall be thrown into prison, so that his sense of family duty will prevail upon him to return; if he persists in his disobedience, secret measures shall be taken to do away with him, wherever he may be."

In spite of all the threats however, by the 16th c. several glass blowers had escaped to Northern Europe, where they soon possessed flourishing businesses. In the 17th and 18th c. ornate mirrors and chandeliers from Venice were so much in demand that France and Bohemia did all they possibly could to recruit glass blowers from Venice, so that they could replace these expensive imports with their own glass manufacture. Increased competition from abroad and the Fall of the Republic in 1797 finally led to a decline in Murano's glass production, which did not experience a revival until the mid-19th c., thanks to the commitment of the Barovier, Seguso, Salviati and Teso traditional glass blowing families. Today there are on the island almost 100 glass workshops with about 6000 employees, mainly working to produce goods for export. So once again Murano glass is a profitable enterprise, producing top-quality luxury articles just as it did centuries ago.

Majestic beauty: the Palazzo Ducale

constructing the south wing with the Sala del Maggior Consilio. The Doge Francesco Foscari initiated this second major phase of building. When the old west wing was demolished, between 1424 and 1438 Foscari had a new one built, in keeping with the new south façade. Foscari decided to add the Porta della Carta to give access to the inner courtyard and as an architectural feature linking St Mark's Basilica and the Doges' Palace. This completed the design of the west façade.

During the third and final phase, the east wing was constructed. As this side of the palace had been substantially destroyed by fire in 1483, the new plans, for which the sculptor Antonio Rizzo was responsible, were for a completely new construction. And so the imposing Doges' staircase, the Scala dei Giganti, which was to become the setting for important ceremonies, came into being. With the completion of the work on this wing, the Doges' Palace acquired its present form. Although fires repeatedly caused major damage to the palace in the 16th c., on the whole these only affected the interior. The layout of the Doges' Palace appears to be based on a square, but actually consists of only three wings: the east side along the Rio di Palazzo, sadly somewhat disregarded, the main façade on the Molo and the west façade overlooking the Piazzetta. The whole is completed by St Mark's Basilica, which links the west side to the east side.

Exterior

This palace (71 m × 75 m), which appears monumental whilst still giving the impression of delicate filigree, achieves this effect by means of its rhythmic construction, architectural material and subdued colour: the pointed arches resting on columns surrounding the building at ground level, above these the open Loggia on the second floor with narrower archways resting on slimmer columns, so that for each arch on the ground flour there are two on the level above, and at the top of the loggia the spandrels have quatrefoil-shaped openings. The marble wall above is roughly the same height as the two lower floors together. Further simple pointed-arch windows and small oculi with narrow quatrefoils are cut into the wall. The central pointed arch on both sides is emphasised by a small balcony and an elaborate external window frame. The appearance of the upper part of the façade is refined by its rhomboidal pattern of white, red and green encrustations, finished off with striking ornamentation of delicate openwork along the top.

The façade overlooking the Rio di Palazza was designed by Mauro Coducci. Along the water's edge is a rusticated base, above which rectangular panels and rectangular windows alternate. Above a continuous cornice, segmented pediments and tondi emphasise the window axis. There are a further three floors, given a rhythmic structure by large round-arched windows, rectangular panels and rectangular openings, with oculi and segmented pediments. Broad cornices emphasise the horizontal line of the building. The central axis is accentuated by the entrance from the water below and by the upper-floor balconies.

East façade

In 1603 Antonio Contin connected the Doges' Palace to the new prison building by means of the famous Bridge of Sighs. Its elegance is achieved by the shape of the arch bearing the crossing, and by the momentum of the gable, which repeats the shape of the arch below, and is embellished with small baroque volutes.

Ponte dei Sospiri

The south façade – facing the lagoon – is the oldest part of the exterior. The flatness of the top part of the construction is interrupted only by the balcony. An inscription marks this as a foundation of the Doge Michele

★★South façade

Corner sculpture on the south side: Adam and Eve

The legendary Bridge of Sighs

Palazzo Ducale

The west façade overlooks the Piazzetta and is decorated with a relief of St. Mark's lion and a figure of Justice.

Steno of 1404. The Doge had himself represented in a devotional picture, which has not survived. The workshop of Pierpaolo dalle Masegne was assigned the task of making the Gothic window frames. Following the fire of 1577 large parts of the ornamentation had to be renewed, and Alessandro Vittoria's "Crowning of Justice" and figures depicting Charity and St. George were added.

The sculptures decorating the corners of the building depict, at the south-east, the archangel Raphael with the young Tobias at the top, whilst below we see the drunken Noah, mocked by his sons. At the south-west corner there is the archangel Michael, overcoming Lucifer, and below the Fall of Adam and Eve. Figures of Virtue (above) and Vice (below) are set in sharp contrast to each other.

The 14th c. capitals of the columns forming the arcade have various motifs: foliage, busts of emperors, animals, allegories of vice and virtue, seasons and the Ages of Man. These are freely combined in no particular strict order. Some of the originals have now been replaced by replicas.

★★West façade

This façade overlooks the Piazzetta and was built between 1424 and 1438 to correspond to the south façade. The frame around the balcony in the top part of the wall is simpler, decorated with a relief of St. Mark's lion (a replacement modelled on the sculpture destroyed in 1798) and crowned by a figure of Justice.

The sculptures at the north-west corner, the archangel Gabriel, and below that the judgment of Solomon, are intended to signify the role of justice at the heart of government. The capitals along this side also deal with allegorical themes or are purely ornamental.

Porta della Carta

The Porta della Carta leads into the inner courtyard of the palace and forms an architectural link between St Mark's Basilica and the Doges' Palace. Together with the Ca' d'Oro, this is regarded as Venice's most important piece of Gothic architecture. The decoration was entrusted to Giovanni and Bartolomeo Bon (1438–42). The entrance and the window above are framed by two large flying buttresses. Above the doorway, the Doge Francesco Foscari kneels before the lion of St. Mark, demonstrating the subordination of the individual to the power of the state. This group was destroyed in 1797, but reconstructed during the 19th c. Vertically above the window, three angels present a tondo of St. Mark, holding up his hand in benediction. The niches contain figures of the virtues, whilst that of Justice dominates the entrance. The portal owes its special character to its filigree ornamentation and small figures.

The Porta della Carta, or "Paper Gate" is thought to be so named from the petitioners who were not allowed to enter the palace, and handed over their written requests and petitions to members of the Council and the Government at this gate. It was also known as the "Porta aurea" (golden gate), because of the gilding of its decorations, now very much faded. The laws of the Republic were proclaimed in front of this gate, at the corner of St. Mark's.

From the Porto della Carta, the internal courtyard of the Doges' Palace is reached through a dark passageway, at the end of which stands the Arco Foscari, constructed like a triumphal arch. The façade opposite the Scala di Giganti was designed specifically to harmonise with that politically important staircase, on which the Doge would kneel at his enthronement, looking towards the Arco. The lower-floor niches contain Antonio Rizzio's figures of Adam and Eve (the figures seen here are replicas; the originals can be seen in the Andito del Amggior Consiglio). On the second floor above the door, there was a figure of the Doge Moro,

★Arco Foscari

The Scala dei Giganti, crowned by the colossal statues of Mars and Neptune from Jacopo Sansovino, was designed by Antonio Rizzio

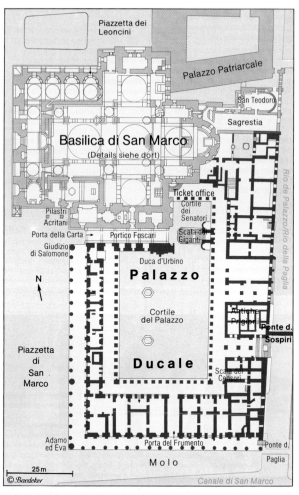

before the Lion of St. Mark, but this was destroyed in 1797. On small turrets and pedestals there are allegories of the virtues and squires. St. Mark, his hand raised in benediction, dominates the gateway. The hierarchical structure reflects the earthly world down below, appealing to the sense and virtue of the Doge in the middle, and the heavenly sphere up above. Columns, arches, niches and turrets form definite verticals, contrasted with a horizontal balustrade and cornices. The Arco was completed under Cristoforo Moro between 1462 and 1471. The facing on the side looking into the courtyard dates from the beginning of the 17th c.

★Scala dei
Giganti

The Scala dei Giganti, opposite the Foscari Arch, was designed by Antonio Rizzio (1483 onwards). This monumental staircase was an important political stage, as the Doge was crowned with the ducal cap on its top step. According to ancient custom, the newly elected Doge had to take the coronation oath, and the embroidered "Zoia" or "corno ducale" in full view of everyone, would be placed on his head. This head-dress was stitched by the nuns of St Zaccharia in the form of a stylised Phrygian fisherman's cap.

The staircase takes its name from the two colossal statues of Mars and Neptune by Jacopo Sansovino (1550), symbolising Venice's dominion over land and water. The winged lion of St Mark with an open book above the rounded archway, which finishes off this "throne" staircase, stands in close relationship to the figures, as regards content, and to the ceremony taking place on the staircase. The relief ornamentation and rich floral Renaissance-style decorations are very fine.

The architecture of the inner courtyard illustrates the different phases in the building of the palace: the south and west wings again take up the two-storey arcade construction of the exterior façades, whilst the upper floors are characterised by brickwork with different window openings. In contrast, the wall behind the Scala dei Giganti, created by Mauro Coducci in the 15th c. is richly decorated, possibly because of the function of the inner courtyard, and also to offer a framework for public appearances of the Signoria. The lower arcades are echoed, with slight variations, in the Gothic sections opposite. The surfaces of the upper-storey walls between the round-arched windows are richly decorated with different kinds of ornamentation. Wide cornices provide divisions between the storeys.

Inner courtyard

The original division into rooms is evident from the external arrangement, with the resulting irregularities that explain the lively character of the façade. In the palace courtyard stand two bronze cisterns, cast by Alfonso Alberghetti and Niccolò dei Conti between 1554 and 1559.

To the left of the main courtyard is the Cortile dei Senatori, with its late Renaissance front: arcades on the ground floor, and on the upper floor, windows crowned by triangular pediments and a balustrade behind which there was originally a small roof terrace. In this small courtyard the Senators used to gather before receptions. The small chapel next to it was the Doges' private chapel (now closed).

Cortile dei Senatori

Rooms in the Doges' Palace

The official rooms of the Doges' Palace can now be viewed, following a marked itinerary. The programme of pictures on display in the rooms is organised iconographically on the basis of the Doges concerned and the City State, and vividly demonstrates the kind of image they wished to project.

Information and advance booking, which is essential, at the Doges' Palace cash desk. Twice daily (10am and noon) there are guided tours of the Itinerari secreti (secret ways) which also take in other important parts of the palace, including the rooms of the chancellors, servants and guards, the writing rooms, the Sala della Cancelleria, the halls of the Capi del Consiglio of the Inquisitori as well as the torture and lead chambers from which Casanova made his dramatic escape. Here visitors can discover the impressive furniture and rich decorations of the unofficial rooms. In addition the tour includes a visit to the attic, to see the extremely complicated system for hanging the Venetian Soffitto, a flat ceiling with paintings. This is to be found in all official buildings and in the Palazzi, where only the painted side can be seen.

Itinerari secreti

In the middle of the east wing a magnificent staircase leads from the Loggia into the former apartments of the Doge, and to the stately upper-storey rooms, that could only be used by members of the Council and

★Scala d'Oro

the Doges' guests of honour. Sansovino was probably responsible for planning these rooms, and P. Guberni for supervision of the works. The decoration of the coffered barrel vaulting consists of stucco work with relief figures and grotesque paintings, emblems and allegories, for which Alessandro Vittoria and Battista Franco were responsible. Sculptures depicting mythological subjects or allegories of the virtues stand in niches and on pedestals – all intended for the glorification of the city of Venice and its government.

Atrio Quadrato

The Scala d'Oro ends in the square anteroom, which still retains its original soffito. As is usual in Venice, this ceiling is divided into sections of various shapes containing oil paintings, surrounded by extravagant frames. The main picture in this room, which was fitted out between 1559 and 1567, is by Jacopo Tintoretto and shows the Doge Girolamo Priuli, with Venetia presenting him with the sword in the presence of his patron saint Jerome and Justice. Venetia, a woman personifying the city, appears in many pictures in the Doges' Palace, and is a central figure in the iconography of the rulers of Venice. The artist has taken into account the fact that the figures will be viewed from various standpoints, and the composition is designed to be seen from different parts of the room.

Sala delle Quattro Porte

The name of this room which may have been designed by Palladio is derived from its four doors, framed with marble columns. A striking feature is the ceiling, which is not flat but slightly vaulted. The sculpted decorations, the sculptures above the portals, the gold-underlaid stucco decorations of the ceiling and the paintings are all of special significance. The soffito, from the studio of Tintoretto, has a centrepiece representing Jupiter conferring mastery of the sea upon Venice, the round pictures show allegories of the power of Venice, and the small ovals depict towns and landscapes in the possession of Venice. The room's most important wall painting, a votive picture of the Doge Antonio Grimani on the north wall, was started by Titian but completed by other artists. The sala was originally used as a meeting room, but after the restoration carried out following the fire in the east wing in 1574, it became an anteroom where the Collegio would gather.

★ Sala dell' Anticollegio

This beautifully furnished sala served as a waiting room for foreign delegations. The wall paintings deserve special attention. The four almost square paintings by Tintoretto have mythological themes: "Minerva separating War and Peace", "Vulcan's Forge", "Mercury and the Three Graces", and "Venus uniting Bacchus and Ariadne in Marriage". The pictures painted in 1577/58 for the Atrio Quadrato are to be interpreted as political allegories, glorifying the city's virtues. In contrast to most of Tintoretto's works, these pictures show only a few figures, whose sensuousness and solidity in a calm, undramatic ambience lend the paintings a solemn, peaceful character.

On the wall opposite the windows hangs the "Rape of Europa" by Paolo Veronese. This highly dramatic and passionate theme is here set at a distance in an idyllic landscape. The foreground, rather than being the scene of the action, is dominated by a display of splendour and luxury.

Next to be seen is "Jacob's Return from Canaan" by Jacopo Bassano. The celebration takes place in an extensive landscape, which dominates the painting.

★ Sala del Collegio

This hall is where the "Collegio" (a kind of council of state) met under the chairmanship of the Doge, and also where the most important visitors were received. What most impresses the visitor about this especially beautiful room are its harmonious proportions and the unity of decoration and furnishings, which are in keeping with its function. In 1574 Antonio da Ponte was commissioned with the design, and he probably consulted with Palladio and Rusconi. On festive occasions, the wall behind the seating (dorsale) of the Tribunal was draped with exquisite tapestries.

In the large wall painting above the throne, Paulo Veronese immortalised the Doge Sebastiano Venier, who was commander in chief of the Venetian fleet in the Battle of Lepanto (1571) as mentioned in an inscription at the bottom left-hand edge. The commander is standing before Christ, surrounded by St Sebastian and St Giustina, on whose feast day the victory was won. The importance of Venetia is especially emphasised by her central position. Several themes are united in this picture: the glorification of the victory takes second place to the votive and devotional picture, and the portraiture.

In the wide picture opposite, the Doge Andrea Gritti is shown kneeling before the Virgin, with St. Mark recommending him to her protection, and the saints Bernard, Alvise and Marina looking on. This composition, like the three votive pictures on the side opposite the windows are attributed to Tintoretto and his workshop. The sequence of ceiling paintings, the drawings for which were produced by Veronese, again deal with the ideals of the State of Venice. On the central axis "Mars and Neptune" represent the power of the City on land and water, the "Personification of Faith" as the foundation of the State, "Venetia with Justitia and Pax" symbolises just and peaceful rule. The borders depict personifications of the virtues: the dog stands for fidelity, the cornucopia for development and success, the crane for vigilance, the spider's web for industry, the eagle for moderation, the dove for peaceableness and the lamb for gentleness.

The Senate, comprising 40, then 60 and later 100 members, met twice weekly in this hall. The Doge and the Collegium sat along the narrow side, whilst the Senators, robed in purple, took their seats on the benches running lengthways down the hall. ★Sala dei Senato

Once again the large wall paintings are designed as votive pictures of the Doges. Above the seating along the narrow side, there is a composition by Jacopo Tintoretto or Palma the Younger (attribution disputed), showing the Doges Pietro Lando and Marcantonio Trevisan praying to the Body of Christ, borne up by angels at the Resurrection. Two Doges are united on this very broad "landscape" format painting, which has a biaxial, strongly symmetrical composition, and thus skilfully catches the eye, wherever the viewer is standing in the room. In the painting on the opposite wall the Doges Lorenzo and Giralamo Priuli worship Christ, who is flanked by the Virgin and St Mark. The chiaroscuro (bright-dark) figures painted in the niches again represent the virtues of government. All the paintings on the longitudinal walls are votive pictures of Doges. The wall clock is intended as a reminder of human mortality.

The Soffito paintings are by Tintoretto and his workshop. In the centre, Venetia is established as ruler of the seas by the Olympic gods, flanked by a representation of minting (coining prerogative) in the Zecca and the veneration of the Eucharist by the Doge Paquale Cigogna. The narrower pictures show the power of arms and the protection of intellectual life and literature. This very large hall appears less austere because of the lively designs of its carved frames, and is made festive by the predominance of the colour gold.

The house chapel (normally only accessible by arrangement, entrance to the right of the Doges' throne) was planned by Scamozzi in 1593. It has a striking sanctuary with a fine Madonna with Christ and John the Baptist as a boy, by Jacopo Sansovino. In the late 18th and early 19th c. the wall and ceiling frescoes, which deal with early Renaissance motifs, were renovated. Private chapel

The Council of Ten, which sat here, was the secret State court. It was in charge of the security services and controlled every aspect of public and private life. In contrast to the other rooms, the seating for the council is arranged in a semi-circle. The middle ceiling picture, of "Jupiter hurling his thunderbolts against the Vices", is in keeping with the room's func- Sala del Consiglio dei Dieci tion. It is surrounded by small paintings with allegorical themes, all by Veronese and his circle. The austere, well-defined design of the ceiling is striking, with unostentatious frames that indicate an early date. The three wall paintings above the semi-circular seating show the "Adoration of the Magi", and to the left of this the arrival of Venetian delegates before Pope Clement VII and Emperor Charles V in Bologna. To the right, Pope Alexander III blesses the Doge Sebastiano Ziano after his victory over Barbarossa.

Sala della Bussola

This room gets its name from the wooden compass in the rear right-hand corner. The doors behind the compass lead into an office and into the Sala del Consiglio dei Dieci. The Sala della Bussola had the function of a waiting room for defendants and witnesses summoned before the Council of Ten.

The wall decoration deals with the history of the City and of the Doges, and the very large main ceiling painting shows St Mark surrounded by the theological virtues (this is a copy, the original being in the Louvre in Paris). There is a famous Bocca di Leone ("lion's mouth") at the entrance, into which written denunciations, accusations or libels could be dropped anonymously.

Sale d'Armi

These rooms contain some of the impressive arsenal of weapons (more than 2200 exhibits) from the time of the Republic. There are well-ordered displays of countless suits of armour and weapons, swords, lances, halberds, firearms, harnesses and trophies, providing a picture of Venetian arms technology and an interesting insight into military history and culture.

Andito del Maggior Consiglio

From the Sale d'Armi a staircase leads up to the second floor, to the Andito del Maggior Consiglio, a passageway used by the members of the Great Council before meetings or during breaks. The gilded beamed ceiling with its ornamental paintings is worth noting. In the rear part of the L-shaped corridor, known as the "Liago", stand Antonio Rizzo's original bronze figures of Adam and Eve (ca. 1470).

Sala della Quarantia Civil Vecchia

The Sala della Quarantia Civil Vecchia is the first room leading off to the left from the Andito. This is where the civil court, a body consisting of forty individuals (quaranta), met. The devotional picture of the Madonna is a late 15th c. fresco. The remaining decorations date from the 17th c.

Sala del Guariento

Arms were originally stored in the second side room leading off the Andito. It now holds fragments of the wall painting by the Paduan artist Guariento (hence the room's name), which was produced for the Sala del Maggior Consiglio in the 14th c. This was seriously damaged by the fire of 1577 in the south wing, and then disappeared under Tintoretto's painting of "Paradise". Not until the beginning of the 20th c. was it rediscovered and moved to its present location. In spite of the damage, the coronation of the Virgin can still be seen in the middle of the many figures in the picture.

★Sala del Maggior Consiglio

The Sala del Maggior Consiglio is impressive not only because of its immense size (54 m long × 25 m wide) but also because of its harmonious proportions and the rhythmic arrangement of its windows. It was made so large not simply in order to be imposing, but also on purely practical grounds, since when the Council was in session it had to accommodate up to 1800 citizens entitled to vote. The Doge and the highest officials sat on the podium along the short east wall, whilst the members of the council occupied the seating then set up in the middle, along the two long walls and against the west wall. In this hall the Republic's important discussions were held and decisions made, includ-

"Apotheosis of Venetia" by Veronese ▶

ing that with the most far-reaching consequences: the decision to dissolve the Republic in 1797.

The hall was built between 1340 and 1355, the first commissions for painting were given to Guariento, and later to Bellini, Carpaccio, Alvise Vivarini, Gentile da Fabriano and Pisanello. However the great fire of 1577 destroyed all but Guariento's fresco (see Sala del Guariento). Building work was quickly started under the supervision of the architect Niccolò da Ponte, and Tintoretto, Veronese, Jacopo Palma the Younger and other artists were commissioned to provide pictures, based on the same themes as those of the pictures that had been destroyed.

The soffito is divided up by a well-defined central axis with three paintings, which are accompanied by four groups each consisting of three pictures. The elaborate frames to these pictures have their own intrinsic value. The central axis begins in the west with "The Provinces paying Homage to Venetia" by Jacopo Palma the Younger, followed by Tintoretto's "Venetia presenting Doge da Ponte with an Olive Branch" and finally the oval painting of the "Apotheosis of Venetia" by Veronese. The glorification of Venice is intended as the climax of this glorious and powerful self-portrait, like Roma residing above the terrestrial globe, as the personification of the eternal state. Venetia hovers before fantastic architecture leading into the depths, surrounded by personifications of the virtues, and by an angel, receiving the crown. The jubilant crowd pushes its way onto the balustrade in the lower part of the picture. However the lower edge of the picture, with its discarded weapons and armour and its armed riders, alludes to the Republic's conflicts with other powers.

The gigantic wall painting "Paradise", behind the Doges' throne, measuring 7 m × 22 m, is the largest painted canvas in the world. It was begun by Veronese, and after he died in 1588, completed by Tintoretto. In the centre is Christ in Majesty, and before him his Mother kneeling, surrounded by seven stars, evoking her seven joys and pains. Christ and his Mother not only occupy the central space, but are also the centre of light, with large numbers of figures grouped around them in concentric circles. These masses of figures appear to hover before an undefinable background. But in spite of the lack of clear structural elements, the composition holds together, as everything is organised around the central point and the figures get smaller towards the centre, focusing attention on Christ.

The large wall paintings show historical events, beginning on the wall opposite the windows next to the picture of Paradise: Doge Sebastiano Ziani (term of office 1172–1178) receives Pope Alexander III. A papal and Venetian legation appears before the Emperor, to present him with an offer of peace. Alexander III makes an offering in San Marco. Unsuccessful peace mission of the papal and Venetian legation to the Emperor. The Pope offers the holy sword to Sebastiano Ziani, who is to set sail with his fleet against the Emperor's troops. The Pope blesses Ziani before his departure to war. The Emperor's son Otto is taken prisoner by the Venetians during a sea battle. The Doge hands over the Emperor's son to the Pope and receives the ring symbolising Venice's marriage to the sea. The Pope releases the Emperor's son. The Doge pays homage to the Pope.

The short west side: Pope and Doge board ship for Ancona. The Doge receives papal gifts in the Lateran.

The paintings along the south side show events connected with the conquest of Constantinople (starting by the picture of Paradise): in San Marco the Doge Dandolo and the crusaders swear the oath of allegiance. Attack on the stronghold of Zara. The surrender of Zara. Alexius asks Dandolo for assistance against his uncle, usurper of the Byzantine throne. Attack on Constantinople. Conquest of the city in 1204. The crusaders elect Baldwin of Flanders the new East Roman Emperor in Hagia Sofia. Baldwin is crowned Emperor. Victory of the Venetians over the Genoese at Chioggia in 1379 (west wall). The frieze along the top of the wall is formed on three sides by portraits of the first 76 Doges who reigned from 697 onwards. The likeness of the Doge Falier who was beheaded for high treason has been painted out and replaced by an inscription commemorating him.

This hall, whose decorations depict justice (17th c.), was where the Civil Court for the cities of the mainland met.

Sala della Quarantia Civil Nova

Initially a library, this large hall was where the numerous public elections were prepared and held. The wall and ceiling paintings, by various Venetian painters, represent the Republic's battles on land and sea, and include Tintoretto's "Victory of the Venetians over the Hungarians before the gates of Zara in 1346". The oil painting of the Last Judgment is by Palma the Younger, and the marble triumphal arch 101694) honours the military commander and Doge Francesco Morosini.

Sala del Scrutinio

In the second floor of the east wing are the private apartments of the Doge, which are however often closed or only used for special exhibitions. The Sala degli Scarlatti, a waiting room from where the Doge was led by dignitaries into the official rooms, has an impressive wooden ceiling and decorated fireplace (1507) by Antionio and Lulli Lombardo. The map room, the Sala dello Scudo, documents the territories under Venetian rule. The Sala Grimani, named after the Doge Marino Grimani, has a beautiful 15th c. ceiling and a 16th c. frieze depicting allegorical themes. The Doge Francesco Erizzo gave his name to the Sala Erizzo, which has a beautiful marble fireplace. A vault with stucco decorations, dating from the 17th/18th c., is the dominant feature of the Sala degli Stucchi. The corridor to the Doges', the Sala dei Filosofi, gets its name from a cycle of paintings which hung here for some time but are now in St Mark's Library.

Apartments of the Doge

As the furnishings of the private apartments were either plundered or destroyed when the Republic was dissolved in 1797, the collection of paintings belonging to the Doge only gives a faint idea of past glory. The most important works include the "Lamentation of Christ", an early work by Giovanni Bellini dating from around 1470, the "Lion of St Mark" by Vittore Carpaccio, dating from 1516, several altarpieces by Hieronymus Bosch and the "Mockery of Christ" by Quentin Massys.

Pinacoteca

The former guardroom contains G.B. Tiepolo's painting of "Neptune presenting Venetia with the Gifts of the Sea".

Sala degli Scudieri

The tour crosses the Bridge of Sighs to the numerous rooms of the former state prison. Originally all the prison cells were inside the Doges' Palace itself, but in the 16th c. a separate building was erected on the opposite side of the Rio di Palazzo. There was no direct connection between the cells and the Doges' Palace until the Bridge of Sighs was built in 1603. Whilst the rooms on the lower floor of the prison were cold and damp (pozzi = fountains), those of the upper storey (piombi = lead chambers) were feared because they were unbearably hot in summer. This may well be the reason for the Venetian gaol's terrifying reputation.

Prigioni

Civil cases were dealt with in this room, which is correspondingly decorated with 17th c. paintings symbolising justice and the judicial office. The 16th c. Byzantine Madonna is very fine.

Sala Censori

The exit leads past the Avogaria (information stand). The Avogaria – three patricians who held office for one year – were responsible for trying cases under constitutional law and keeping the Golden Book.

Avogaria

One of the most famous contestants of the "Women's Regatta on the Grand Canal" was Maria Boscolo, who won four times (Vedute by Gabriele Bella, 18th c.)

★Palazzo Pesaro Degli Orfei

with the Museo Fortuny   J 5

Location
San Benetto

Quay
Sant'Angelo

Currently closed
for restoration
(tel. 041 5200995)

On the pretty square in front of the Benedictine Church, which has a picture of St Francis by Tiepolo, the visitor's gaze falls upon this Gothic palace with its seven-arched central window. From 1899 until his death in 1950, the Spanish fashion designer Mario Fortuny, famed for his pleated clothes, lived here. Born in Granada, he trained as an artist in Paris before coming to Venice, where he designed one of the most beautiful women's dresses of all times: soft, elegant and erotic, the Delphos dress of 1907, the specially woven fabric flattered the woman's figure without any need for a restricting corset! Fortuny also designed materials printed with arabesque designs, like those still manufactured on La Giudecca (see entry) today.

The museum set up in Fortuny's artistically furnished studio in the Piano nobile of the Palace graphically describes the life, work and ideas of this all-round genius.

The legendary pleated dresses and oriental-style lamps handpainted to Fortuny's designs are available from Venetia Studium (Calle Larga XXII Marzo 2403), and Fortuny fabrics from V. Trois (Campo San Maurizio 2666).

★Palazzo Querini-Stampalia

with library and gallery   L 5

From the 13th c. until the beginning of the 16th c., the arid Greek island of Stampalia (now Astypalaia) was in the possession of the

Querinis, who had this beautiful Renaissance Palace built in the mid-16th c. In 1868 the property, together with the Querini Library and Art Collection passed into the ownership of the City. In the 1970s the ground floor and garden were redesigned by the Venetian architect Carlo Scarpa (1906–1978). The inner courtyard was transformed into a green area showing Arabian and Japanese influences such as cherry, magnolia and pomegranate trees. Thanks to Mariapia Cunico's restoration, completed in 1993, the garden has regained its delightful atmosphere.

Location
Campiello
Querini-Stampalia

Quay
Rialto

★**Biblioteca Querini-Stampalia** The well-stocked library is on the first floor, and has more than 120,000 volumes and manuscripts, predominantly from the Venetian area (open Mon.–Sat. 2.30–11.30pm, Sun. 3–7pm).

★**Pinacoteca Querini-Stampalia** The second floor holds a valuable collection of Venetian paintings from the 14th–18th c., most of which were acquired by Giovanni Querini-Stampalia. Of special interest are the views by Gabriele Bella painted during the first half of the 18th c., including the famous "Women's Regatta on the Grand Canal", and the "Holy Thursday Carnival on the Piazzetta". Also represented are Donato Venetiano ("Coronation of the Virgin", 1372), Giovanni Bellini ("Madonna and Child" and "Presentation of Christ in the Temple"), Palma the Elder, ("Portrait of Francesco Querini and his Wife") and Lorenzo di Credi ("Virgin and Child with John the Baptist) and Pietro Longhi, with almost 30 scenes of the same genre (open Tue.–Sun. 10am–1pm, 3–6pm, Sat. until 10pm).

★★Piazza San Marco   K 5

St Mark's Square, dubbed "the most beautiful salon in Europe" by Napoleon, is the point around which Venetian life revolves. It is known as "la Piazza" for short, all other squares being called "Campo". No other city in the world has an entrance that can compare with this one. The first sight of the city for approaching visitors is the Piazzetta flanked by the Campanile and Doges' Palace, and behind them the magnificent Basilica of St Mark, clock tower, Procuratie Vecchie and Procuratie Nuove, an impressive and unforgettable sight. In its splendour the layout of the square provides a perfect picture of the former power and size of Venice, with the Republic's centres of political and religious life grouped around. The arcades around three sides of the square provide architectural unity: on the north side the Clock Tower and the Procuratie Vecchie with the Cafés Lavena and Quadri, on the west the Napoleonic wing with the Museo Correr, on the south the Procuratie Nuove with the Museo Archeologico, the Café Florian and the Biblioteca Nazionale Marciana. From San Marco Basilica the square becomes narrower as it approaches the Ala Napoleonica, which appears to give it considerably greater depth; over an average length of 175 m, it narrows from 82 m at the Church to 56.6 m by the Napoleonic Wing. The square's east side is dominated by the monumental façade of the Basilica di San Marco (see entry). The towering Campanile with its elegant Loggietta stands where the square meets the Piazzetta. Otherwise the square, paved with trachyte and marble slabs, is complete open, without a single monument or roadway to detract from the unbroken architectural unity. The only traffic is the visitors and the famous pigeons, which live here in their thousands.

Quay
San Marco

Until the fall of the Republic the St Mark's Square was above all a market place. Today it is a place to stroll and an "auditorium" for concerts and theatrical productions. Every visitor should at least once enjoy the pleasure of sitting in one of the concert cafés around the square, and

The Procuratie Vecchie and the Ala Napoleonica

listening to waltz melodies and perennial favourites over a cup of coffee. The pigeons of St Mark's are also part of the scene, and old and young alike can have fun feeding them. Whatever their origins – whether descended from the pigeons brought to the lagoons in the 5th c. by the Venetian forefathers fleeing before Attila, or from the pigeons set free by the Doges each Palm Sunday, or even from the carrier pigeons that brought the news of the capture of Constantinople in 1204, they are an institution.

Building history Originally the Piazza was full of fruit trees, with a canal running across it. The completion of the Basilica and the enlargement of the Doges' Palace also saw a start made on landscaping the square. The Campanile was begun in 912, and the Procuratie Vecchie in 1204. The fruit trees disappeared, the canal was filled in and in 1267 the square was paved over. The Procuratie Nuove were built in 1583, and the square was paved with marble in 1735; the large white squares originally marked the sites where the individual craftsmen's guilds were allowed to erect their market stalls. The square finally acquired its present aspect with the building of the Napoleonic Wing.

★Procuratie (Procurators' Office)

The north and south sides of the St Mark's Square are bordered by the Procuratie, the former offices of the Procurators, the chief officials of the Republic. The Procurator, elected to office from the 10th c. onwards, was the most important man in the Republic after the Doge, and did not have to answer to anyone, even the Grand Council. He was the "Custodian of St Mark" and administered the wealth that accumulated in the church coffers from public and private gifts, bequests and regular income. The sums in question were enormous, as a donation was always made to St Mark as a matter of course in thanksgiving for a successful and profitable enterprise. With this huge fortune the State financed all its possessions, the building of San Marco and all its welfare institutions: hospitals, alms distribution, hostels for the homeless, homes for the aged and orphanages. It soon became impossible for one person to shoulder alone the burden of the work that came to be involved in administering the public purse; in the 13th c. there were already four Procurators, in 1319 six and in 1442 nine.

In 1204 there was a two-storey building on the present-day site of the Procuratie Vecchie. The present three-storey building, in early Renaissance Venetian style, dates from between 1480 and 1517. The architect was Mauro Codocci and the building work was completed by Bartolomeo Bon. This fine building, which houses the illustrious ★**Caffè Quadri** and ★**Caffè Lavena**, has arcades along the length of the façade (150 m), 50 on the ground floor and 100 on each of the upper floors.

Procuratie Vecchie

The magnificent clock tower was planned by Mauro Coducci in Renaissance style to finish off the Procuratie Vecchio, and built between 1496 and 1499. The top storey with the star-studded blur mosaic and the lion of St. Mark was added by Giorgio Massari in 1755. The two bronze Moors on the platform, which strike the bell on the hour were cast by Paolo Ranieri between 1494 and 1497, and visitors who climb to the roof terrace of the clock tower can see them at close quarters. The great clock from which the tower gets its name is also a work of Ranieri and of his son. It shows the hour, the phases of the moon and the position of the sun in the signs of the zodiac. In the adjacent square a gilded Madonna is to be seen. During Ascension Week and at Epiphany an angel leads the Three Kings past the Madonna, on the hour.

★**Torre dell'Orologio**

Currently closed for restoration

When the Procuratie Vecchio became too small, the building of the Procuratie Nuove was begun in 1583 on the south side of the square.

Procuratie Nuove

Popular meeting places are the historic cafés under the Baroque arcades of the Procuratie

The architect Vincenzo Scamozzi used his teacher Sansovino's library as a model, adding another storey and topping it with a cornice instead of a balustrade. Baldassare Longhena completed the building in 1650 in accordance with Scamozzi's original plans. Between 1805 and 1814 Napoleon I lived in the Procuratie Nuove whenever, in his capacity as "King of Italy", he visited Venice, his second Italian seat of residence after Milan. Today the ★**Caffè Florian** on the ground floor is a major attraction with its waltz music and irresistible pastries.

Museo Archeologico

Opening times:
Daily 9am–2pm

Housed in the east part of the Procuratie Nuove, the Archaeological Museum dates back to the 16th c. when Cardinal Domenico Grimani and Giovanni Grimani made a significant gift of Greek and Roman finds. The exhibits include eleven Classical Greek korai dressed in chitons (5th c.), ancient gems carved with figures, Roman busts from the time of the Republic and of the Empire, Byzantine ivory carvings (St John the Evangelist and St Paul, 10th c.), Assyrian reliefs (8th–7th c. BC) and reliefs of centaurs by T. Aspetti (entrance to the Biblioteca Marciana).

Lavena, Quadri and Florian

The historical cafés under the Baroque arches of the Procuratie are the traditional meeting places of Venice. During the summer months each of these three cafés has its own band, playing familiar melodies that enhance the special atmosphere of St Mark's Square.

The Café Florian, now classified as an historical monument, opened in 1720 with the name "Venetia trionfante" before it assumed the name of its founder, Floriano Francesconi. The thematically decorated rooms inside, the Chinese, Turkish and Senate rooms have for a long time held a place in world literature, and famous writers who have drunk their coffee here include Goethe, Honoré de Balzac, Marcel Proust, Thomas Mann, Ernest Hemingway and Mark Twain. During the 19th c. the Café Florian and the other cafés mirrored the political antagonism, with the Venetian patriots Manin and Tommaseo preferring the "Florian" whilst the Austrian officers patronised the "Quadri". The Quadri, only half a century younger than the Florian and equally famous for its irresistible pastries, also exudes the atmosphere of past times. It takes its name from its former owner Giorgio Quadri, a Levantine from Corfu, who in his time knew how to prepare the best "Turkish coffee". The Café Lavena, established in 1750 and lovingly restored in 1990, is nostalgically furnished in a style reminiscent of imperial and royal times when it was still known as "Ungheria". It was frequented by Giuseppe Verdi and Richard Wagner, with his wife Cosima and father-in-law Franz Liszt.

Ala Napoleonica

The western side of the square is formed by the Ala Napoleonica which was built in 1810 by order of Napoleon. The work was entrusted to the architect Giuseppe Soli who simply continued the first two storeys of the Procuratie Nuove, omitted the third floor so as not to spoil the proportions of the Procuratie Vecchie, and topped his building with a broad band fronted by statues to bring it up to the height of the Procuratie Vecchie. Although scarcely a work of art, the building nevertheless adds something to the square.

★Museo Civico Correr

Opening times: daily 9am–5pm
A wide outdoor staircase leads up to the Correr Collection, brought into being by Teodoro Correr (1750 to 1830), which is now an interesting collection illustrating the cultural history of Venice, with its own significant art gallery. The first-floor rooms are devoted to local history, and the

anteroom has a view of the city by Jacopo de' Barberi, which dates from 1500. Next there are two halls with views by Antonio Canova, who also produced the marble groups "Orpheus and Eurydice" and "Daedalus and Icarus" for the ballroom, and the painting "Cupid and Psyche" and the portrait of Amedeo Svajer in the dining hall. The two adjacent rooms have works illustrating the history of the Doges of Venice, including a portrait of Francesco Foscari. Next comes the library, the costume room containing robes of office and an important coin collection with exhibits from the 12th – 18th c. Venice's naval power is brought back to life in the following rooms whose exhibits include a model and the remains of the last 35 m long and 7 m wide "Bucintoro", the magnificent vessel on which the Doges were rowed out to the Lido (see entry) every year on the Sunday following Ascension Day for the "Marriage with the Sea". Also remarkable are several historical depictions of the Battle of Lepanto (1571). The extensive collection of weapons follows, with the 17th c. armour and ceremonial swords of the conqueror of the Turks, Francesco Morosini, who was Doge from 1688 to 1694.

The art gallery on the second floor has important works including, first of all, the Venetian-Byzantine panel paintings by Paolo and Lorenzo Venetiano, "Presentation of the Keys" (1369) and a Gothic "Madonna and Child" by Jacobello del Fiore. The early Renaissance is represented by Cosmé Tura's powerful "Pietà" and Baldassare Estense's "Portrait of a Young Man". The works of the Venetian Bartolomeo Vivarini are represented by his "Madonna and Child in Majesty", and two Madonna reliefs by Jacopo Sansovino are on display. The three Bellinis have a whole room to themselves, with Giovanni Bellini's "Christ with Two Angels", and Gentile Bellini's portrait of the Doge Giovanni Mocenigo. Also worthy of note are Alvise Vivarini's "St Anthony" (ca. 1480), Marco Basaitis "Madonna and Child" (ca. 1502) and Vittore Capaccio's highly original picture "Two Venetian Noblewomen" (ca. 1510). Finally the beautiful 16th Majolica works are not to be missed.

The Museo del Risorgimento adjoins the Museo Civico Correr and contains documents and illustrations of the political development of Venice from the fall of the Republic (1797) to its union with the Kingdom of Italy (1866), with extensive material from the Napoleonic era and on Venice's struggle for freedom under the leadership of Daniele Manin.

Museo del Risorgimento

See entry.

**Basilica di San Marco

The rectangular, towering Campanile links St Mark's Square to the Piazzetta. The building was begun in the 10th c. and work continued until the 12th c. The pointed roof was finally added in the 15th c. It could be seen from afar by approaching ships and it guided them home with its gilded pinnacle. On 14 July 1902 the tower collapsed, smashing the Loggetta at its foot as well as a considerable part of Sansovino's Libreria Vecchia. By 1912 it had been painstakingly rebuilt. The Campanile is just under 99 m high; a lift goes up to the Belfry from where there is a magnificent view of the city.

*Campanile

Opening times: daily 9am–7pm

The small marble hall built by Sansovino between 1537 and 1540 was initially intended for the members of the Great Council, to protect them from rain and snow whilst they were gathering outside, ready to go in to meetings. But as early as 1569 this elegant building, a work of art in itself, had been demoted to a guardroom for the Doges' Palace guards. It fulfilled this function until the Fall of the Republic in 1797. In 1902 the Loggetta was severely damaged when the Campanile collapsed, but it was possible to rebuild it using the original stones and sculptures. Restored to its former glory, it now serves the large numbers of tourists waiting for the Campanile lift. Of special interest are Sansovino's four bronze statues of Minerva, Apollo, Mercury and Peace between the pairs of columns.

Loggetta

This charming square is where Venice receives its visitors. It is open to the sea with the two columns on the Molo, bordered on the right by the Moorish–Gothic Palazzo Ducale (see entry), and on the left by the Libreria Vecchia with the Campanile towering up behind. It provides a splendid entrance to the St Mark's Square, and Venetians consequently regard it as part of that square. The Piazzetta did not acquire its present shape until the library was built. In the early middle ages a broad branch canal, sheltered from storms, still ran alongside the Doges' Palace up to the Basilica of St Mark's.

★★Piazzetta

The Doge Michieli brought back three columns from Tyre (modern-day Lebanon) in 1125. However during unloading, one of them fell into the sea and sank into the depths of the lagoon. The other two were erected on the Molo: one was crowned by the lion of St Mark – probably an early medieval legendary beast from Persia, which was given wings and had a book placed between its paws. Until well into the 18th c. the bronze statue, which was restored between 1985 and 1991, was gilded. A statue of St Theodore was placed on the second column, the first patron saint of Venice until he was replaced by St Mark. The dazzling white statue is probably a composite work, the head having been taken from a Roman emperor and the rest, including the dragon, from an early St George.

Colonne di Marco e Teodoro

The time-honoured library on the west side of the Piazzetta opposite the Palazzo Ducale (see entry) is the masterpiece of the architect and sculptor Sansovino (see Famous People) who commenced work on this magnificent secular building in 1536. After Sansovino's death Vincenzo Scamozzi completed the construction in accordance with the master's original plans from 1583–1588.
  The library represents the real turning-point of Venetian architecture and the final break with Gothic Venice. Sansovino was a Florentine; he leaned towards the art of that region and towards Classical Rome. With this structure of Baroque-Roman arcades, arches, columns, balustrades and sculptures, Venice lost its own individual form of architecture, since from then on almost all new buildings were modelled on this particular innovation. This style of architecture also became known throughout Europe as a result of Scamozzi's theoretical work "Idea dell'architettura universale" (Idea of a Universal Architecture) which appeared in 1615. The library itself is a unique work of art, elegant, harmonious and yet majestic.

★Libreria Vecchia di San Marco

The Library of St Mark dates back to 1468 when Cardinal Bessarion donated a collection of manuscripts. The central portal built 1533–1554 by Alessandro Vittoria gives onto the staircase, also decorated by Vittorio. The ceiling painting "Wisdom" (1560) in the anteroom is by Titian. The Golden Hall has 21 ceiling medallions, three of them, "Geometry", "Arithmetic" and "Music", by Veronese, and on the walls are 12 portraits of philosophers, five of them by Tintoretto. The exhibition rooms contain an astonishing collection of gems, manuscripts, calligraphy and book illuminations, including the Grimani Breviary (1510–1520) which alone has 831 pages of Flemish miniatures. The actual library of St Mark with over 750,000 volumes is today housed in the former Mint (Zecca), also built by Sansovino, which is connected to the exhibition rooms.

Biblioteca Marciana (Tours by appointment, tel. 041 5208788)

★Ponte di Rialto   K 4

The Rialto Bridge was for a long time the only footbridge over the Grand Canal; the Ponte dell'Accademia was not built until 1854 and the

Location
Canal Grande

◀ Imposing entrance to the Lagoon City; the Piazzetta with its Campanile

On the constantly busy Rialto Bridge visitors can buy jewellery or souvenirs, or just admire the view

Quay
Rialto

Ponte Scalzi near the station is 20th c. The name "Rialto" is derived from "Rivus Altus" (high bank) which was the name given to the earliest settlement on the island. The first wooden bridge was built on this spot as long ago as 1180, probably by Nicolò Barattieri, later to be replaced by a drawbridge which collapsed in 1444 under the weight of a crowd of people who had gathered on the bridge to watch a boat procession.

Towards the middle of the 16th c. famous architects were invited to submit plans for a stone bridge, among them Sansovino, Vignola and Andrea Palladio. However in 1588 the commission was finally awarded to Antonio da Ponte with his single-arched structure, and by the beginning of September 1590 the 28 m long marble bridge of could already be crossed. It is supported by 6000 oak piles driven into the muddy subsoil on each side, and its arch is 28 m in span and 7.5 m high. Two rows of leather, jewellery and souvenir shops divide pedestrian traffic into three lanes. From the upper platform of the bridge there is a magnificent view of the hustle and bustle on the Grand Canal and along its banks.

San Bartolomeo   K 4

Location
Campo San
Bartolomeo

This was the church of the German merchants in Venice for which Albrecht Dürer painted his famous "Feast of the Rosary" in 1506. A century later the painting was acquired by Emperor Rudolf II and taken to Prague where it is now on display in the National Gallery in the Palais Sternberg. The church was dedicated to St Bartholomew in the 12th c. and remodelled at the beginning of the 18th c. Today it is used for special art exhibitions. The high altarpiece "Martyrdom of St

Bartholomew" by Palma the Younger and, in the choir, paintings of four saints by Sebastiano del Piombo (ca. 1485–1547) on the former organ wings are of special interest.

★San Francesco della Vigna   N 4

As the name suggests, the site occupied by this church was once a vineyard, before the Franciscans built a monastery here in 1253. Work on the large church was started by Sansovino (see Famous People) in 1543, but was not completed until 30 years later by Andrea Palladio (see Famous People). He was responsible for the epoch-making design of the façade, modelled on a classical temple front using columns, entablature and pediment, which are also central structural features of Palladio's later churches, San Giorgio Maggiore (see entry) and II Redentore (see La Giudecca).

Location
Campo San
Francesco della
Vigna

Quay
San Zaccaria

The interior is in the form of a hall with side chapels. The south transept has Antonio Negroponte's altarpiece "Madonna in Majesty" (ca. 1470) and the Cappella Santa, which is accessible via the north transept, has a "Madonna with Saints" (1507) by Giovanni Bellini (see Famous People). The sacristy houses a 15th c. triptych by Antonio Vivarini, and the fifth chapel on the left has a "Madonna with Saints" (1551) by Paolo Veronese (see Famous People). The cycle of sculptures (ca. 1500) in the cappella Giustiani to the left of the High Altar is ascribed to Pietro Lombardo.

San Giacomo dell'Orio   H 4

The foundation stone of this church, whose name is thought to be derived from Lauro (= laurel), was laid in the 9th or 10th c. The building was completely remodelled in about 1225, when the Romanesque Campanile was added. The church, which stands in a pretty square, full of plane trees, received its present form at the beginning of the 15th c. but the presbytery was not added until the mid-16th c.

Location
Campo San
Giacomo dell'Orio

Quay
San Staè

Inside, the church has a richly carved wooden ceiling. The High Altarpiece by Lorenzo Lotto "Sacra Conversazione" (1546) is especially interesting, and the Old Sacristy contains works by Palma the Younger. The New Sacristy lies outside the church building and has magnificent ceiling painting by Paolo Veronese.

★San Giobbe   H 4

The church of San Giobbe, dedicated to Job, is an excellent example of Venetian sacred architecture of the Early Renaissance. It was built by Antonio Gambello (from 1450) who began the church with the Campanile still in Late Gothic style, and Pietro Lombardo, who continued the building from 1471 in Renaissance style, with the portal, the choir cupola and the Cappella Martini.

Location
Campo San
Giobbe

Quay
Ferrovia (Station)

Especially interesting are Paris Bordone's "St Peter" dating from the 16th c. in the fourth side-altar on the right, and, in front of the High Altar, the fine tomb-slab of the Doge Cristoforo Moro, the church's founder, whose term of office lasted from 1462 to 1471. In the Sacristy is a triptych by Antonio Vivarini (ca. 1445) which can be seen on request. The glazed terracottas in the Cappella Martini are associated with the workshop of the Florentine della Robbia.

★San Giorgio Maggiore L/M 6/7

Quay
San Giorgio

The first church dedicated to St. George came into being within the framework of a Benedictine monastery as long ago as the end of the 10th c. However the existing church building goes back to a model completed by Andrea Palladio (see Famous People) in 1563. The foundation stone was laid in 1566 and in 1579 the church was complete, except for the façade which was finished by Simon Sorella between 1597 and 1610, many years after Palladio's death, to slightly modified plans. Viewed from a distance, San Giorgio Maggiore provides an important architectural focus in the lagoon of Venice with a picturesque group consisting of Campanile, dome, nave and façade, which viewed from the Piazzetta and the Doges' Palace, makes a strong visual impression due to the charming play of light and shade. As with his other churches, San Francesco della Vigna (see entry) and Il Redentore (see La Giudecca), Palladio based the design of his façade on a classical temple front with colossal columns and a pediment that, when seen from a short distance, appears somewhat out of proportion.

Interior

Palladio drew heavily on the architectural ideas of Roman antiquity in his design for the white-grey interior, with reliefs using columns, piers, pilasters and entablatures. The basilica has a nave and two aisles, transepts with semi-circular apses and a central cupola above the crossing, which is connected to a square presbytery to the east, which ends in a monastic choir, also with an apse. The focal point of the interior is the High Altar (1591–1593) in the presbytery, a masterpiece by Girolamo Compagna, a pupil of Sansovino. The terrestrial globe, symbolising the burden and endeavour of earthly existence, is crowned by a statue of God the Father. Below this, a dove symbolises the Holy Spirit. Christ is

A harmonious group of stately buildings on San Giorgio Maggiore

represented on the cross, flanked by the four evangelists. The side walls of the sanctuary are decorated by two large-scale works by Tintoretto. The depiction of the "Shower of Manna" (1594) on the left shows a rural idyll with people engaged in various occupations. e.g. women spinning and washing, a smith and a shoemaker, whilst the miracle of the manna appears of secondary importance, but is clearly intended to demonstrate God's provision for human needs in general. Moses, who resembles Christ, is pushed into the lower right corner of the picture, accompanied by his brother Aaron and a donor. Tintoretto's Last Supper (1594), the final version of many, is unusual in that the table is seen from a diagonal perspective. At the same time, the drama of the action is enhanced by the flickering light. Whilst the group of servants to the right of the picture represent everyday worldly existence, on the left the ranks of the apostles with their glowing haloes lead up to the calm figure of Christ, who is bathed in light. Thus the Son of God as a heavenly apparition, is made the central point of the painting. The magnificent stalls in the monastic choir (1594–1598) are made from walnut, and carved with scenes from the life of St Benedict.

A passageway to the left of the monastic choir leads to the Campanile lift. This bell tower was originally part of the buildings of 1470. However it later collapsed and was rebuilt in 1791, modelled on the tower in St Mark's Square. The view of the lagoon from the belfry is breathtaking.

Campanile

Today the cloister area is part of the Fondazione Cini and is not open to the public. Of the two cloisters, the one at the rear was built between 1520 and 1540, whilst that at the front was started by Andrea Palladio in 1579 and finally completed by Baldassare Longhena, who also added the Early Baroque staircase and the library (1641). The dormitory is however an older building, dating from 1488–1521.

Cloisters

San Giovanni in Bragora   M 5

The church was given its present Late-Gothic form between 1475 and 1479, and the presbytery was added between 1485 and 1494. The interior, with its nave and two aisles has a wooden roof truss and houses three masterpieces of Venetian early Renaissance painting. In the choir apse is Cima da Congegliano's "Baptism of Christ" (1490) in a marble frame. This painting unites an idyllic rustic atmosphere with a harmonious arrangement of figures. In the left choir chapel is a triptych by Bartolomeo Vivarini, depicting Mary, John the Baptist and St Andrew (1478) and in the first side chapel next to the entrance a "Resurrection" (1498) by Alvise Vivarini. Over the entrance is an interesting work by Palma the Younger, "Christ before Caiaphas" (1600). The choir walls have pictures of the "Washing of the Feet" and "Last Supper" by Paris Bordone (1500–1571), a pupil of Titian.

Location
Campo Bandiera
e Moro

Quay
Arsenale

San Giovanni Crisostomo   K 4

This domed Renaissance-style church, is one of the masterpieces of Mauro Coducci who built it between 1479 and 1504 on the foundations of an earlier church. It is dedicated to St John Chrysostom, one of the four Greek Doctors of the Church. Of interest in the interior are a late work by Giovanni Bellini, "St Jerome, St Christopher and St Augustine" (1513) in the first side chapel on the right and, over the High Altar, Sebastiano del Piombo's "Madonna and Saints" (including St John Chrysostom; 1509–1511). Also of interest is the marble bas-relief by Tullio Lombardo on the second altar on the left.

Quay
Rialto

San Moisè   K 5/6

Location
Calle Largo 22
Marzo

Quay
San Marco

Even though many art connoisseurs find the Allessandro Tremigno's façade (1668) too rich and over-ornate, the people of Venice love the church of San Moisè, dedicated to Moses in the 9th c. and remodelled in 1632, with a typical Venetian bell-tower. The interior has a "Washing of the Feet" by Tintoretto and a "Last Supper" by Palma the Younger, and on the sacristy altar a bronze relief depicting the Entombment, produced by the Roccatagliata brothers in 1633. Heinrich Meyring's Baroque sculpture on the High Altar depicts Moses receiving the Tablets on Mount Sinai.

San Nicolò   S 3

Location
Lido

Quay
San Nicolò

This church was founded on the Lido (see entry) in 1044, but was reconstructed in the Baroque style in the 17th c. and has an unfinished façade. It was once thought that this church contained the remains of St Nicholas that Venetian sailors had stolen from the cathedral of the town of Myra, which belonged at that time to the Byzantine Empire) on the south coast of Asia Minor (opposite Rhodes). Sometime after their return had been celebrated, and the monastery and church had been founded, the Venetians discovered that the people of Bari in Apulia had made away with the remains of the "real" St Nicholas. This legend is depicted by Giovanni da Crema's beautiful choir stalls, which date from 1635. The "Marriage of the Doge with the Sea". which was celebrated annually from 1177 until the Fall of the Republic in 1797, culminated in a festival service in this parish church.

San Nicolò da Tolentino   F 4

Location
Campo dei
Tolentini

Quay
Piazzale Roma

The church was built between 1591 and 1601 by Vinzenzo Scamozzi, whose designs for the choir and domed crossing were based on plans by Andrea Palladio. The façade is 17th c. In the interior, to the left of the entrance, Bernardo Strozzi's "St Lorenz" (1581–1644) is of interest, and to the left of the choir arch "The Inspiration of St Jerome" a significant late work by Johann Liss of Oldenburg (1597–1630).

San Pietro di Castello   Q 5

Location
Campo San Pietro

Quay
Giardini

On the eastern edge of the city is the island of San Pietro di Castello, linked to Venice by two bridges. This is the site of Olivolo, one of the lagoon's earliest settlements, and of Venice's episcopal church of the same name. According to legend, the 7th c. Bishop Magnus of Altimum had a vision of St Peter who ordered him to build a church "where he found sheep and goats grazing". So from 775 onwards the Church of San Pietro was the episcopal church, and between 1451 and 1807 it was the church of the Patriarchs of Venice. This function was not taken over by the Basilica of St Mark until after the fall of the Republic.

The present building dates from the 17th c. Its façade is thought to be based on plans by Andrea Palladio (see Famous People). The Campanile was designed by Mauro Coducci (1482–88) in Early Renaissance style. The original tower roof collapsed in 1670. Inside the basilica, with its domed crossing, the choir frescoes (1735) by Girolamo Pellegrini next to the Baroque High Altar (1649), an altarpiece depicting St John the

Evangelist, St Peter and St Paul, and the "Cattedra di San Pietro", the
seat of St Peter, are of interest. According to tradition this marble throne
was used by St Peter in Antioch. Baldassare Longhena was responsible
for the rich sculptures in the Cappella Vendramin.

San Polo · San Paolo   H 4

The original Late Gothic church was reconstructed and drastically
altered in the 19th c. Only the 14th c. Campanile survives unaltered. Of
interest inside is the "Last Supper" by Tintoretto (see Famous People)
which he painted in 1568–69. This is his third version of the theme, the
first, dating from 1547 being in the church of San Marcuola, and the
second in San Trovaso (see entry). He produced yet another version for
the High Altar of San Giorgio Maggiore (see entry). Also of interest in
San Polo are the 16th c. bronze statues near the High Altar by Alessandro
Vittoria. The painting of the "Madonna with St John of Nepomuk" was
produced by Giovanni Battista Tiepolo (see Famous People) in 1751, and
the stations of the cross in the sacristy were painted by his son
Giandomenico.

Location
Campo San Polo

Quay
San Silvestro

★San Salvatore   K 5

The church of the Augustinian monastery which was founded in
Carolingian times was reconstructed in Renaissance style by Tullio
Lombardo and Giovanni Sansovino between 1507 and 1534, and given its
present Baroque façade by Giuseppe Sardi between 1663 and 1700. It can
justifiably be assumed that the architects of San Salvatore wanted to
create a church that could rival St Mark's in size and magnificence.
However San Salvatore has only three domes, whereas St Mark's has
five.

The sumptuous Renaissance furnishings include monuments such as
the magnificent memorial to the Doge Francesco Venier after the second
altar on the left. This memorial was designed by Sansovino in 1556. The
Corner family's wall tombs are situated in the front walls of the
transepts, among them the tomb of Caterina Cornaro (1454–1510),
Queen of Cyprus. The outstanding paintings are the two works by Titian:
"The Annunciation" on the third altar on the right, with a marble frame
by Sansovino, and "The Transfiguration of Christ" on the High Altar.
Also of interest are Paris Bordone's "Martyrdom of St Theodore" and
"Christ in Emmaus", which is thought to be by Giovanni Bellini, on the
choir chapel walls.

Location
Calle Mazzini

Quay
Rialto

★San Sebastiano   F 6

The Renaissance Church of San Sebastiano was built between 1505 and
1546. **Paolo Veronese** (see Famous People) is buried here to the left of
the choir. His epochal reputation was founded on the ★★**cycle of pictures** which he produced here from 1553 onwards. Among his most
important works are the ceiling paintings in the sacristy the "Coronation
of the Virgin" and the "Four Evangelists", and in the nave, scenes from
the story of Esther: "Esther taken before Ahasuerus", the "Esther
crowned Queen" and the "Triumph of Mordecai". The wall paintings in
the nave are by Paolo Veronese and his brother Benedetto. The organ-
case was also designed and painted by Paolo Veronese. His paintings
"St Sebastian before Diocletian" and the "Martyrdom of St Sebastian"
in the nun's choir date from around 1558. On the High Altar is one of the

Location
Campo San
Sebastiano

Quay
Ca' Rezzonico

artist's later works "Madonna in Majesty with Saints Sebastian, Peter, Catherine and Francis".

Sant'Angelo Raffaele

This church, a few paces to the north-west, was founded in the 7th c. but the present, somewhat plain, church goes back to the 17th c. Inside the building, the organ loft is decorated with a sequence of ★**pictures** illustrating the story of Tobias, an 18th c. masterpiece by **Antonio Guardi**.

San Silvestro   J 4

Location
Campo di San
Silvestro

Quay
San Silvestro

This church was originally founded in the 9th c., although the present building dates from 1836–1843 and the classical façade was only completed in 1909. In the first side-altar to the right is Jacopo Tintoretto's (see Famous People) monumental "Baptism of Christ" (ca. 1580). In contrast to his representation of the same biblical theme in the Scuola Grande di San Rocco (see entry) this painting is restricted to a very personal encounter between John the Baptist and Christ, who is illuminated by the Holy Spirit in the form of a dove.

San Trovaso · Santi Gervasio e Protasio   G 6

Location
Campo San
Trovaso

Quay
Accademia

This church is in fact dedicated to Saint Gervase and Saint Protase, but their names were finally abbreviated to Trovaso. The interior is simple but it has several paintings by well-known artists: Tintoretto's "The Last Supper" in the north transept – the second of four versions based on this theme – and "The Temptation of St Anthony" (ca. 1557) in the left choir chapel and Michele Giambono's altarpiece "St Chrysogonus (ca. 1440) in the right choir chapel. The most important works of art in the church are the marble altar reliefs in the south transept, by an unknown artist, which are thought to date from about 1470.

★Squero di San Trovaso

On the Rio di San Trovaso is one of Venice's last remaining gondola yards, the Squero di San Trovaso where these gleaming black symbols of Venice are still built using traditional methods (see Baedeker Special p. 80). The low wooden houses with their pretty flower-covered balconies are a reminder of the origins of many Veneto boat-builders, who came to Venice from the valleys of the Dolomites, near Cortina d'Ampezzo.

★San Zaccaria   L/M 5

Location
Campo San
Zaccaria

Quay
San Zaccaria

This church is thought to have been founded as early as the 9th c. The present building dates from between 1460 and 1500 and is by the two great master builders Antonio Gambello and Mauro Coducci. Its huge façade is an astounding example of the transition from Gothic to Early Renaissance architecture. It is one of the most important achievements of the Venetian Renaissance before it lost its individuality with Sansovino and adopted the forms of the mainland. The Campanile is still Byzantine, the choir already Gothic and the nave is in the style of the Early Renaissance. Of special interest inside the church are Giovanni Bellini's (see Famous People) magnificent late work "Madonna in majesty with St Peter, St Catherine, St Lucy and St Jerome (1505) on the second side altar on the left, and Andrea del Castagno's frescoes (1452) on the vaulting of the Cappella di San Tarasio.

San Zaccaria was considered the most worldly of all the convents in the lively city of 18th c. Venice. The parties held at the convent and the love-affairs indulged in by the nuns were the talk of the city. This was probably because most of San Zaccaria's nuns were the daughters of noble families sent there for dynastic or financial reasons. Cheated out of their lives, they found their own way of avenging themselves.

Santa Maria della Fava   K 4

This 18th c. church has a dome and a single nave with reliefs and statues by Giovanni Bernardi, the teacher of Antonio Canova. It also contains, in the first side chapel on the right, an early work by Giambattissta Tiepolo "Anne, Joachim and Mary" and, in the second side altar on the left, a masterpiece by Piazzetta, "St Filippo Neri begging for the Poor".

Location
Campo della Fava

Quay
Rialto

★Santa Maria Formosa   L 4/5

Mauro Coducci built this church between 1492 and 1500 on the foundations of an older, probably 11th c. church. The façade overlooking the Campo and the Baroque bell-tower were added in the 17th c. The almost free-standing Renaissance church building has an interior which, with its slender columns, little cupolas and barrel vaults, is completely covered with excellent Renaissance ornamentation. The most important works of art are Bartolomeo Vivarini's altarpiece "Madonna of Mercy" (1473) and an early 16th c. "St Barbara" by Palma the Elder in the chapel to the right of the high altar. The name "Formosa", which in the Venetian dialect

Location
Campo Santa
Maria Formosa

Quay
Rialto

Campo Santo Maria Formoso on which stands the church of the same name

means "fat", goes back to the legend that Bishop Magnus had a vision of the Virgin in the form of a corpulent matron, who ordered him to found the church.

Until the Fall of the Republic it was traditional for the Doge to visit the church every year at Candlemas. This commemorated a day in 944 when a group of girls on their way to church were seized and abducted by Slavs from Dalmatia. They were rescued by the Scuola dei Casselleri (Guild of Makers of Marriage Coffers), who had their oratory in the church. As their reward they asked the Doge to make an annual visit to the church at Candlemas. "But what shall I do if it rains?" asked the Doge. "We shall give you a hat." "And what if I am thirsty?" "We shall give you wine." From then on every year at Candlemas the Doge was given a straw hat and a flagon of wine at the Church of Santa Maria Formosa. One of the hats can be seen in the Museo Civico Correr (see entry).

Campo Santa Maria Formosa Every morning the wide square around the church is the scene of a fruit market. The square, which is surrounded by beautiful palace façades, is bordered by canals on two sides.

★★Santa Maria Gloriosa dei Frari • I Frari   G 4/5

Location
Campo San Rocco

Quay
San Tomà

Opening times
Mon.–Sat.
9am–6pm; Sun.
1pm–6pm

As there was little space in the San Marco and Rialto quarter for the building of large churches for the mendicant orders of the Franciscans and Dominicans, in the mid-13th c. the Doges of Venice left these two preaching orders plots of land in the sparsely populated west and north of the city on which to build their monumental Gothic churches. The Franciscans ("frari" in Venetian dialect is equivalent to "frati" in Italian) soon found the first church of their order inadequate, so in about 1340 they began building a new choir and transept area, but it was only during the course of the 15th c. that the nave was replaced with a basilica with a nave and two aisles. The simple Gothic brick building, reflecting the Franciscan ideal of poverty was finally completed with the dedication of the High Altar in 1469. The interior, which gives the impression of spaciousness, is divided into a somewhat dark nave and aisles, and a straight chancel with light shining through the wall of the main choir chapel, which is framed by three narrow, low chapels on both sides. The magnificent interior with monuments and altarpieces depicting their donors, represents a pantheon of Venetian history.

Nave Above the main portal on the inside of the façade is the resplendent black and white marble monument to Giralomo Garzoni, who died in the war against the Turks in 1688. The deceased is shown crowned by a guardian angel and flanked by the personifiction of Religion (left) and Venice (right). The monument to its right honours the Procurator Pietro Bernardo (d. 1538), while the tomb to the left is the last resting place of Procurator Alvise Pasqualino, (d. 1528).

In the second recess of the left nave, is the Antonio Canova's (1757–1822) pyramid-shaped monument which he designed himself, and which was built by his pupils. The heart of Canova, the most important sculptor of Classicism, rests here, whilst his body is buried in the Mausoleum in his birthplace, Possagno. The next monument, which was designed by Baldassare Longhena, is that of the Doge Giovanni Pesaro (d. 1659). The next altar has a famous picture by Titian, known as the Pesaro Madonna (1519/1526), an outstanding composition that makes effective use of diagonals and juxtaposition of colours, making it

*The "Assumption of the Virgin Mary" by Titian
in the main choir chapel in I Frari* ▶

Santa Maria Gloriosa Dei Frari · I Frari

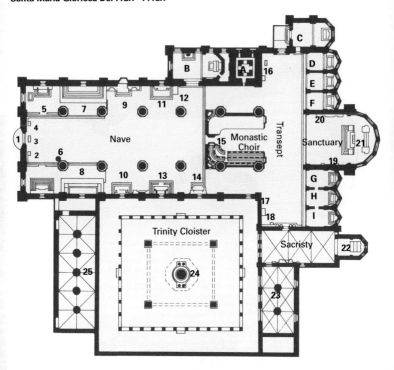

1 Main portal
2 Tomb of Alvise.
   Pasqualigo († 1528)
3 Tomb of Girolamo Garzoni (1688)
4 Tomb of Pietro Bernardo
   († 1538)
5 Crucifixion altar
6 Holy water basin with
   statuettes by
   G. Campagna (1593)
7 Tomb of A. Canova
   († 1822)
8 Monument to Titian
   († 1576)
9 Tomb of Doge Giovanni Pesaro
   († 1659)
10 Altar of Purification
11 "Madonna di Ca Pesaro" Titian
   (1526)
12 Tomb of Bishop Iacopo Pesaro (†
   1547)

13 Altar of St Joseph of Copertino
14 Altar of St Catherine
15 Choirstalls of 1468
16 Monument to Genero Orsini
17 Tomb of General I.
   Marcello († 1484)
18 Tomb of Beato Pacifico Buon (†
   1437)
19 Tomb of Doge Francesco Foscari
   († 1457)
20 Tomb of Doge Niccolò
   Tron († 1473)
21 High altar with Titian's
   "Assumption of the Madonna"
   ("Assunta", 1516–18)
22 "Madonna Enthroned
   with Saints" by G. Bellini (1488)
23 Chapter House
24 Trinity Fountain (1713–14, G
   Trognon)
25 Refectory

A   Bell Tower

CHAPELS
B   Emiliani
C   Corner: Marble statue of John
    the Baptist (1554); altarpiece by
    Bart. Vivarini (1474)
D   Milanesi: Tomb of Claudio
    Monteverdi († 1643); altarpiece
    by Al. Vivarini
E   Trevisan: Melchiore Trevisan (†
    1500)
F   San Francesco
G   Fiorentini: wooden statue of
    John the Baptist by Donatello
    (1451)
H   Sacramento: Wall-tomb of the
    Florentine Ambassador Duccio
    degli Alberti († 1336)
I   Bernardo: Altar painting by Bart.
    Vivarini (1482)

possible to combine a devotional picture with a secular group portrait. Framed by a standard-bearer and a Turkish prisoner, the donor Jacopo Pesaro appears kneeling on the left of the picture. He fought against the Turks in the service of the Pope and is being commended by St Peter to the Madonna. His brother Francesco and younger members of the family appear opposite, being commended to the Virgin by St Francis.

From the nave, the attention is drawn to the choir screens, which were created between 1468 and 1475 by Bartolomeo Bon and Pietro Lombardo in a transitional style between Late Gothic and Early Renaissance. Particularly striking are the fine reliefs of the prophets which contrast with the naturalistic depictions of the Fathers of the Church, arranged in pairs.

In the **main choir chapel** Titian's monumental altarpiece depicts the Assumption of the Virgin in flaming reds (1518). In the lower part of the picture the powerful figures of the apostles show widely differing reactions to this incomprehensible event, whilst in the centre the graceful Mother of God floats heavenward in a sun-like aureola on an inverted arch made up of thronging winged putti, to be received by God the Father. Of the Doges' monuments in the main choir chapel, the Late Gothic monument created by Antonio and Paolo Bregno for Francesco Foscari (d. 1457), on the right wall, is of special interest. Foscari extended Venetian rule to the mainland (terra ferma). Two shield-bearers have pulled the canopy aside to reveal the reclining body of the deceased, who is surrounded by the virtues of a ruler. On the left-hand wall, the monument to Doge Nicolò Tron (d. 1473) was created by Antonio Rizzo in Early Renaissance style with antique figures in the niches.

Left transept In the Cappella San Francesco, off the left transept, Bernardino Licinio's early 16th c. altarpiece "Madonna in Majesty with Saints", with its strong Titian influence, is especially impressive. The adjacent Cappella Trevisan contains the early 16th c. monument to Melchiore Trevisan by Lorenzo Bregno. In the Cappella Milanesi, the grave panel commemorates the composer Claudio Monteverdi (1567–1634), St Mark's first director of music and founder of the Venetian Opera, with works such as "Orfeo" (1607) and "L'incoronazione di Poppea" (1642). The altarpiece depicts "St Ambrose and other Saints" and a "Coronation of Mary" (ca. 1503) by Alvise Vivarini. The Cappella Corner is decorated by a holy-water font with a figure of John the Baptist (ca. 1554) by Jacopo Sansovino and the triptych "St Mark with other Saints" (ca. 1474) by Bartolomea Vivarini.

Right transept The Cappella Fiorentini in the right transept has an fascinating and impressively coloured wooden statue by the great master Donatello, depicting John the Baptist (1451), patron saint of Florence, in stark naturalistic style as an ascetic and a compelling preacher. In the adjacent Cappella del Sacramento is the wall tomb of the Florentine envoy Duccio degli Alberti, (d. 1336) whilst the Cappella Bernardo has a surprising altar panel in several sections (1488) with the Virgin and saints in a beautiful Renaissance frame, by Bartolomeo Vivarini.

Above the way through to the sacristy is the monument to Admiral Benedetto Pesaro (d. 1503), in the form of a triumphal arch, and on the wall to the right of it are the Early Renaissance-style monument to General Jacopo Marcello (d. 1503) and the monument to General Paolo Savelli (d. 1405), the first monument in Venice in the form of a rider on horseback.

Sacristy In the sacristy, the apse has a masterpiece by Giovanni Bellini, a triptych commissioned by the Pesaro family for their family vault in

1488. The central panel depicts the Virgin in majesty with the Christchild, whilst the left wing depicts St Nicholas and St Peter, and the right wing St Benedict and St Mark, the saints for whom Pietro Pesaro, the father, and his sons Nicolò, Marco and Benedetto were named. The strongly individual, lifelike figures of the saints radiate dignity, intelligence, and worldly wisdom. Bellini has also skilfully incorporated the surrounding architectural pilasters and arches into the painting, and has set the Virgin against a gold-painted domed vault, like a nimbus. The peace and harmony emanating from this altarpiece, with its vibrant, saturated colours, also fascinated Albrecht DÅrer who saw the painting in Venice in 1495 and later used it as a model for his famous "Four Apostles" (1526; Alte Pinakothek, Munich).

★Santa Maria dei Miracoli K/L 4

Location
Calle delle Erbe

Quay
Rialto

Santa Maria dei Miracoli is a masterpiece of Early Renaissance architecture by Pietro Lombardo (1481–1489) built for the veneration of a miraculous picture of the Virgin. Instead of decorating the exterior with sculpture, Lombardo used cleverly matched coloured marble arranged to form rosettes, circles, octagons and crosses on the façade. The hall-like, barrel-ceilinged interior is embellished in the same way, with the golden domed ceiling achieving a much greater effect above the grey and coral marble walls as a result. The raised chancel is partitioned off by an exquisite Early Renaissance balustrade decorated with figures. This interior is one of the most beautiful of all Venetian Renaissance buildings and since 1970 this endangered church has been restored with money donated by the Association of German Scientists.

★Santa Maria del Rosario · Chiesa dei Gesuati G/H 6

Location
Fondamenta
Zattere dei
Gesuati

Quay
Accademia

This church belonged in the 15th c. to the Order of the Gesuati (not to be confused with the Gesuiti, or Jesuits), and, when that order was dissolved, it was taken over by the Dominicans. The present church was built for them by Giorgio Massai between 1726 and 1736, an architectural gem with a hall, side chapels and a façade reminiscent of Palladio.

The interior has impressive ceiling frescoes (1738) by G.B. Tiepolo (see Famous People) depicting "St Dominic taken up to Heaven", "The Virgin Mary instituting the Rosary", "The Glorification of the Dominican Order" and the altarpiece "The Virgin in Majesty with the Dominican Saints Catherine of Siena, Rose of Lima and Agnes". Piazzetta painted the altarpiece "St Dominic" (ca. 1743) on the second altar to the right and, on the third altar to the right, the picture of Dominican saints Vincent Ferrer, Ludovico Bertrando and Giacinto. Sebastian Ricci created the altarpiece "Pope Pius V. and the Dominican saint Thomas of Agnin and St Peter martyred (ca. 1733) on the first altar to the left, and Tintoretto (see Famous People) provided the painting of the Crucifixion (ca. 1560) on the third altar to the left.

★★Santa Maria della Salute J 6

Location
Fondamenta dell
Salute

Quay
Salute

This magnificent Baroque domed church was built to commemorate the liberation from the plague epidemic of 1630 which claimed 40,000 victims in Venice alone. Baldassare Longhena began the work in 1631 on foundations of over one million wooden piles. It was not completed until 1687, five years after his death. Longhena's design was only accepted by

Masterpiece of Baroque: Santa Maria della Salute

the Senate because it "would make a grand impression without costing too much".

Santa Maria della Salute (The Church of our Lady) depicts Mary as "Ruler of the Sea" (Capitana del Mar); the statue of the Virgin on the top of the dome carries the staff of command of a Venetian Admiral of the Fleet.

The broad flight of stairs leading up to the church and its two huge domes not only gives it an astounding breadth but also enhances the whole cityscape. Seen from the sea (the true "View of Venice") Santa Maria della Salute perfectly offsets the Basilica of St Mark's, the Palazze Ducale and the Campanile (see entries).

The eight pillars of the monumental central area support a huge dome. Of the building's many sculptures – believed to number more than 120 figures – the group on the High Altar by Juste Le Court is probably the most important: the Madonna complying with the fervent request of Venetia and driving out the plague. The faithful commemorate the end of the plague and the founding of the church by holding a solemn service and procession every year on November 21st, the Feast of the Salvation. The paintings in the Great Sacristy to the left of the choir are also interesting: Tintoretto's "The Wedding at Cana", and Titian's ceiling paintings "Cain and Abel", "The Sacrifice of Abraham" and "David and Goliath" (1542–1544).

Santa Maria Zobenigo · Santa Maria del Giglio   J 6

The church was founded in the 9th c. by the Zubanico family, after which it was named. The interior was restored in 1660 and the Baroque façade was added in 1678–83 by Giuseppe Sardi on the orders on

Location
Campo Santa
Maria Zobenigo

Santi Apostoli

Quay
San Marco

Antionio Barbaro who had his own immortality ensured in return: he stands carved in stone above the main portal, with, underneath, some of his ancestors. The lower plinths are decorated with reliefs showing panoramas of the cities in which Antonio Barbaro had served: Padua, Candia in Crete, and Zara (left), Rome, Corfu and Spalato (right). The interior is a hall framed by chapels with a "Last Supper" by Palma Giovane above the entrance and a Pietà on the High Altar by Giuliano dal Moro. In the sacristy are early works by Tintoretto (see Famous People), "The Four Evangelists" (1552–57), originally part of an organ case.

Santi Apostoli   K 4

Location
Campo dei Santi
Apostoli

Quay
Ca' d'Oro

This 14th c. church, which was reconstructed in the 18th c., is remarkable for the superb Corner family chapel in the right aisle. This square, vaulted space was created towards the end of the 15th c. by Mauro Coducci and counts as one of the finest examples of Venetian Renaissance architecture. It was originally intended as the burial place of Catarina Cornaro, the Queen of Cyprus. The richly carved columns and the light cupola achieve an astonishing harmony, enhanced by Giambattista Tiepolo's (see Famous People) excellent altarpiece "The Communion of St Lucy" (1748).

★★Santi Giovanni e Paolo · San Zanipolo   L 4

Location
Campo Santi
Giovanni e Paolo

Quay
Rialto

The imposing brick church of the Order of the Dominicans, dedicated to the martyrs John and Paul by Emperor Decius in the middle of the 3rd c., and known as Zanipolo for short, is part of a magnificent complex of Gothic and Renaissance buildings which also includes the adjacent Scuola Grande di San Marco, which is still used as a hospital, and the Celleoni Monument on the forecourt. Having been started at the end of the 13th c., construction of this Dominican church, which with a length of 101.5 m, is the largest in Venice, continued until well into the 15th c. According to an inscription, the nave was completed in 1369, the transept was built towards the end of the 14th c. and the high, well-proportioned and light-filled choir did not appear until the first half of the 15th c. The crossing was finally vaulted in about 1450. In keeping with the Dominican ideal of poverty, the exterior is plain, but nevertheless monumental, having no bell-tower or special façade ornamentation. The church owes its civic importance to the fact that no fewer than 27 Doges are buried here.

Interior

The church has a nave and two aisles, with high, round pillars supporting the groined vaulting. Typically Gothic vertical supports are also a feature of the transept, cupola and choir chapels. Originally, from the fourth pair of pillars onwards, a screen separated the monastic choir from the nave and it is only since its removal that there has been a clear view through to the light-flooded choir with its two chapels on both sides.

Above the portal, on the wall inside the façade, there are magnificent monuments to right and left, commemorating the Doges Pietro, Giovanni and Alvise Mocenigo. Pietro Mocenigo's Renaissance-style monument (ca. 1481) goes down to the ground, and the plinth has reliefs depicting Hercules. This work by Pietro Lombardo no longer shows the Doge in the traditional reclining position, but in the attitude of a hero. Tullio Lombardo's monument to Giovanni Mocenigo, completed in about 1500 is characterised by classical strength and the triumphal arch motif is replaced by columns. In contrast, the colossal tomb (1580–1646) of Alvise Mocenigo who died in 1577, which incorporates the church portal, has decorative Baroque features.

Left aisle The marble statue of the kneeling St Jerome on the first altar in the aisle was designed by Alessandro Vittoria (1525–1608). Level with the second round pillar is Pietro Lombardo's monument (1481) to Doge Nicolò Marcello, with plinth, columns, pilasters and entablature. This is adjacent to the monument created by Tuscan sculptors for the Doge Tommaso Mocenigo in a transitional style between Late Gothic and Renaissance, using for the first time a canopy with rocaille niches and a reclining figure of the deceased. A little further along is the wall-tomb of the Doge Pasquale Malipiero in Pietro Lombardo's Early Renaissance style, adorned with a Pietà relief, griffins and a canopy. The adjacent late 16th c. sacristy with 17th c. furnishings has beautiful wall carvings made from walnut and a ceiling painting by Marco Vecellio with "St Dominic and St Francis worshipping the Virgin" and an altarpiece of the Crucifixion by Palma the Younger. In the left transept on the front wall near the entrance to the Cappella del Rosario are three monuments to Doges belonging to the Venier family: Antoni (who held office from 1382–1400), Francesco (1554–1556) and Sebastiano (1577–1578). One of the oldest monuments in the church, that of the Doge Giovanni Dolfin, who held office from 1356–1361, is let into the left wall of the church. This is a simple sarcophagus with the ducal couple before Christ, the

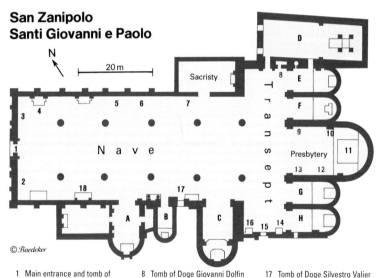

San Zanipolo
Santi Giovanni e Paolo

© Baedeker

1 Main entrance and tomb of Doge Alvise Mocenigo (d. 1577)
2 Tomb of Doge Pietro Mocenigo (d. 1476)
3 Tomb of Doge Giovanni Mocenigo (d. 1485)
4 A. Vittoria: St Jerome
5 Monument to Doge Nicolò Marcello (d. 1474)
6 Monument of Doge Tommaso Macenigo (d. 1423)
7 Wall tomb of Doge Pasquale Melipiero (d. 1462)

8 Tomb of Doge Giovanni Dolfin (d. 1361)
9 Tomb of Doge Marco Corner (d. 1368)
10 Tomb of Doge Andrea Vendramin (d. 1478)
11 High Altar dated 1619
12 Tomb of Doge Leonardo Loredan (d. 1521)
13 Tomb of Doge Michele Morosini (d. 1382)
14 Altar-piece by Rocco Marconi
15 Altar-piece by Lorenzo Lotto
16 Panel by A. Vivarini

17 Tomb of Doge Silvestro Valier (d. 1700)
18 Altar with panel by Giovanni Bellini
A Cappella dell' Addolorata
B Cappella della Pace
C Cappella di S. Domenico
D Cappella del Rosario (burnt down in 1867, renovated 1912–28)
E Cappella Cavalli (di S. Pio V)
F Cappella della Trinità
G Cappella della Maddalena
H Cappella del Crocifisso

Cappella del Rosario in San Zanipolo   *Monument of Condottiere Colleoni*

Adoration of the Magi and the Death of the Virgin. In the Cappella del Rosario, the votive chapel built in 1582 to commemorate the sea Victory of Lepanto (1571), following the fire of 1867, which destroyed the original decorations, ceiling paintings by Paolo Veronese (1528–1588) have been incorporated into a new carved ceiling. These include "The Adoration of the Magi", "The Assumption of the Virgin", and "The Adoration of the Shepherds". The rear wall of the chapel is adorned by "The Nativity".

In the **presbytery**, the High Altar (1619), which is in the form of a triumphal arch, was designed by Baldassare Longhena with figures (ca. 1660) of St John and St Paul, the church's patron saints. On the left side wall attention is drawn to the Gothic monument with the reclining figure of the Doge Marco Corner, who died in 1368, set against a five-panelled retable with a figure of the Madonna by the Tuscan sculptor Nino Pisano. The following Renaissance monument (ca. 1492) to Doge Andrea Vendramin (term of office: 1476–1478), a masterpiece by Tullio Lombardo, is in the form of a classical triumphal arch, standing out from the surface of the wall. The reclining figure of the deceased, watched over by servants, rests on a sarcophagus with personifications of the virtues. The Virgin in Majesty appears in the arch relief above, whilst in the side niches, there are statues of young warriors in classical pose. The opposite wall is adorned by the 1572 monument to the Doge Leonardo Loredan, who held office between 1501 and 1521. He is shown as a statesman and peacemaker between Venetia (left) and the League of Cambrai (right). The adjacent Gothic monument to Doge Michele Morosini, who died in his election year, 1382, is typical of 14th c. monumental art, in the way that it combines architecture, painting and sculpture. The front wall of the right transept is decorated by "Christ bearing the Cross" (15th c.) by Alvise Vivarini, the "Coronation of the Virgin" (16th c.) by Giovanni da Udine and the Lorenzo Lotto's sensitively painted altarpiece (1542), whose composition and colouring were strongly influenced by Titian, "St Antonius Pieruzzi giving Alms". (St Antonius Pieruzzi, of the Dominican Order, was Archbishop of Florence. He died in 1459 and was canonised in 1523). The brilliant stained glass in the large window (post 1470) is from Murano and represents saints George, John, Paul and Theodore.

Right transept In the Cappella di San Domenica is a fascinating 18th c. Rococo masterpiece, which is unusually rich in movement and bathed in unreal light: Giovanni Battista Piazzetta's ceiling fresco (1682–1754) depicting the apotheosis of St Dominic (1727).

Further towards the exit is the somewhat theatrical Baroque monument to Silvestro Valier, who died in 1700, the last Doge to be buried in Zanipolo. The adjacent Cappella della Pace has a Byzantine icon, which was presented to the Dominicans in 1349. The Lady chapel next to it is fundamentally Late Gothic, painted during the 17th c. and with a 19th c. altarpiece depicting the Descent from the Cross. A few steps further on is a recently restored triptych (ca. 1475–1480) in Early Renaissance style, attributed to Giovanni Bellini, with a beautiful, original frame. The central panel depicts St Vincent Ferrer, a Spanish Dominican, whilst the side panels show St Sebastian and St Christopher, and the predella below shows scenes from the life of St Vincent (1346–1419).

The Colleoni Monument on the forecourt, the second epoch-making equestrian statue after Donatello's Gattamelata statue in Padua, was modelled by the Florentine Renaissance sculptor Andrea del Verrochio between 1481 and 1488, and cast by Alessandro Leopardi in 1496. On a pedestal decorated with reliefs, and somewhat reminiscent of a tomb chamber, horse and rider are innovatively depicted just as they are moving, inviting the observer to walk round the statue. The figure itself has little in common with the real General Bartolomeo Colleoni (1400–1475), rather it represents the ideal of a Condottiere – proud and powerful.

★**Monumento di Colleoni**

Colleoni led the wars for the Republic on the mainland from 1448 onwards, accumulating huge wealth in the process. On his death bed he bequeathed his whole estate to the State, on condition that he would have a monument "in front of San Marco". As the State, which had never before approved a public monument, did not wish to forego the money, it had the requested monument put up in front of the Confraternity House of San Marco. After all the dying man had not specified that it had to be the "Church" of San Marco!

The Scuola, directly next to the Zanipolo church, was the house belonging to the rich guild of goldsmiths and silk merchants. Today it is a municipal hospital. The lower part of the building was started by Pietro Lombardo in about 1490; his son Tullio created the reliefs and the two lions. Mauro Coducci finally completed the building (ca. 1500) by adding the stepped round gables crowned with figures. Though not so light as Santa Maria dei Miracoli and not so powerful as San Zaccaria (see entries) the façade nevertheless counts as one of the most outstanding examples of Venetian Renaissance. The illusionistic design of the wall on the ground floor, the arches and figures decorating the gable are highly effective. Also of interest is Bartolomeo Bon's relief depicting St Mark above the entrance. The sculptor was one of the masters who created the Porta della Carta at the Palazzo Ducale (see entry).

Scuola Grande di San Marco

Santo Stefano   H/J 5

The Late Gothic brick church at the top end of the Campo Santo Stefano

Location
Campo Santo
Stefano

Sculpture above the doorway of the Scuola Grande di San Marco

Quay
Accademia

was completed in 1374. The perilously crooked bell-tower, the gables on the façade, the choir and the impressive wooden vaulting in the nave were added 150 years later.

Two important Venetians are buried in the simple interior. In the nave is the tomb-slab of Doge Francesco Morosoni, who held office from 1688–1694 and recaptured the Peloponnese for Venice, but at the same time blew up the Parthenon on the Acropolis which was used by the Turks to store their gunpowder. The composer Giovanni Gabriele (ca. 1555–1612) is buried in front of the first altar on the left. After being court musician in Munich from 1575–1579, he was organist at St Mark's from 1586 onwards and is regarded as a pioneer of Early Baroque music. Santo Stefano also contains some valuable paintings by Venetian artists. In the sacristy are three paintings by Tintoretto (see Famous People): "The Last Supper", "Christ Washing the Disciples' Feet" and "Christ on the Mount of Olives", a crucifix dating from around 1330 by Paolo Veronese (see Famous People) and Bartolomeo Vivarini's "St Nicholas and St Laurence". The church also has interesting Late Gothic choir-stalls in the Presbytery and the fragments of a choir screen (both ca. 1488). The fine 16th c. monastery cloister (entrance at the east end of the north aisle) is also worth seeing.

Campo San Vidal

The lower end of the broad Campo Santo Stefano merges into the Campo San Vidal , bordered on the east side by the elongated **Palazzo Loredan**, which was built at the beginning of the 16th c. for the Doge Leonardo Loredan (term of office: 1501–1521, and today houses the Istituto Veneto di Scienze, Lettere e Arti. The Early Baroque narrow side was completed by Grapiglia in 1618

In front of the Palazzo is a **monument** to the writer Niccolò **Tommaseo** (1802–1874).

Across the square stands the Palazzo Morosini Gatterburg, built for the Doge Francesco Morosini, who governed from 1688 to 1694. The ornamentation around the main and side entrances testifies to his victories over the Turks.

A few steps to the south stands the recently restored, magnificent Baroque palace of the Pisani, which was started in 1614 by Bartolomeo Monopola. A few alterations were carried out by Girolama Frigimelica in 1728; a second floor was added and a new courtyard laid out, connected to the first courtyard by open loggias. Today this is the head office of the City Conservatoire.

This church was founded in 1084, and the Campanile dates from the 12th c. The single nave, the apsed chapels and altars in the side walls were added by Antonio Gaspari in the 17th c. The Contarini family commissioned Andrea Tirali to design the façade (1734–1737). Today the church is used as a gallery, exhibiting valuable paintings, including works by Carpaccio and Piazzetta.

To the north of the Campo Santo Stefano lies the picturesque Campo Sant'Angelo, named after a church dedicated to the Archangel Michael, which was demolished in the 19th c. and of which the only part to survive was the Moroni family's little Oratorio Annunziata. The north-east corner of the square is dominated by the ornate façade of the Palazzo Duodo, where the composer Domenico Cimarosa (1749–1801), the master of the "Opera buffa", spent the last years of his life.

Decorated palace façades on the Campo Sant'Angelo

★Scuola Grande dei Carmini F 5

Location
Campo Santa
Margherita

Quay
Ca' Rezzonico

Opening times:
Mon.–Sat.
9am–6pm Sun.
9am–1pm

The Scuola of the Carmelites was formerly one of the six most important confraternities in Venice. The Scuole were not schools but meeting
places and houses of prayer for religious fraternities where Venetian citizens banded together. They were organised either according to country
of origin or according to occupation, had specific religious or charitable
aims and above all provided mutual assistance and charitable benefits.
They were often very rich, and this is demonstrated by their splendid
confraternity houses.

The Scuola dei Carmini belonged to a lay confraternity of the Order of
the Carmelites, which had its origin in a community of hermits established by crusaders in Palestine in the 13th c. The Carmelites could
nevertheless afford to commission such important artists as
Giambattista Tiepolo and Nicolò Bambini to decorate their house for
them. In the flat-ceilinged ground-floor hall Bambini painted scenes
from the life of Mary in monumental colours.

★Ceiling painting
by Tiepolo

In the hall on the upper floor Tiepolo (see Famous People) created
nine ceiling paintings between 1739 and 1744, including his most
mature work "Mary handing St Simon the Scapular of the
Carmelites", in which the Virgin appears radiant among a group of
angels. In the corners there are personifications of the virtues and
scenes from the life of the blessed Simon Stock. Tiepolo was only
paid 400 shekels for this fresco. Piazzetta's painting "Judith and
Holofernes" (ca. 1743) in the corridor leading from the guest hall to
the archive is also of interest.

Santa Maria del
Carmine
(Il Carmini)

The Gothic church across the square, with its high 17th c. bell-tower was
built at the end of the 13th, and beginning of the 14th c. Like the Scuolo
Grande dei Carmini, this also belonged to the Carmelites. Inside the
church are very beautiful paintings, also depicting scenes from the history of the Order. The most valuable works of art include Cima da
Conegliano's "Adoration of the Shepherds" (ca. 1504) on the second
wall altar on the right and Lorenzo Lotto's "St Nicholas with John the
Baptist and St Lucy" (ca. 1523) in the left aisle.

Palazzo Zenobio

A short distance to the west, at the Fondamenta, lies the Baroque
Palazzo Zenobio, built by the architect Antonio Gaspari between 1680
and 1685. The simple design of the Baroque façade already displays
elements of classical style. Today the palace is the head office of the
Armenian Moorat-Raphael priests' college. The festival hall, painted by
Tiepolo, can be viewed by prior arrangement (tel. 041 5228770).

★★Scuola Grande di San Rocco G 4/5

Location
Campo San Rocco

Quay
San Tomà

Opening times:
daily 9am–5.30pm

In the immediate vicinity of the Church of San Rocco, the meeting house
of the lay fraternity of St Roch was commenced by Bartolomeo Bon in
1517 and completed by Antonio Abbondi in 1549 in High Renaissance
style. The fraternity was established in 1489 by middle-class citizens,
craftsmen and merchants for the purpose of caring for the sick. As its
patron saint it chose St Roch, who nursed the sick during an outbreak of
the plague, and whose relics were brought to Venice in 1485. The painter
Tintoretto, himself a member of the Scuola, was commissioned to decorate the interior from 1564 onwards. By 1588 he had created one of the
most comprehensive series of Italian paintings on biblical themes, representing the history of salvation from the story of Adam and Eve, to the
redemption of mankind through the sacrificial death of Christ.

Ground floor

The Scuola is entered on the ground floor through the spacious, colonnaded hall where the poor were fed and the sick cared for. The room has a flat wooden ceiling, on which ★★**Tintoretto's cycle of paintings of the life of the Virgin** begins at the long, left wall with the Annunciation. Against the historical background of the Counter-Reformation, Tintoretto stresses the mystical, the miraculous and the mysterious by strongly contrasting light and dark, moving colours, and by means of dramatic gestures. For example, in the midst of a tumult of angels, the Archangel Gabriel, enveloped in cloud, descends into Mary's earthly chamber, which has been transformed into a ruin, in a dazzling beam of light. The "Adoration of the Magi", which comes next, is a complicated diagonal composition, showing Mary with the Christchild surrounded by light and seated on the arch of a bridge whilst receiving homage. "The Flight into Egypt" shows a landscape and figures bathed in twilight, that still appear naturalistic. The drama of the Slaughter of the Innocents in Bethlehem, the details of which remain in darkness, is enhanced by a swirling composition. The pictures of Mary Magdalene and Mary of Egypt, in upright format, have a serious, melancholy atmosphere, emphasised by the wilderness surrounding the two figures, which are detached from the world. The cycle finishes with depictions of the Circumcision and the Assumption.

The staircase with pictures of the plague in Venice leads to the magnificent ★★**large hall** on the upper floor. On the walls the New Testament cycle continues with scenes from the life of Christ, starting with the Nativity on the long wall. The traditional scene includes the Adoration of the Shepherds, and the individual figures are represented with psychological sensitivity, exemplified by the contemplative demeanour of the older shepherd and the joyful excitement of the younger. Unlike traditional representations of the theme, the Baptism of Christ is here shown in the midst of a large crowd of people, and the deeply bowed Saviour, whose face is in shadow, already prefigures his later bearing of the cross. In contrast the Resurrection is shown as a great visionary manifestation of light. The scene on the Mount of Olives departs from tradition, showing Christ in the sleep of the angels as in a dream, whilst Peter awakes and looks for the henchmen. In "The Last Supper", the table divides the space diagonally, with Christ and Judas (front right) the tight group ofappearing at opposite poles. The isolation of Judas is

Upper floor

Scuola Grande di San Rocco

Ceiling painting in the large hall
of the upper floor

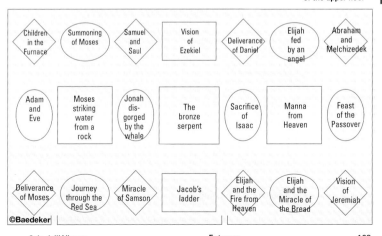

contrasted with disciples huddled around Christ, with the beam of light shining on Christ identifying him as the source of their strength. The next, narrow side of the room includes the altar of St Roch, framed by Girolamo Campagna's statues of St Sebastian and John the Baptist. Titian's lovely Annunciation (ca. 1526) and Tintoretto's "Meeting of Mary and Elizabeth" (1588), a late work, full of feeling, rest here on easels. Giovanni Domenico Tiepolo's two paintings of 1732, "Hagar in the Desert, comforted by Angels", and "Abraham and the Angels" have been in the Scuola only since 1789. The Christ cycle continues on the entrance side with the miracle of the feeding of the five thousand, bathed in a sphere of supernatural light. This is followed by the "Raising of Lazarus", the "Ascension", the "Pool at Bethesda" and the "Temptation of Christ".

The 21 ceiling paintings, especially designed to be viewed from below, are particularly interesting. They show scenes from the Old Testament in artistically framed panels, which on the one hand relate to the pictures on the wall, e.g. the "Sacrifice of Isaac" and the "Death of Christ", or the miracle of the manna and the feeding of the five thousand, and on the other hand to the charitable tasks of the fraternity, such as feeding the poor and caring for the sick. The central ceiling panel depicts the miracle of the brass snake with Moses saving those killed by snakebite. In the scene in which Moses is striking water from the rocks, he appears as a Christ-like figure, referring to the source of life in terms of the history of Redemption. Also fascinating is Tintoretto's "Jacob's Ladder", in an extremely high format, transformed into a magnificent heavenly staircase, with light playing around it.

On entering the ★Sala dell'Albergo, the smaller room adjoining the great hall which was used by the fraternity's trustees, attention is drawn to Tintoretto's large Crucifixion, in which the body of Christ, bathed in light, already proclaims the victory over death and the Redemption of Mankind. On the entrance wall are scenes from the Passion: "Christ before Pilate", the "Man of Sorrows" and "Christ bearing the Cross". The ceiling paintings (1564) were amongst Tintoretto's earliest commissions, and show the Apotheosis of St Roch in the centre, with the panels adjacent to it depicting allegorical figures symbolising the other five major fraternities of Venice, as well as the Virtues and the Seasons. The painting of "Christ bearing the Cross" on the easel is now believed to be by Giorgione rather than Titian.

★Scuola di San Giorgio degli Schiavoni　　M 5

Location
Calle dei
Furlani/Ponte dei
Greci

Quay

San Zaccaria

Opening times:
Tues.–Sat.
10am–12.30pm
3pm–6pm Sun.
10am–12.30pm

The confraternity house of St George was the Scuola of the Dalmatian merchants, the "Schiavoni" (Slavs). Between 1502 and 1508 Vittore Carpaccio decorated its walls with a magnificent cycle of pictures, which still survive complete and which, alongside his pictures in the Galleria dell'Accademia, the Museo Civico Correr and the Ca' d'Oro (see entries), rank as the most important work of this inspired Renaissance painter who was skilled in blending realistic detail with a sense of the decorative. The scenes on the left wall show "St George killing the Dragon", and "St George bringing the Dragon into the City". To the left and right of the altar are "St George Baptising a heathen King and Queen" and "St Tryphon Exorcising the Emperor's Daughter". On the right wall is "The Agony in the Garden", "The Calling of St Matthew", "St Jerome leading his Lion into a Monastery", "The Funeral of St Jerome" and "St Jerome in his Study".

★Teatro La Fenice　　J 5

The famous Teatro La Fenice, surrounded by three canals, is Venice's

Location
Calle delle Veste

Quay
Santa Maria del
Giglio

Reopening
scheduled for
2001

opera-house. A luxurious theatre was built between 1790 and 1792 to replace its predecessor, the popular San Benedetto Opera House, which burned down in 1773, and thus was symbolically called "La Fenice" having arisen from the ashes like the phoenix. On 16th May 1792 the theatre reopened with Giovanni Paisello's "I Giochi di Agrigento". In 1836 this opera house, too, was destroyed by a devastating fire, to be rebuilt only a year later in its original Neo-Classical style, but even more elegant and sumptuous than before. The interior was richly decorated with gold, pink and white stucco, carvings and gilding. The house survived in this form until 1996, only the auditorium which had been able to seat 1200 was reduced to just 820 seats. In February 1996 the theatre burned down almost to its foundations walls. However, by 2001, it will have been restored to its full Neo-Classical glory, just as it was after the first fire. The estimated costs, one-third of which have been covered by international donations and a special UNESCO fund, run into tens of millions. Temporary premises have been used to stage operatic performances in the mean time.

This grand theatre owes its reputation as "Queen of the World of Opera", which goes back to the 19th c., to its well-considered statutes and Venice's rich musical tradition. Its statutes stipulate that two new operas must be staged every year, an artistic idea that helped establish the Fenice's standing as a first-rate opera theatre. Rossini, Bellini, Donizetti and Verdi composed important operas especially for this theatre, which thus saw the first performances of Rossini's "Tancredi" (1813), "Sigismondo" (1814) and "Semiramide" (1823), as well as Bellini's "Capuleti ed i Montecchi" (1839) and "Beatrice di Tenda" (1833) and Donizetti's "Anna Bolena" (1830), "Maria di Rudenz" (1839) and "Belisaro" (1836), not to mention no less than five of Giuseppe Verdi's operas: "Ernani" (1844), "Attila" (1850) "Rigoletto" (1851), "La Traviata" (1853) and "Simone Boccanegra" (1857). Incidentally, the rapturous reception for Verdi and the incessant chants of "Viva Verdi" at the performances were not simply on grounds of artistic merit. VERDI spelt out the clarion call of Italian opposition to Austrian rule and stood for "Vittorio Emanele Re d'Italia" (Victor Emmanuel, King of Italy). In the second half of the 19th c. Richard Wagner's works were performed on the Venetian stage. The Fenice's theatre-goers experienced "Rienzi" in 1873, "Lohengrin" in 1881, and in 1882 Wagner himself directed his Symphony of Youth in C Major here. Shortly after the death of this celebrated composer, the Ring Cycle was performed for the first time in Italy at the Fenice. During the 20th century the Fenice has seen first performances of Igor Stravinsky's "The Rake's Progress", directed by the composer himself in 1951, to be followed by Benjamin Britten's "The Turn of the Screw", Sergei Prokofiev's "Fiery Angel" and Bruno Maderna's "Hyperion". In 1985 Pina Bausch achieved a major triumph here with her highly original choreography, and it is undoubtedly thanks to the special atmosphere of the theatre, with its perfect acoustics, that singing stars from Caruso to Pavarotti, conductors such as Leonard Bernstein and producers from Giorgio Strehler to Luca Ronconi have been only too willing to work here.

There is every reason to think that in the future the Fenice's productions will once again be regarded as epitomising the very best in Italian opera.

★Torcello R 1

Location

Torcello is the real precursor of Venice, and it is believed that it was already inhabited in Roman times. The town of the same name was founded in the 7th c. and in the 12th c. was still a flourishing commercial and episcopal town with palaces and churches, shipyards and docks, its own laws and a large population. Why this large town should have vanished, leaving only two churches and a handful of houses dotted over this large island, is a mystery.

★Santa Maria Assunta

Today only the former cathedral, a colonnaded basilica with nave and side aisles, built in the Venetian-Byzantine style, bears witness to Torcello's former importance. Dedicated to the Assumption of the Virgin between 639 and 641, it was reconstructed in Carolingian times and the portico and two lateral apses were added in the 9th c. The height of the nave was raised and the bell-tower added at the beginning of the 11th c. The basilica's greatest treasure is its mosaics.

To see the ★**mosaics** in chronological order, start with the right side apse, where the oldest mosaics, dating from the 11th c. are to be found. The angels carrying a medallion of the Lamb of God (vaulting of the apse) still show strong Byzantine influence. The Fathers of the Church, Gregory, Jerome, Ambrose and Augustine were added later, as was the

Detail from a mosaic from the Last Judgement in Torcello Cathedral

Santa Fosca: important building of the 11th c.

"Christ in Majesty between two Archangels" (concha of the apse). The main apse, with stepped priests' stalls from the reconstruction phase of 834 is decorated with mosaics dating from the 12th c.: the Madonna and Child above a frieze of the Twelve Apostles, their incorporeal, strongly elongated forms on a gleaming gold ground producing an impression of otherworldliness.

The **presbytery** screen still has beautiful relief panels with peacocks and lions (11th c.) and an iconostasis of Mary and the Apostles dating from the 15th c. The high altar was originally 7th c. but was restored in 1929. The pulpit was assembled in the 13th c. from earlier fragments.

The whole west wall of the church is covered by the tiers of a ★**mosaic of the Last Judgment** produced by Byzantine artists. The top tier shows the anastasis, Christ's resurrection and descent into Hell, to liberate the souls there. With his staff in hand, Christ stands at the shattered gates of Limbo, and leads out Adam and Eve, followed by David and Solomon, whilst John the Baptist, surrounded by prophets, points to Christ. At the edges there are large figures of the archangels Gabriel and Michael. The second tier shows Christ in Majesty in the mandorla on a double rainbow, supported by Mary and John the Baptist, and surrounded by apostles and the prophets, as he separates the Blessed from the Damned. The river of fire passes between two wheels from Christ's feet towards Hell. In the centre of the third tier Christ's empty throne is seen with Adam and Eve kneeling, and angels sounding trumpets. Above the door arch are Mary at prayer and Michael weighing souls, whilst on either side of the door are the Blessed (clothed) and the Damned (naked).

Next to the basilica stands the small church of Santa Fosca, a significant **Santa Fosca**

167

Torcello

centrally planned building dating from the 11th c. surrounded by a 12th c. arcade. The square interior – like an ancient tomb – with its adjacent rectangular choir serves as a memorial to St Fosca, a martyr from Ravenna, and is of unusually harmonious proportions.

Museo dell'Estuario

The museum next door exhibits archaeological finds from Torcello, including funeral steles from the 1st c. BC and the silver altar-covering from the former cathedral (open: daily 10am–12.30pm, 2pm–5.30pm).

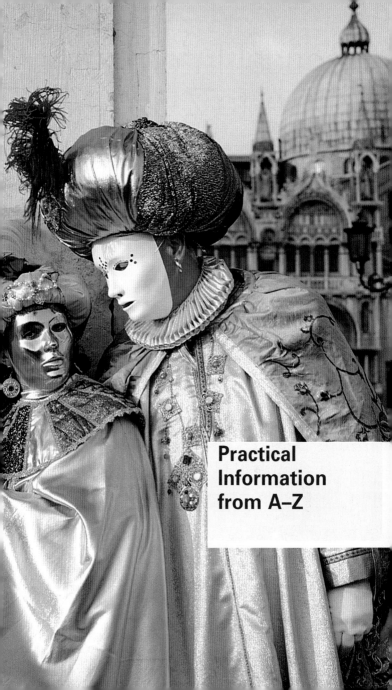

**Practical
Information
from A–Z**

Practical Information from A to Z

Airport

Venice's airport is Marco Polo International Airport near Tessera, 13 km north of the city. Transport to and from Venice is by bus or motor launch (see Getting to Venice). Nicelli airport in San Nicolò di Lido can only be used by small aircraft.

Airport information

Tel. 041 2606111/2381590

Airlines

Alitalia
Aeroporto Marco Polo,
tel. 041 2609260
Piazzale Roma, tel. 041 5205530
Via Sansovino 7, Mestre, tel. 041 2581333, fax 041 5216246

British Airways
Riva degli Schiavoni, San Marco 4158;
tel. 041 5282026

TWA (general sales)
San Marco 1475;
tel. 041 5203219 and 041 5203220

Air Transport

See Getting to Venice

Cafés

The first person in Italy who spoke or wrote about coffee was Francesco Morosini, the Doge's ambassador at Constantinople 1582–85. "In Turkey they drink a black water which is produced from a seed called samen and which, so they say, is able to keep people awake". The first coffee house in Venice opened in 1647 and in the 18th c. coffee drinking became so popular that eight coffee houses were established in St Mark's Square alone. Anyone strolling through Venice will now find a café or patisserie in all the larger squares. The enticing pastries, delightful cream cakes, biscottini, pasticcini and other delicacies can be enjoyed at any time of day as a snack to accompany a cup of coffee or a glass of wine.

St Mark's Square

The famous coffee houses around St Mark's Square are also the most expensive; but they number among the most beautiful cafés in the world. Many illustrious personalities have taken coffee in the Florian, Quadri or Lavena.
★Florian, Piazza di San Marco 56, tel. 041 5205641
★Lavena, Piazza di San Marco 133, tel. 041 5224070
★Quadri, Piazza di San Marco 120, tel. 041 5222105/5289299

◀ Carnival – the Festival of Mask with fantastically-clothed figures

Other cafés and ice-cream parlours (selection)
Causin, Dorsoduro, Campo Santa Margherita 2996, tel. 041 5236091
(irresistible ice-creams)
Chioggia, Piazzetta San Marco 11, tel. 041 5285011 (with a view of the
Doges' Palace)
Dal Col, San Marco, Calle dei Fabbri, tel. 041 5205529 (delightful aroma
of pastries and hot croissants on Saturdays)
Harry's Dolci, Giudecca, Fondamenta San Biagio 773, tel. 041 5224844
(first-class selection of Venetian pastries)
★Nico, Dorsoduro, Zattere ai Gesuiti 922, tel. 041 5225293 (unrivalled
ice-cream)
★Rosa Salva, San Marco, Campo San Luca 4589, tel. 041 5225385 (a
must for the cappuccino fan and the sweet toothed)
★Zorzi, San Marco, Calle dei Fuseri 4357, tel. 041 5225350 (try the cream
puff pastries or the sweet baicoli with hot chocolate)

Camp Sites (campeggi)

★★★★Camping Alba d'Oro, Via Triestina 214/B, tel. 041 5515102, fax 041   Ca' Noghera
920312 (open: middle of Apr.–middle of Oct.)

★★Campeggio Fusina, Via Moranzani 79/bis, tel. 041 5470055, fax 041   Fusina
5470050 (open all year)

★★Campeggio Serenissima, Via Padena 334, tel. 041 920286 (open: Malcontenta
Apr.–Oct.)

★Camping Jolly, Via A. De Marchi 7, tel. 041 920312, fax 041 920312   Marghera
(open: Mar.–Oct.)

★★Campeggio Venezia, Via Orlando 8, Loc. Campalto, (4 km east of   Mestre
Mestre) tel. 041 5312828, fax 041 975928 (open: May–Sept.)
★Campeggio Rialto, Via Orlando 16, Loc. Mestre, tel. 041 900785 (open:
June–Sept.)

★Campeggio Marco Polo, Via Triestina 167, tel. 041 5416033, fax   Tessera
5415346 (open: Feb.–Nov.)

There are nearly 30 camping sites on the Cavallino peninsula opposite   Cavallino
the northern end of the Lido. The annual brochure, "Venezia, Hotels –
Camping", from the tourist information office (see Information) contains
details about these sites.

Chemists (farmacie)

Chemists are usually open Mon.–Fri. 9am–1pm and 4pm–8pm.   Opening times
    They close in turn on Wednesdays and Saturdays.

Chemists who take it in turns to provide a service at night and on   Farmacie di turno
Sundays and public holidays are listed in the booklet "Un Ospite di
Venezia" (A Guest in Venice) and the local paper "Il Gazzettino" under
"Farmacia di turno".

Please give me	Mi puó dare	Useful
a thermometer	un termometro	expressions
a plaster	un cerotto	
medicine for	una medicina per	
constipation	costipazione	
a cough	tosse	
diarrhoea	diarrea	

a fever	febbre
influenza	influenza
a headache	mal di testa
a sore throat	mal di gola
stomach ache	mal di pancia
sun burn	scottatura solare
tooth ache	mal di denti

Churches

Since 1988 in order to secure the resources to maintain the churches with their important art treasures and to keep them open daily visitors have had to pay a fee to enter thirteen sacred buildings. The fee is about £1 per church; locals and those attending holy mass enter free as before. The late Gothic Frari Church, San Giacomo dall'Orio, Madonna dell'Orto, Santa Maria Formosa, Redentore and the treasury of the Basilica di San Marco alone have 400 valuable paintings, among them works by Veronese, Tintoretto, Titian and Tiepolo.

Conversions

To convert metric to imperial multiply by the imperial factor; e.g. 100 km equals 62 mi. (100 × **0.62**).

Linear measure	1 metre	**3.28** feet, **1.09** yards
	1 kilometre (1000 m)	**0.62** mile
Square measure	1 square metre	**1.2** square yards, **10.76** square feet
	1 hectare	**2.47** acres
	1 square kilometre (100 ha)	**0.39** square mile
Capacity	1 litre (1000 ml)	**1.76** pints (**2.11** US pints)
Weight	1 kilogram (1000 grams)	**2.21** pounds
	1 metric ton (1000 kg)	**0.98** ton

Temperature

°C	°F		°C	°F
−5	23		20	68
0	32		25	77
5	41		30	86
10	50		35	95
15	59		40	104

Currency

The unit of currency is the 'lira (plural 'lire. There are banknotes for 1000, 2000, 5000, 10,000, 50,000 and 100,000 lire and coins in the denominations of 50, 100, 200 and 500 lire.

Euro

On January 1st 1999 the Euro became the joint currency of eleven European countries. It is used in stock-exchanges and cashless transfers; it will become the official means of payment on January 1st 2002.

Import/Export of currency

Currencies from other member states of the European Union can be imported and exported without restrictions. But a declaration is required for sums exceeding 20 million lire, either in foreign or in Italian currency.

It is advisable to have sufficient cash in lire available for early payments, e.g. motorway tolls. Money can be exchanged at the borders, larger hotels and railway stations. The exchange offices in travel agencies are the most expensive because of their administration charges.

Changing money

Travellers' cheques in lire or foreign currency can be changed in banks. Eurocheques can be used up to a value of 300,000 lire. A cash charge is deducted for each cheque.

Traveller's cheques, Eurocheques

The issuing centre should be informed immediately about loss of Eurocheques or cheque cards.

Loss of Eurocheques/ cheque cards

Banks, the larger hotels and restaurants, car rental firms and many shops accept the leading international credit cards, preferably Visa, Eurocard and American Express. Inform the issuing company if you loose your credit card (note the telephone number before leaving home).

Credit cards

Banks are open Mon.–Fri. between 8.30am–1.30pm. The opening times in the afternoon vary (usually. 2.30–3.30am). Banks close at 11.20am on the days before public holidays (prefestivi).

Banks

You can withdraw money with credit or Eurocheque cards at the many cash points (bancomat) which are open 24 hours a day. A maximum of 500,000 lire per day can be taken out with a Eurocheque card, and no more than 3,000,000 lire may be taken out per month and card. The individual banks have different maximum amounts.

Cash points

Customs Regulations

Within in European Union, the import and export of goods for private use is to a large extent free of customs duties. In order to distinguish between private and commercial use the following maximum amounts apply: 800 cigarettes, 400 cigarillos, 200 cigars, 1 kg pipe tobacco, 10 litres of spirits, 20 litres of fortified wine, 90 litres of table wine (max. 60 litres of sparkling wine) and 110 litres of beer. In the event of spot checks, it is important to be able to show that the goods are essentially for private use.

EU

Travellers aged 17 and over from outside the EU may bring into Italy 200 duty-free cigarettes or 100 cigarillos or 50 cigars or 250 g pipe tobacco, 2 litres each of table and sparkling wine, or 1 litre of spirits with more than 22 vol.% alcohol, 500 g of coffee or 200 g of coffee extract, 100 g of tea or 40 g of tea extract, 50 g of perfume or 0.25 litre of toilet water. Gifts not exceeding £175 in value are also duty free.

Bringing goods into Italy from outside the EU

Disabled Access

The free town map, issued in several languages by the tourist information office (see Information), shows the easiest access for wheel-chair users, toilets for the disabled and conveniently located hotels.

Venezia per tutti

Electricity

The voltage is 110 or 220 V AC, sometimes also 125 V AC. Standard European equipment plugs can only be used if their contact pins are thin. It is recommended that you take your own adapter.

Embassies and Consulates

United Kingdom Embassy	Via XX Settembre 80A I-00187 Roma (Rome) tel. (06) 4825441, 4825551
USA Embassy	Via Vittorio Veneto 119A I-00187 Roma (Rome) tel. (06) 46741
Canada Embassy (Consular Section)	Via Zara 30 I-00198 Roma (Rome) tel. (06) 4402991

Emergencies

Emergency call	Tel. 113 (polizia soccorso pubblico)
Police	Tel. 112 (carabinieri)
Fire brigade	Tel. 115 (vigili del fuoco)
Car breakdown	Tel. 116 (soccorso stradale ACI)
Medical assistance	tel. 118 (and see entry)

Events

The daily paper "Il Gazettino", the brochure "Un Ospite di Venezia" and the tourist information offices (see Information) have details about events.

January

In the early hours of January 1st brave swimmers take their first plunge of the new year at the Lido beach.

Regate des Befane: "Witches' regatta" on the Grand Canal on January 6th (Epiphany)

February

Carnevale di Venezia: the traditional Venetian carnival begins on February 7th, the day after Epiphany, and lasts until Shrove Tuesday. But the main events with colourful processions, masked balls, theatre performances and concerts are concentrated into the last 10 days before Ash Wednesday (see Baedeker Special "The Festival of the Masks", page 42). The end of the carnival is symbolised by the burning of Pantalone on the pyre. Afterwards masked participants walk along the Riva degli Schiavoni to the Church of Mercy where the midnight Ash Wednesday concert (Concerto delle Ceneri) – the only concert which can be attended in masks – takes place.

March

Su e zo per i Ponti: a cross-city marathon for all ages on a Sunday in the middle of March.

Easter

Benedizione del Fuoco: the "blessing of the flame", late in the afternoon of Maundy Thursday is the high point of Passion Week. The holy flame is lit in the atrium of the completely dark St Mark's Basilica, the procession then walks slowly through the building lighting all the candles on the way until the whole cathedral is bathed in brilliant light.

April

Festa di San Marco: the feast of the city's patron, St Mark, on April 25th.

During the days of the Republic this was a state ceremony with a procession. Today it is celebrated with High Mass in St Mark's Basilica. During the afternoon the gondolieri have their "Regata dei Traghetti" on the Grand Canal. Following an old custom, on this day Venetian men give their loved ones a rose bud, the "bocolo".

La Sensa: on the Sunday after Ascension Day when, according to legend, the Serenissima (Venice city) married the sea. On this day, until the end of republic in 1797, the Doge in his magnificent state galley, the "bucintoro", was rowed out to the Lido where he threw a precious gold ring into the waves as a sign of the eternal bond with the sea. Merchants from all over Europe visited the city for an exhibition which lasted fourteen days and ended with a celebration banquet for the diplomats. Today a historic procession takes place in St Mark's Square. The burgomaster plays the role of the Doge and is accompanied by representatives of the church and the military. Thousands watch from Riva degli Schiavoni as the historic fleet crosses to the Lido where a simple laurel wreath is thrown into the water.
Vogolanga: a rowing regatta on the Sunday after Ascension Day. The boats start at 8.30am in St Mark's bay and return there via the islands of Sant' Erasmus, San Frencesco del Deserto, Burano and Mazzorbo. — *May*

Biennale d'Arte: international biennial art exhibition open until October (2001, 2003 etc.; see Baedeker Special "Biennial Festival of Contemporary Art", page 111).
Sagra di San Pietro di Castello:in the last week of June, small stalls selling wine and Venetian specialities are erected in front of San Pietro; the Sunday ends with a large tombola. — *June*

Il Redentore: the Feast of the Redeemer on the third Sunday recalls the end of the plague of 1576. High point: on the previous evening there is a festive procession of boats on the Canale della Giudecca which is crossed by a temporary floating bridge where hundreds of illuminated craft rock while awaiting the great fire-work display. The Giudecca shore is lined with richly laid tables where traditional dishes such as roast duck, snails and marinated sardines are served. The celebration ends in the early hours of the morning on the Lido beach where people await the sunrise with singing and dancing. — *July*

Mostra Internazionale d'Arte Cinematografica: International film festival on the Lido, a media spectacle with many VIPs (see page 116).
Concerto dell'Assunta: concert on 15 August in the Santa Maria Assunta Basilica on Torcello, to celebrate the assumption of the Blessed Virgin Mary. — *August*

Regata storica: the historical gondola regatta which takes place on the Grand Canal on the first Sunday in September is one of the high points of the year. Book your tribune, balcony or window seat in good time at a travel agency. Before the start there is a magnificent procession with historical figures from the heyday of the Serenissima such as the Doge, his wife, the Dogaressa, the Queen of Cyprus and ambassadors. Between 2.30pm and 7pm there four different races: youth regatta, women's regatta, regatta with caorlina (type of boat from the adjacent Caorle) and a regatta with small gondolas.
Sagra del Pesce di Burano: fish and wine stalls, where you can fortify yourself before the Burano regatta, are erected in Burano on the third Sunday. — *September*

Festival di Musica Contemporaneo: festival of contemporary music. — *September to October*

Festival del Teatro: theatre festival — *October*
Sagra del Mosto di Sant'Erasmo: the wine festival of St Erasmus island

with new wine (mosto) and small delicacies, music, dancing and the only regatta in which both men and women jointly participate, takes place on the first Sunday.

Marathon on the second Sunday: from the Brenta Canal to the Salute Church in Venice.

November

Festa dei Morti: on Commemoration Sunday it is customary for men in love to give the objects of their desire "fave", small pieces of coloured shortbread.

Festa di San Martino: on November 11th, the feast of St Martin, children walk through the city beating cooking pots with spoons and singing about the good deeds of the holy St Martin. One gives them a small tip for their performance or, more likely, to put a stop to their drumming. Bakeries sell St Martin on a horse, all made out of short bread with a colourful sugar coating.

Festa della Madonna della Salute: on November 21st here is a large pilgrim procession in memory of the salvation from the plague of 1630. The route is from St Mark's Basilica, via a pontoon bridge on the Grand Canal near the Campo Santa Maria del Giglio, to the Santa Maria della Salute Church. "Castradina", prepared from lamb and cabbage, is the traditional meal on this day.

Excursions

★Chioggia

See entry

★★Laguna

Islands in the lagoon: Burano, La Giudecca, Lido, Murano, San Giorgio Maggiore, Torcello (see entries)

★Venetian villas

These are a lively heritage from antiquity: the country houses in the hills behind Venice and on the navigable Brenta canal (about 30 km-link to Padua) parallel to the A4 between Mestre/Marghera and the regional capital.

The particular attraction of the Venetian villas is the fusion of Roman styles with Renaissance architecture. Their location in the vineyards and fruit farms at the foot of the Dolomites is their greatest charm. This is one of the most economically prosperous regions in Italy and visitors can still sense the aristocratic poise and the opulent comfort of those days when the Doges came here in the summer to relax. Unfortunately, many extremely ugly industrial sites have been developed around Venice; Mestre and Marghera are prime examples. There are many new buildings, factories and petrol stations within the precincts of Treviso and Vincenza where the plans of Roman citadels can still be recognised. But only a few miles away in the hills one finds shady alleys of planes, vine garlands between mulberry trees and attractive sandstone goddesses in overgrown gardens with ponds and grottos.

★★Villa Barbaro

Some Venetian villas can be visited. The Villa Barbaro in Maser is famous for the frescos of Paolo Veronese and the beautiful stucco work by Alessandro Vittoria (open: March–Oct. Tue., Sat., Sun. 3pm–6pm; Nov.–Feb. Sat., Sun. 2.30pm–5pm, tel. 0423 923004). The home of the Barbaro family, it reflects the characteristics of the Palladian country house: an entrance with tall Ionic columns and a side wing with a pillared hall. Many villas, such as Palladio's La Rotonda with its four temple facades, can only be admired from the outside.

In some villas, which have been converted into hotels or restaurants, the "sweet life" of the Renaissance patricians can be tasted at quite reasonable prices. These refuges for connoisseurs make a pleasant base for trips to Venice during the hot months. In the evening when it is hot and humid at the lagoon guests can return to an airy country house. The price of a good hotel on the mainland buys only a rather mediocre room in Venice itself. The Villa Revedin near Osoppo, which has a good fish restaurant, the Villa Ducale in Dolo on the Brenta Canal and the Villa Michelangelo in Arcugnano near Vicenza are very reasonably priced. The Villa Cipriani in Asolo and the Villa Al Toulà in Ponzano Veneto near Treviso (with a first-class restaurant) are luxurious and consequently expensive. In the Villa Giustinian in Portobuffol, near Treviso, tourists can stay in small reasonably priced rooms or in luxurious suites and enjoy the pleasures of an elegant restaurant. The villa is surrounded by a pewter-covered wall and towers with features from the middle ages.

The beautiful Brenta countryside can be explored by car or by excursion boat, the Burchiello. Approximately 70 magnificent country houses are concentrated in a small area along the canal bank. ★Brenta Canal

One of these the Villa La Malcontenta which Palladio built (1550–1560) for the Foscari family. It is said that in the 14th c. a noble Foscari lady was burnt here in solitary atonement for an extravagant life; hence the name "the malcontent" (open: Apr.–Oct., Tue., Sat. 9–12am or by agreement, tel. 041 5470012) ★Villa La Malcontenta

Napoleon once resided in the magnificent Villa Nazionale in Stra, the house of Doge Alvise Pisani (18th c.) which has over 100 rooms. Mussolini and Hitler had their first meeting here (open: Daily 9am–4pm, tel. 049 502074) ★★Villa Nazionale (Villa Pisani)

High in the hills near Thiene stands Andrea Palladio's first villa, named after the founding family "Piovene Porto Godi" and still owned by their successors. The house is plain and elegant and stands in a wonderful 19th c. garden. Its spaciousness is a Venetian luxury. Villa Piovene Porto Godi

Food and Drink

The Italians do not eat breakfast; a cup of strong coffee "un caffè e via" is enough in the morning. They consider a breakfast with cheese, yoghurt and ham, not to mention muesli, to be barbarous. Although most hotels now serve a full continental breakfast, the Italians themselves are content with a quick expresso coffee or cappuccino in a bar, accompanied perhaps by a pastry (pasta). It is best to forego hotel breakfasts, which are usually insignificant and relatively expensive, and to buy a roll with ham or salami in a bar in much more interesting surroundings. The 'normal' Italian coffee is also much better than an hotel's expensive tourist version. Lunch (pranzo) is usually taken at 12.30 or 1pm and dinner (cena) never before 8pm. An Italian lunch or dinner always consists of a first course (primo) with pasta or soup and a second course (secondo) with a meat or fish dish. Consequently, a foreigner can sometimes be misunderstood if he is satisfied with a plate full of spaghetti as a main course. Those who are very hungry can ask for a cold or warm starter (antipasto) before the primo. For those with a sweet tooth, a piece of cake, soft ice-cream (dolce) or ice-cream (gelato) is served after the secondo.

Brodetto di pesce: fish soup with onions, tomato juice, white wine, parsley, bay leaves and oil.
Broèto: eel soup
Panada veneziana: bread soup with olive oil, garlic, bay leaves and parmesam
Risi e luganega: rice soup with pork sausages

Food and Drink

Starters Venetian cuisine Soups	**Arancino:** rice balls filled with minced meat or ham coated with bread-crumbs and deep-fried **Bovoleti:** snails with garlic and parsley **Bruschetta:** toasted bread with olive oil, garlic and tomatoes **Castraure:** artichokes cooked in oil and garlic **Cicheto:** tasty morsels of small octopuses, meat balls or marinated sardines **Gnocchi alla Fontina:** semolina dumplings with grated Fontina cheese **Risi e bisi:** rice with fresh peas, bacon cubes and ham **Risotto de peoci o de cape:** rice with shellfish, crabs, shrimps, etc. **Sopressa:** Venetian sausage **Spaghetti con cozze/peoci:** spaghetti with mussels **Spaghetti alle vongole:** spaghetti with clams

Meat dishes

Braciolo alla veneziana: pork steak braised in wine vinegar

Castradina: lamb cooked with cabbage; traditional dish for the Madonna della Salute celebrations.

Fegato alla veneziana: Venetian style calf's liver braised in oil with onion rings

Museto: pork sausages usually prepared with lentils and mashed potatoes.

Fish dishes

Bacala manteca: dried cod cooked with milk and cream and stirred to a cream

Caparosoli = Vongole: clams

Cape sante: scallops

Caragoli: sea snails

Coda di rospo ai ferri: grilled anglerfish

Filetti di San Pietro fritti: fillets of St Peter's fish, coated in egg and flour and fried

Go: fish from the Venetian lagoon

Granseola: sea spider

Mansanete: shrimps fried in oil

Molèche col pien: soft-shelled crayfish fried in egg dough

Sarde in soar: sardines fried in fat and marinaded in vinegar with onions, raisins and pine kernels

Sepe nere con polenta: octopus cooked in its own liquid with maize dough

Sogliola alla casseruola: casseroled sole with mushrooms

Desserts

Baicoli: Venetian speciality, thin, sweet biscuits which are dipped into coffee or hot chocolate

Buraneli: round, egg-dough biscuits from Burano dipped into wine before eating

Bussolai ciosoti: round, egg-dough biscuits from Chioggio (similar to those from Burano)

Croccantini: a caramel-almond mixture eaten with sweet wine and biscuits

Crostoli: carnival biscuits

Fritole: carnival doughnuts with raisins and pine kernels

Fugassa: yeast cake

Nicolota: biscuits with raisins and aniseed

Persegada: quince bread in the shape of a horse and rider offered on St Martin's day

Pinsa: fruit-bread sweet for Epiphany

Drinks

Wines from all over Italy are served in Venice. "Spriz", a mixture of white wine, Campari, Aperol and mineral water, is a Venetian speciality. The best-known Venetian white wines are the dry Breganze bianco, Bianco di Conliano and Gambellara, those with a fine bouquet Barbarano bianco, Tocai and Verdiso, the semi-sweet Soave and the smooth Recioto. Veneto dry reds include Barbarano rosso, Breganze rosso, Cabernet di Treviso, Friularo, Bardolino, Merlot, Ricioto, Amarone and Valpantena. Redioto rosso, Rubino della Marca and Rubino del Piave have a fine bouquet. Sweet Moscato di Arqua is often drunk with desserts. Table wine is served open in litre, half-litre and quarter-litre carafes (un litro, mezzo litro un quarto) and by the glass (un bicchiere). Those who do not wish to drink wine with their meal can order beer (better fresh from the bottle than stale from the cask) or mineral water (carbonated: acqua gassata)

Everyone in Italy drinks caffè espresso at the end of a meal. A good caffè is like us, "hot, strong and sweet", say Italian men modestly. However, foreign visitors much prefer cappuccino, a strong coffee with plenty of hot milk and the famous milky foam on top. An espresso machine is the heart of a coffee bar. There are few seats so customers stand at the bar. The furnishings are sparse but the choice of the correct coffee is a science in itself. Espresso, simply called caffè in Italy, is served double (doppio), "corrected" (corretto) with grappa, brandy or bitters,, and even weak and diluted (ristretto). There are even more varieties of cappuccino: light or dark (chiaro or scuro), at different temperatures and with more or less foam. Caffelatte or macchiato (speckled) is a simple milky coffee.

Caffè and cappuccino

Grappa is the proper conclusion to a rich meal. It must be strong, dry and smell pleasantly of fruit. The best grappa comes from South Tyrol, Trentino, Friaul, Veneto or Piemont.

Grappa

See entry

Restaurants

Menu

English	Italian
Menu	listino
Wine list	lista dei vini
Meat broth	brodo
Thick vegetable soup	minestrone
Starters	antipasti
Meat dishes	piatti di carne
Roast	arrosto
Veal	vitello
Rabbit	coniglio
Lamb	agnello
Pork	maiale
Scallop	scaloppina
Wiener Schnitzel	costoletta alla milanese
Liver	fegato
Duck	anatra
Goose	oca
Chicken	pollo
Wild boar	cinghiale
Sausage	salsiccia
Ham	prosciutto
Fish	pesce
Fried fish	fritto di pesce
Boiled	bollito
Seafish	frutti di mare
Prawns	granchi
Crab	gambero
Salmon	salmone

Food and Drink

English	Italian
Lobster	ragosta
Clams	vongole
Mussels	cozze
Sole	sogliola
Octopus	calamare
Vegetables	verdure, legumi
Aubergines	melanzane
Cauliflower	cavolfiori
Beans (white)	fagioli
Beans (green)	fagiolini
Peas	piselli
Potatoes	patate
Peppers	peperoni
Mushrooms	funghi
Mixed salad	insalata mista
Spinach	spinaci
Tomatoes	pomodori
Noodles	pasta
Rice	riso
Potato dumplings	gnocchi
Dessert	dessert, dolce
Ice-cream	gelato
with fruit	con frutta
with crystallised fruit	fruit cassata
Fruit salad	macedonia
Cheese	formaggio
Whipped cream	panna montata
Fruit	frutta
Apple	mela
Orange	arancia
Banana	banana
Pear	pera
Strawberries	fràgole
Cherries	ciliege
Peach	pesca
Plums	prugne
Water melon	cocómero
Grapes	uva
Drinks	bevande, bibite
Beer	birra
Fruit juice	succo di frutta
Freshly pressed orange juice	spremuta d'arancia
Coffee, Espresso	caffè
Lemonade	aranciata
Milk	latte
Mineral water	acqua minerale
Cream	crema
Tea	tè
Water	acqua
Wine	vino
White wine	vino bianco
Red wine	vino rosso
Dry	secco
Sweet	amabile
Bread	pane

English	Italian
White bread	pane bianco
Roll	panino
Biscuits	biscotti
Cake	torta
Macaroons	amaretti
Marmalade, jam	marmelata
Honey	miele
Salt	sale
Pepper	pepe
Butter	burro
Sugar	zócchero
Vinegar	aceto
Oil (olive)	olio (d'oliva)
Soft-boiled egg	un uovo alla coque
Omelette	frittata, omeletta
Scrambled egg	uovo strapazzato
Fried egg	uovo al tegame

Galleries

Works by modern Italian and Venetian artists can be found in the following galleries:

Il Capricorno, San Marco, San Fantin 1994, tel. 041 5206920 (renowned avant-garde gallery)

Junck, San Marco, Calle delle Botteghe 3463, tel. 041 5286537 (glass works)

Naviglio, San Marco, Calle della Piscina 1625, tel. 041 5227634 (modern classical artists)

Riarte, San Polo, Campo Bella Vienna 216, tel. 041 5226532 (drawings and watercolours)

Santo Stefano, San Marco, Campo Santo Stefano 2953, tel. 041 5234518 (Venetian masters such as De Chirico)

Totem – Il Canale, Dorsoduro, Accademia 878/b, tel. 041 5223641 (contemporary works from Northern Italy)

Il Traghetto, San Marco, Campo Santa Maria del Giglio 2456, tel. 041 5221188 (modern art from Italy and North America)

Getting to Venice

Although the island city of Venice can be reached via the European motorway system and from the mainland over the road bridge Ponte della Libertà (4 km), travelling by car is not recommended as cars can only be taken as far as the Lido.

By car

Parking fees are very high and cars should be left only in supervised car parks because of the danger of theft. Illegally parked cars are towed away. During the main holiday season the car parks on the island of Tronchetto (tel. 041 5207555) and the rather expensive multi-storey car parks near the Piazzale Roma (tel. 041 5222308, 041 5232213) are usually full. It is better therefore to leave the car on the mainland near the road bridge in the car parks at San Giuliano and Fusina; or for a longer stay in Punta Sabbioni, Treporti, Mestre or Marghera which can be reached by bus or boat from Venice.

Parking

Hotels

Breakdown service	ACI, Piazzale Roma, tel. 041 5206235
By coach	There are numerous package tours by coach either direct to Venice or including Venice in a longer circuit.
By rail	From London to Venice the fastest route, leaving London (Victoria Station) at 9am, takes just over 24 hours. Also, every Thursday (and sometimes Sunday) from mid March to mid November, the legendary Orient Express (restored) departs from London for Venice via Paris, Zurich and Innsbruck. Trains arrive at the railway station, Stazione Santa Lucia, which has been connected to the mainland by a railway bridge since 1846. It lies to the north of the Grand Canal where visitors can embark on a scheduled boat which brings them without problems to St Mark's Square.
Reduced tickets	Italian railways have favourable offers for international travellers such as small groups, senior citizens (carta res) and young people (Eurotrain Twen tickets; Inter Rail; BIJ). Euro Domino tickets (or Euro Domino Junior for people under 26 years) qualify holders for unlimited travel within Italy on 3, 5 or 10 freely chosen days. In addition, the fare from the place of residence to the border is reduced by 25 per cent.
By sea	Venice has connections to all the major Adriatic ports plus Rhodes and Piraeus. Information can be obtained from the harbour office (tel. 041 5203044) or harbour customs office (tel. 041 5200938). Venice is also a favourite place of embarkation for cruises. Zattere and Riva degli Schiavoni are the preferred quays. Those with their own boats can dock in the ports of S. Elena or S. Giorgio.
By air	Aeroporto Marco Polo There are scheduled flights from London daily and from Manchester twice weekly to Marco Polo International Airport (13 km north-east of Venice). Buses run to Piazzale Roma (route 5) and motor-boats to St Mark's Square. Water taxis provide the fastest, but also the most expensive, service (tel. 041 5235775, 041 5222303). Private flights land at Nicelli Airport in San Nicolò di Lido which has a motor-boat service to Riva degli Schiavoni.
Airlines	See Airport

Hotels

Categories	Hotels are officially classified in five categories, from luxury (5 stars) to hotels or pensions with modest amenities (1 star). The hotels in the following list are divided into four price categories:

Category		Double room, rate for 2 persons
★★★★★	L	from 350,000
★★★★	I	from 260,000
★★★	II	from 180,000
★★	III	from 120,000

The prices vary depending on the season. In the high season they can double. r. = room, sp. = swimming pool, pb. = private beach.

Reservations	Since Venice has many visitors all year round, and particularly during the high season, the carnival and larger events, it is absolutely necessary to make a reservation. Hotels can be booked directly or through travel agencies, tour operators etc.
★★★★★ L	Bauer Grünwald & Grand Hotel, San Marco 1465, Campo San Moisé, tel.

An oasis of luxury in Neo-Moorish style – the Cigahotel Excelsior on the south side of the Lido, with its wide sandy beach

041 5207022, fax 041 5207557; 202 r. (just a few steps from this luxurious hotel on the Grand Canal to St Mark's Square, restaurant with panoramic view)

Danieli, Riva degli Schiavoni, Castello 4196, tel. 041 5226480, fax 041 5200208; 243 r., sp., pb. (top-class hotel with superior interior in the Gothic Palazzo Dandolo style from the late 14th c. Diners in the much-praised panorama restaurant have an unforgettable view across the lagoon to San Giorgio Maggiore and the Lido)

Excelsior, Lungomare Marconi 41, Lido, tel. 041 5260201, fax 041 5267276; 197 r.; sp.; pb. (luxury oasis in neo-Moorish style on the south-side of the Lido; Ciga hotel boat transfer from the Lido to St Mark's Square)

Gritti Palace, Campo Santa Maria del Giglio, San Marco 2467, tel. 041 794611, fax 041 5200942; 93 r., sp., pb. (Doge Andrea Gritti built the palace at the beginning of the 16th c.; in 1585 the splendid building was presented to Pope Sixtus V who turned it into a residence for his ambassadors; Hemingway wrote about it; first-class Club del Doge restaurant)

Cipriani, Giudecca 10, tel. 041 5207744, fax 041 5203930; 98 r., sp. (one of the best hotels in Venice with a magnificent garden, yacht harbour and a private boat service to St Mark's Square)   ★★★★ I

Cavalletto & Doge Orseolo, Calle Cavalletto, San Marco 1107, tel. 041 5200955, fax 041 5238184; 82 r. (first-class hotel in a romantic setting on a gondola harbour behind the Old Law Courts)

Des Bains, Lungomare Marconi 17, Lido, tel. 041 5265921, fax 041 5260113; 196 r., sp., pb. (top-class hotel in the Bell Epoche style, famous because of the novel "Death in Venice", which Visconti filmed here; gourmets find an exquisite menu in the Liberty restaurant; boats to St Mark's Square)

Hotels

Hotel Europa ...   *... and Hotel Bauer Grünwald*

Europa & Regina, Via XXII Marzo, San Marco 2159, tel. 041 5200477, fax 041 5231533; 199 r., sp., pb. (one of the traditional city hotels; popular VIP meeting place; pure romanticism; a candle-light dinner in the elegant Tiepolo restaurant with a view of gondolas drifting past the Santa Maria della Salute)

Gabrielli-Sandwirth, Riva degli Schiavoni, Castello 4110, tel., 041 5231580, fax. 041 5209455; 105 r. (historical palace with stylish furniture; 5 minutes on foot to St Mark's Square)

Londra Palace, Riva degli Schiavoni, Castello 4171, tel. 041 5200533, fax 041 5225032; 59 r. (elegant city hotel with British atmosphere; Tchaikovsky composed his fourth symphony here; view over the beach promenade to the lagoon)

Luna Baglioni, Calle Vallaresso, San Marco 1243, tel. 041 5289840, fax 041 5287160; 118 r. (oldest hotel in Venice with magnificent furnishings; absolute comfort and perfect service)

Metropole, Riva degli Schiavoni, Castello 4149, tel. 041 5205044, fax 041 5223679; 72 r. (recommended for romantics; stylish atmosphere in an 18th c. grain store)

Monaco & Grand Canal, Calle Vallaresso, San Marco 1325, tel. 041 5200211, fax 041 5200501; 74 r. (charming hotel for those who demand the best, with gourmet restaurant)

Saturnia & International, Via XXII Marzo, San Marco 2399, tel. 041 5208377, fax 041 5207131; 97 r. (stylish 14th c. palace of a Venetian admiral; beautiful inner court and roof terrace)

★★★II   Ala, Campo Santa Maria del Giglio, San Marco 2494, tel. 041 5208333, fax 041 5206390; 86 r. (pleasant hotel near St Mark's Square)

Ateneo, San Fantin, San Marco 1876, tel. 041 5200777, fax 041 5228550; 22 r. (charming, small hotel with family atmosphere)

186

Hotel Regina, one of the most traditional city hotels in Venice

Hotel Rialto: in the very heart of the Lagoon City

Bisanzio, Calle della Pietà, Castello 3651, tel. 041 5203100, fax 041 5204114; 39 r. (elegant hotel in an historic 16th c. building, just 300 yards from St Mark's Square)

Boston, San Marco 848, tel. 041 5287665, fax 5226628; 47 r.

Centauro, Calle della Vida 4297, tel. 041 5225832, fax 041 5239151; 32 r. (Venetian style rooms; close to St Mark's Square)

Flora, Via XXII Marzo, San Marco 2283/a, tel. 041 5205844, fax 041 5228217; 43 r. (romantic hotel with a beautiful garden)

Pausania, Dorsoduro 2824, tel. 041 52220836, fax 041 5222989; 27 r. (carefully renovated 14th c. palace; start the day slowly with a breakfast on the veranda in the garden)

Rialto, San Marco 5149, tel. 041 5209166, fax 041 5238958; 72 r. (comfortable hotel next to the Rialto Bridge)

★★lll

La Residenza, Campo Bandiera e Moro, Castello 3608, tel. 041 5285315, fax 041 5238859; 14 r. (stylishly furnished patrician palace)

Seguso, Zattere 779, tel. 041 5286858, fax. 041 5222340; 18 r. (scene of "Venice Can Be Very Cold" by Patricia Highsmith; view of La Giudecca Church)

Wildner, Riva degli Schiavoni 4161, tel. 041 5227463, fax 041 5265615; 16 r. (central position and reasonably priced)

Information

Central tourist office

Azienda di Promozione Turistica di Venezia
Castello 4421, tel. 041 5298711, fax 041 5230399
Internet: www.provincia.venezia.it

Other tourist offices

Uffici Informazioni Assistenza Turistica (I.A.T.)
Venezia, San Marco, tel. 041 5208964
Venezia, Ferrovia Santa Lucia, tel. 041 5298727, fax 041 719078
Lido, Viale Santa Maria Elisabetta, tel. 041 5265721, fax 041 5298720
Marghera, Rotatoria autostradale, tel. 041 937764
Ca' Savio, Via Fausta 79/G, tel./fax 041 966010
Dolo, Arino Sud, Autostrada Padova–Venezia, tel. 041 413995

Tourist guides

Authorised tourist guides (Guide Turistiche) are available from the Associazione Guide Turistiche, Castello, tel. 041 5209038, 041 5239902.

Language

Italian

As a rule English is spoken in the larger hotels, restaurants and shops. Otherwise, some of the terms below will help.

As the direct descendant of Latin, Italian comes closer to it than any of the other Romance languages. Italian had many dialects, not least because of the country's past political divisions, but the great 13th/14th c. writers, especially Dante, used Tuscan and this is still the recognised medium of communication. The language of educated Florentines is the purest Italian.

Venetian dialect

The Venetians speak a distinctive Italian dialect of their own. Not only is their pronunciation more softened than in any other part of the country, they also change actual words of Italian: brothers, for example is "frari" instead of "frati", house is "ca" instead of "casa", angel "anzelo" instead of "angelo", fish is "pesse" instead of "pesce". The Venetian dialect is also found throughout Venice on the nameplates of streets, canals, buildings etc.

The stress is usually on the penultimate syllable. Where it falls on the last syllable this is always indicated by an accent (perché, città). Where the stress is on the last syllable but two an accent is not officially required, except in certain doubtful cases, but it is sometimes shown as an aid to pronunciation (chilòmetro, sènapa), é and ó are the closed sound, è and ò the open sound.

Consonants: c before c or i is pronounced ch, otherwise like k; g before e or i is pronounced like j, otherwise hard (as in "go"); gn and gl are like n and I followed by a consonantal y (roughly as in "onion" and "million"); h is silent, qu as in English, r is rolled; s is unvoiced (as in "so") at the beginning of a word before a vowel, but has the sound of z between vowels and before b, d, g, l, and vv; sc before e or is is pronounced sh; z is either like ts or ds. Vowels are pronounced in the "continental" fashion without the diphtongisation normal in English; e is never silent. The vowels in a diphthong are pronounced separately (ca-usa, se-i).

0	zero	19	diciannove
1	uno, una, un, un'	20	venti
2	due	21	ventuno
3	tre	22	ventidue
4	quattro	30	trenta
5	cique	31	trentuno
6	sei	40	quaranta
7	sette	50	cinquanta
8	otto	60	sessanta
9	nove	70	settanta
10	dieci	80	ottanta
11	undici	90	novanta
12	dodici	100	cento
13	tredici	101	centuno
14	quattordici	153	centocinquantatre
15	quindici	200	duecento
16	sedici	1000	mille
17	diciassette	5000	cinquemila
18	diciotto	1 million	un milione

1st primo (prima)
2nd secondo
3rd terzo
4th quarto
5th quinto
6th sesto

7th settimo
8th ottavo
9th nono
10th decimo
20th ventesimo/vigesimo
100th centesimo

½ un mezzo (mezza)
⅓ un terzo

¼ un quarto
¹⁄₁₀ un decimo

Good morning, good day! — Buon giorno!
Good evening! — Buona sera!
Goodbye — Arrivederci
Yes, no — Si, no!
I beg your pardon — Scusi
Please — Per favore
Thank you (very much) — (Molte)grazie!
Not at all (you're welcome) — Prego
Do you speak English? — Parla inglese?
A little, not much — Un poco, non molto
I do not understand — Non capisco
What is the Italian for ...? — Come si dice ... in italiano?
What is the name of this church? — Come si chiama questa chiesa?
The cathedral — Il duomo
The square — La piazza

Language

	The palace	Il palazzo
	The theatre	Il teatro
	Where is the Via ...?	Dov'è la via ...?
	Where is the road (motorway)	Dov'è la strada (autostrada)
		to ...? per ...?
	Left, right	A sinistra, a destra
	Straight ahead	Sempre diritto
	Above, below	Sopra, sotto
	When is (it) open?	Quando è aperto?
	Today	Oggi
	Yesterday	Ieri
	The day before yesterday	L'altro ieri
	Tomorrow	Domani
	Have you any rooms?	Ci sono camere libere?
	I should like ...	Vorrei avere ...
	A room with bath (shower)	Una camera con bagno (doccia)
	With full board	Con pensione completa
	What does it cost?	Qual'è il prezzo? Quanto costa?
	Bill, please (to a waiter)	Cameriere, il conto!
	Where are the lavatories?	Dove si trovano i gabinetti?
		(il servizi, la ritirata)
	Wake me at six	Può svegliarmi alle sei!
	Where is there a doctor	Dove sta un medico
	(dentist)?	(un dentista)?

At the post office	Address	Indirizzo
	Airmail	Posta aerea
	Letter	Lettera
	Post box	Buca delle lettere
	Postcard	Cartolina
	Stamp	Francobollo

Travelling	Aircraft	Aeroplano
	Airport	Aeroporto
	Arrival	Arrivo
	Baggage (luggage)	Bagagli
	Booking office	Sportello
	Bus (tram) stop	Fermata
	Change (trains)	Cambiare treno
	Connection	Coincidenza
	Departure (air)	Partenza (decollo)
	Departure (rail)	Partenza
	Fare	Prezzo di biglietto (tariffa)
	Flight	Volo
	No smoker	Non fumatori
	Porter	Portabagagli (faccino)
	Smoker	Fumatori
	Station	Stazione
	Stop	Sosta
	Ticket collector	Conduttore
	Timetable	Orario
	Track	Binario
	Waiting room	Sala d'aspetto

Days of the week	Monday	Lunedi
	Tuesday	Martedi
	Wednesday	Mercoledi
	Thursday	Giovedi
	Friday	Venerdi
	Saturday	Sabato
	Sunday	Domenica
	Day	Giorno

Weekday	Giorno feriale	
Holiday	Giorno festivo	
Week	Settimana	
January	Gennaio	Months
February	Febbraio	
March	Marzo	
April	Aprile	
May	Maggio	
June	Giugno	
July	Luglio	
August	Agosto	
SeptemberSettembre		
October	Ottobre	
November	Novembre	
December	Dicembre	

See Chemists

Language, illness

See Food and Drink

Language, restaurant

Lost Property offices

Riva del Carbon, Palazzo Farsetti (city hall), Campo S. Luca, tel. 041 2708225

Municipal lost property office

ACTV (city public transport), tel. 041 780310, 041 984144

Municipal transport

Stazione Santa Lucia, tel. 041 716122, 041 716211

Railway station

Aeroporto Marco Polo, tel. 041 661266

Airport

Medical Assistance

Everywhere in Italy: tel. 112

Emergency call

Pronto Soccorso (first aid): tel. 118

Medical assistance

Ospedale Civile, Venezia, Fondamenta dei Mendicanti/Campo dei SS. Giovanni e Paolo, tel. 041 5294516/7
Ospedale al Mare, Lido, Lungomare d'Annunzio 1, tel. 041 5261750
Ospedale di Mestre, Via Circonvallazione 50, tel. 041 988988

Hospitals

See entry

Emergency services

Under EU Social Security Regulations, travellers are entitled to health care on the same basis as Italians during a stay in Italy, but they must obtain a certificate of entitlement (E 111) before leaving home.

Health insurance

Medical treatment by doctors and hospitals of the state health insurance (Unit ... Sanitaria Locale, U.S.L.) is given under the regulations valid in Italy. The hotel, local council or tourist information office will provide the address of the appropriate U.S.L. office. On presentation of a completed and signed form E 111, the U.S.L. will provide a coupon book with certificates for free treatment by the doctors. Generally the patient has to pay a part of the cost of medical treatment and the prescribed medicines him/herself (retain receipts for presentation to your insurer). Privately insured persons must submit the invoices from the doctor and chemist to their insurer for a refund.

Museums

Since museum opening times are changed very frequently it has proved to be impossible to keep the details up-to-date, despite great effort. Avoid finding a museum closed by telephoning to ask when it is open.

Aquarium
Calle Albanesi, tel. 041 5207770
Open: daily 9am–7pm

Biblioteca Manfrediana
See A–Z, Piazza di San Marco, Piazzetta
Casa Goldoni (Palazzo Centani)
Campo San Tom ..., San Polo 2793
Closed at present because of renovation
Information: tel. 041 5236353
The comedy playwright Carlo Goldoni (1707–1793) was born here. The building contains memorabilia and interesting items of theatre history. It also houses the theatre institute.

Collezione Cini (Palazzo Cini)
San Vio, Dorsoduro 1050, tel. 041 5210755
Open: Tue.–Sun. 10am–1pm, 2pm–6pm
Collection of 13th–16th c. Tuscan art including valuable pieces of period furniture, ebony carvings, paintings by Taddeo Gaddi, Piero della Francesca, Filippo Lippi and Lorenzo di Niccolò.

Collezione Peggy Guggenheim
See A–Z

Galleria d'Arte Moderna
See A–Z, Ca' Pesaro

Gallerie dell' Accademia
See A–Z

Galleria Franchetti
See A–Z, Ca' d'Oro

Museo Archeologico
See A–Z, Piazza di San Marco

Museo d'Arte Orientale
See A–Z, Ca' Pesaro

Mueso d'Arte Vetrario
See A–Z, Murano

Museo Civico Correr
See A–Z, Piazza di San Marco

Museo Comunit ... Ebraica
See A–Z, Il Ghetto

Museo Diocesano
Ponte della Canonica (in the former Sant' Apollonia monastery), Castello 4312, tel. 041 5229166
Open: Mon.–Sat. 10.30am-12.30pm
Liturgical vessels, silverware and paintings are among the museum's treasures. The exhibits of contemporary religious art range from architectural designs to glass paintings.

Museo Dipinti Sacri Bizantini Ist. Ellencio, Ponto dei Greci, tel. 041 5226581

Open: Mon.–Sat. 9am–12.30pm, 1.30pm–4.30pm, Sun. 10am–5pm.
An interesting walks leads through the Greek quarter with trattorias and hidden bars, all in the shadow of the Orthodox church of San Giorgio dei Greci. From the middle ages until the end of the republic, Greeks always played an important role because of the Venetian possession of Crete, Cyprus and the Ionic islands. Today the community has just about 3000 inhabitants. To the left of the church is the former Scuola di San Niccolo dei Greci in the Palazzo Flangini (17th c.) which houses a small icon museum (Ist. Ellenico, Ponte dei Greci). Apart from about 80 14th–18th c. icons, magnificent liturgical robes with rich embroidery and a collection of liturgical vessels are displayed.

Museo dell' Estuario
See A–Z, Torcello

Museo Fortuny
See A–Z, Palazzo Pesaro degli Orfei

Museo Marciano
See A–Z, Basilica di San Marco

Museo del Risorgimento
See A–Z, Piazza di San Marco

Museo del Settecento Veneziano
See A–Z, Ca' Rezzonico

Museo di Storia Naturale
See A–Z, Fondaco dei Turchi

Museo Storico Navale
Riva S. Biagio, tel. 041 5200276
Open: Mon.–Fri. 8.45am-1.30pm
The maritime museum on the Rio dell'Arsenale, opposite the church of San Biagio, exhibits the impressive spoils of the Republic's numerous sea wars. By means of ships models, navigational instruments, uniforms and documents it gives an interesting view of ship building and ship types from the beginning of Venice's maritime power to its end in 1797. The decorated sides of a 16th c. galley can be seen together with the remains of a 17th c. "Bucintoro", the magnificent state galley of the Doges which was destroyed by fire in 1798.

Palazzo Ducale
See A–Z

Palazzo Mocenigo
Centro Studi di Storia del Tessuto e del Costume
San Staè 1992, tel. 041 721798
Open: Mon.–Sat. 8.30am-1.30pm
The costume museum in a patrician palace furnished with original items displays exquisite textiles.

Pinacoteca Querini-Stampalia
See A–Z, Palazzo Querini-Stampalia

Scuola di Merletti
See Baedeker Special "Lace and More Lace", page 70

Music

Operas and ballet are performed in temporary buildings pending the   Opera/ballet

Nightlife

re-opening (expected in 2001) of the Teatro La Fenice (see A–Z) burnt down in 1996. The tourist office has information (see Information).

Concerts

There are concerts throughout the year. They are often the only chance to see the otherwise inaccessible interiors of many city palaces. Since 1930 there has been an annual festival of contemporary music (Festival di Musica Contemporaneo) in September.

Gondola serenades

Gondola trips with music on the Grand Canal and the twisting side canals are the embodiment of Venetian romanticism. However, they are expensive; for departures see Public Transport.

Nightlife

General

Most pubs close not later than midnight. Night-owls may choose between various restaurants, bars in large hotels (see Hotels), some night-clubs, discotheques and the casino. The brochure "Fuori orario" published by the city council has the addresses of pubs, discos and bars, which are active after 10pm.

Casino

Municipale (gaming casino)
October to March: Palazzo Vendramin-Calergi, Calle Larga Vendramin, Cannaregio 2040, tel. 041 720044 (daily 4pm–4am)
April to September: Pallazo del Casino, Lungamare G. Marconi 4, Lido, tel. 041 5297111 (daily 4pm–3am)

Bars, night-clubs and discotheques (selection)

Acropolis, Lungomare Marconi 22, Lido, tel. 041 5260466 (meeting place for disco fans)

Harry's Bar: a must for cocktail lovers

★Antico Martini e Martini Scala, San Marco, Campo San Fantin 1983, tel. 041 5224121 (piano-bar; small snacks are offered until 3.30am)
Club El Souk, Dorsoduro, Calle Contarini Corf- 1056a, tel. 041 5200371 (stylish disco with current hits)
Devils' Forest, Rialto, Campo San Bartolomeo, tel. 041 523 66 51 (pub with live music)

★Harry's Bar, San Marco, Calle Vallaressa 1323, tel. 041 5285777 (opened by Giuseppe Cipriani and Harry Pickering in 1931 and made famous by the accomplished drinker, Ernest Hemingway, in his novel "Across the River and into the Trees". Illustrious VIPs meet in the legendary cocktail bar (open until 2am) and the gourmet restaurant on the first floor – cocktails and snacks are very expensive)

Taverna La Fenice, San Marco 1938, tel. 041 5223856 (meeting place of artists next to the Teatro La Fenice where guests can dine in style)

Opening Times

No opening times can be given for retail shops as they open at various times. Generally, it can be assumed that shops are open from 9am–1pm and 4pm–8pm and are closed on Sundays and public holidays.

Retail shops

See entry

Chemists

See Currency

Banks

See entry

Postal services

Postal Services

Post offices deal only with letters, parcels and postal bank services, they have no public telephones (see telephones). They are usually open Mon.–Sat. 8.10am–1.25pm; the main post office 8.10am–7.25pm.

General

Italian letter boxes are red. Stamps (francobolli) can be bought at post offices and also at tobacconists, identifiable by a sign with a "T" above the entrance.

Letter boxes

Public Holidays

January 1st (New Year's Day, Capo d'anno); January 6th (Epiphany, Epifania); Easter Monday (Pasqua); April 25th (Liberation Day 1945 and St. Mark's Day); May 1st (Labour Day, Festa del primo maggio); August 15th (Assumption, Ferragosta: a family celebration, the high point of the Italian summer holiday migration); November 1st (All Saints, Ognissanti); December 8th (Immaculate Conception, Immaculata Concezione) December 25th and 26th (Christmas, Natale).

Public Transport

Vaporetti (canal steamers) of the Municipal Transport Services ACTV provide city connections along the Grand Canal and to the islands in the lagoon. Although single tickets are available, the "Venezia Card" for 24

Lagoon services

hours, 72 hours or one week is recommended. It is valid on all lines and can be bought at the stops. Free maps showing the boat services are available from tourist information offices (see Information) and the ACTV, Piazzale Roma. The vaporetto services usually operate from 6am to 11pm; some such as line 1 even through the night, but only once an hour after 1am.

Grand Canal

The vaporetti of lines 1 and 82 (and line 3 in the morning during the summer) operate in both directions between St Mark's Square and Santa Lucia railway station (Ferrovia) on the busiest thoroughfare, the famous Grand Canal (see entry).

Stops on the
Grand Canal

Piazzale Roma (lines 1, 82, 52)
Ferrovia (lines 1, 82, 52)
Riva di Biaso (line 1)
San Marcuola (lines 1, 82)
San StaS (line 1)
Ca' d'Oro (line 1)
Rialto (lines 1, 82)
San Silvestro (line 1)
San Angelo (line 1)
San Tom ... (lines 1, 82)
San Samuele (line 82)
Ca' Rezzonico (line 1)
Accademia (lines 1, 82)
Santa Maria del Giglio (line 1)
Salute (line 1)
San Marco (lines 1, 82)

Boat lines

Linea 1
Piazzale Roma–Ferrovia–Riva di Biaso–San Marcuola–San Staè–Ca' d'Oro–Rialto–San Silvestro–San Angelo–San Tomà–Ca' Rezzonico–Accademia–Santa Maria del Giglio–Salute–San Marco–San Zaccaria–Arsenale–Giardini–Santa Elena–Lido
Linea 3 (only in the morning in summer)
San Zaccaria–Canale della Giudecca–Tronchetto–Ferrovia–Rialto–San Samuele–San Marco–San Zaccaria
Linea 4 (only in the afternoon in summer)
San Zaccaria–San Marco–San Samuele–Rialto–Ferrovia–Tronchetto–Canale dell Giudecca–San Zaccaria

Linea 6
San Zaccaria–Lido

Linea 10
San Zaccaria–Grazia–San Clemente

Linea 12
Fondamenta Nuove–Murano–Mazzorbo–Burano–Torcello

Linea 13
Fondamenta Nuove–Murano–Vignole–San Erasmo–Treporti

Linea 14
San Zaccaria–Lido–Punta Sabbioni–Treporti–Burano–Torcello

Linea 16 (only in summer)
Fusina–Zattere

Linea 17 (car ferry)
Tronchetto–Lido–Punta Sabbioni (only in summer)

Linea 20
San Zaccaria–San Servolo–San Lazzaro

Linea 52
Piazzale Roma–Ferrovia–Canale di Cannaregio–Fondamenta Nuove–San Michele–Murano–San Zaccaria
Ferrovia–Piazzale Roma–Canale della Giudecca–San Zaccaria–Santa Elena–Lido/Santa Maria Elisabetta–Casinò (only in summer)

Linea 82
Tronchetto–Piazzale Roma–Ferrovia–San Marcuola–Rialto–San Tomà–San Samuele–Accademia–San Marco
Tronchetto–Sacca Fisola–San Basilio–Zattere–San Eufemia–Palanca–Redentore–Zitelle–San Giorgio–San Zaccaria–Giardini–Lido (only in summer)

Apart from the three pedestrian bridges, it is possible to cross the Grand Canal quickly by gondola:
San Marcuola–Fondaco dei Turchi
Santa Sofia/Ca d'Oro–Pescheria
Riva del Carbon–Riva del Vin (Rialto)
Ca' Garzoni–San Tomà
San Samule–Ca' Rezzonico
Santa Maria del Giglio–San Gregorio

Gondola ferries

To travel in the narrow black gondolas, the most famous trademark of the city (see Baedeker Special "The Gondola – a quaint conveyance", page 80), is the embodiment of romanticism. Visitors see Venice at its

Gondolas

An unforgettable experience: a gondola trip on the Canal Grande and through the labyrith of side canals

most impressive – from its celebrated canals. However, goods and people are mainly transported by motor launches today. Though the prices for travel by gondola are fixed, it is nonetheless recommended to agree the price at the start (about 120,000 lire per hour).

Gondola stations

Bacino Orseolo, San Marco, tel. 041 5289316
Calle Vallaresso, San Marco, tel. 041 5206120
Campo San Moisè, San Marco, tel. 041 5231837
Campo Santa Sofia, Cannaregio, tel. 041 5222844
Danieli, Riva degli Schiavoni, Castello, tel. 041 5222254
Ferrovia, San Simon Piccolo, Santa Croce, tel. 041 718543
Molo, San Marco, tel. 041 5200685
Piazzale Roma, tel. 041 5221151
Riva del Carbon, Rialto, tel. 041 5224904
Santa Maria del Giglio, San Marco, tel. 041 5222073
San Tomá, San Polo, tel. 041 5205275
Tronchetto, tel. 041 5238919

Water taxis
(motoscafi)

Together with the canal service boats, motoscafi are now the most widely used transport. They have fixed prices which are shown at the stops.

Water taxi ranks

Aeroporto Marco Polo, tel. 041 5415084
Ferrovia, tel. 041 716286
Fondamenta Nuove, tel. 041 5237313
Lido, Viale Santa Maria Elisabetta, tel. 041 5260059
Piazzale Roma, tel. 041 716922
Rialto, tel. 041 5230575
San Marco, tel. 041 5229750
Tronchetta, tel. 041 5211444

Buses

Buses provide transport between Venice and the mainland.
Route 5: Piazzale Roma–Aeroporto Marco Polo
Routes 2, 4, 7, 12: Piazzale Roma–Mestre
Route 6: Piazzale Roma–Marghera
Route 19: Piazzale Roma–Favaro

On the Lido

Buses connect the landing stage at Santa Maria Elisabetta with the casino at Lungamare Marconi and the Via Colombo (route A) as well as connecting the stop at Santa Maria Elisabetta with Malamocco and San Nicolò (route B) or Alberoni (route C). There is also a connection between Santa Maria Elisabetta and Alberoni, San Pietro in Volta, Pellestrina and Chioggia (route 11)

Taxis

Since Venice is pedestrianised, taxis go only as far as the Piazzale Roma (radio taxi, tel. 041 5237774) on the road to Mestre and Marghera on the mainland (radio taxi, tel. 041 936222) and on the Lido (radio taxi, tel. 041 5265974, 041 5265975).

Restaurants

In Venice, as elsewhere in Italy, people like to eat well. Everything you desire is available, from a gourmet restaurant to a simple osteria, from a bistro with light snacks to a fantastic fish restaurant. Since Venice is always busy it is advisable to book well in advance.

Pizzeria, osteria,
trattoria

Hungry people watching their purse should visit a pizzeria. The waiter will not be offended if you only have a pizza and a glass of beer. Unfortunately, there are now few cosy, reasonably-prized osterias where

a small selection of hearty meals is served and a jug of simple, tasty wine stands on the table. Unless you have the misfortune to stumble into a stylish food boutique carrying the same name, two hours in an osteria give you a far more genuine impression of Venetian life than a visit to an expensive ristorante. The trattoria provide a fast and reasonable service; a starter, a main course, a bottle of wine, coffee and "il conto per favore" (may I have the bill please).

A meal in a ristorante is slightly more expensive and sophisticated; white table-cloth, good atmosphere, selected wines and carefully prepared meals. The proprietor expects the guests to order several dishes: antipasto, starter, main meal (ladies are allowed to skip either), dessert and coffee. Parties can sometimes choose between a combination of different starters, an offer which should always be accepted. Since most places are now called ristorante it is hardly possible to distinguish them in this conventional way.

Ristorante

On entering an Italian restaurant you wait until the waiter shows you to your seat. Tips are placed separately from the payment on the plate. The "menu turistico" offered in many restaurants is often better than might have been expected and is usually a reasonably-priced chance to taste Venetian cuisine.

Did you know?

Categories
Category A – over 80,000 lire
Category B – approx. 60,000 lire
Category C – approx. 40,000 lire

Selected Restaurants

These categories for an à la carte meal without wine are intended to be a guide to prices. If noble wines or expensive specialities are ordered the bill will certainly be higher.

★Antico Martini, San Marco, Campo San Fantin 1983, tel. 041 5224121, A (A favourite meeting place for artists and intellectuals since the opening of La Fenice Opera next door. The Baldy family took over the elegant restaurant with the Vino winebar and Martini Scala piano-bar in 1921)

Upper price category

★Alla Borsa, San Marco, Calle delle Veste 2018, tel. 041 5235434 (first-class gourmet restaurant with a pleasant atmosphere)

★La Caravella, San Marco, Calle XXII Marzo 2397, tel. 041 5208901, A (gourmet meeting-place with superior risotto and heavenly fish specialities; a romantic, candle-lit dinner between figure heads and models of three-masted ships)

★La Colomba, San Marco, Piscina Frezzeria 1665, tel. 041 5221175, A (Works by Carrà, Chagall, De Chirico, Kokoschka etc. decorate the walls of this gourmet restaurant. The proprietor, who was interested in the arts, asked his patrons, at that time little-known artists, to pay with paintings and not lire – lucky for us)

Corte Sconta, Castello, Calle del Pestrin 3886, tel. 041 5227024, A (fish dishes in all variations, particularly popular during the mollusc season)

★Do Forni, San Marco, Calle dei Specchieri 457, tel. 041 5237729 (top-class restaurant with a bar in Orient Express style)

★Harry's Bar (see entry)

★Harry's Dolci, Giudecca, Fondamenta San Biagio 773, tel. 041 5208337, A (on warm summer evenings customers sit under a white canvas roof on the Fondamenta; superb seafood salad, Venetian liver and various pastas from Cipriani)

Osteria da Franz, Castello, Fondamenta San Giuseppe 754, tel. 041 5220861, A (imaginative cuisine, scallops au gratin and spaghetti with rocket and mantis shrimps are recommended)

★Vini da Arturo, San Marco, Calle de la Verona 3656, tel. 041 5286974, A (a small gem with unsurpassed beef steaks)

Medium price category

★Antiche Carampane, San Polo, Rio Terra delle Carampane 1911, tel. 041 5240165, B (very cosy; the mussel soup and croccatini with sweet wine are a must)

★Fiaschetteria Toscana, Cannaregio, San Giovanni Crisostomo 5719, tel. 041 5285281, B (try the tasty lagoon fish and the heavenly zabaione)

Da Fiori, San Polo, Calle del Scateler 2202, tel. 041 721308, B (traditional dishes such as mantis shrimps, dried cod puree and breaded artichokes are served in the two restaurants)

Haig's, San Marco, Santa Maria del Giglio 2477, tel. 041 5232368, B (warm dishes until the early hours of the morning)

★Osteria ai Coristi, San Marco 1995, tel. 041 5226677, B (traditional Venetian restaurant with enchanting inner court near La Fenice theatre)

★Osteria da Alberto, Cannaregio, Calle Giacinto Gallina 5401, tel. 041 5238153, B (at Alberto Ferrari's heavy copper pans hang from the roof and bulbous bottles from the walls; only food in the best Venetian tradition is served)

★Poste Vecie, Rialto, Pescheria, tel. 041 721822, B (oldest trattoria in Venice with enchanting garden and stylish dining room; fish dominates the menu)

Lower price category

All' Angelo, San Marco, Calle Larga San Marco 403, tel. 041 5209299, C (super pizza from a wood-fired oven resembling a grotto)

Alle Botte, San Marco, San Bartolomeo 5482, tel. 041 5209775, C (the lasagne and Venetian liver with sweet onions are recommended)

★Ai Gondolieri, Dorsoduro, Fondamenta delle Torreselle 366, tel. 041 5286396 (well selected wines; taste the liver paté, deer fillet in madeira and the home-made confectionery)

Al Mondo Novo, Castello, Salizzada San Lio 5409, tel. 041 5200698, C (cosily furnished with a small garden; fish specialities)

Boldrin, Cannaregio, Salizzida San Canciano, tel. 041 5237859, C (much visited snack bar with culinary titbits)

Canottieri, Cannaregio, Fondamenta del Marcello 690, tel. 041 715408, C (tasty pasta dishes; cabaret on Tuesdays; concerts on Thursdays)

★L'Olandese Volante, Castello, Campo San Lio 5658, tel. 041 5289349, C (sit on the small campo, sip an aperitif or beer from a vast selection and order imaginative sandwiches, salads or pasta)

Da Zorzi, San Marco, Calle dei Fuseri 4359, tel. 041 5225350, C (vegetarian restaurant with heavenly crème caramel)

★Galuppi, Via B. Galuppi 468-470, 30012 Burano, tel. 041 730081, B (excellent fish dishes and local specialities)   Burano

Antica Trattoria Muranese, Fondamenta Cavour (near the glass museum), tel. 041 739610, C (pleasant trattoria with pretty garden)   Murano

★Locanda Cipriani, tel. 041 730150, A (international VIPs visit Giuseppe Cipriani's gourmet restaurant which meets the highest standards)   Torcello

Shopping and Souvenirs

Venice is famous for its masks, beautiful marbled paper, elegant Burano lace and intricate glassware from Murano. There is also an extremely wide range of exclusive fashion articles, high-class leather goods and   Shopping

Window shopping in the Lagoon City: carnival motives can be seen all year

Venetian bacari – an *ombra* with a *cicheti* –

It is known that the Venetians trace their name back to the Veneti people, a derivative of Eneti (from the Greek 'enos', meaning wine), and therefore regard themselves as wine people par excellence. 'Bacari', reminiscent of Bacchus, the god of wine, is the name given to the typical Venetian wine-bars serving vins ordinaires and simple 'cicheti', tasty morsels made from local ingredients.

The Venetians are in their element in these places where, seated at age-old wooden bars, they sip the wine like actors in a shadow play from a 100 ml glass called an "ombra" and nibble some choice morsel. A bacaro is a thoroughly democratic establishment where a guest is treated just like the regular patrons, there are no class distinctions, no language problems, no signs of disapproval, just relaxed communication between all and sundry. Anyone wishing to go on an "ombre-crawl" (giro de ombre) and explore the real heart of the city is recommended to try some of the following bacari:

Al Bacaretto, San Marco, Calle delle Boteghe; tel. 041 5289336 (not far from the Palazzo Grassi with well-patronised tables inside and outside; mixed clientele; highly imaginative cicheti)

Al Mascaron, Castelo, Calle Lunga Santa Maria Formosa 5225; tel. 041 5225995 (one of the original wine-bars; recommended are the spaghetti with crayfish and the traditional 'castradina con verze sofegae', smoked mutton with savoy cabbage braised with bacon fat)

Al Volto, San Marco, San Luca, Calle Cavalli 4081; tel. 041 5228945 (popular with the younger set of Venice; well-stocked wine-cellar and superb choice of 'crostini' (toasted savouries)

Antiche Cantine Ardenghi, Cannaregio, Calle della Testa 6369; tel. 041 5237691 (a regular haunt of gondoliers; try the Venetian calf's liver with sweet onions)

Antico Dolo, San Polo, Ruga Vecchia San Giovanni 798; tel. 041 5226546 (Bruno Ruffini's really intimate and cosy wine-bar near the Rialto market has only three tables; in the tiny kitchen he prepares some magic local delicacies, including a substantial 'tripa rissa' and pickled sardines)

Da Alberto, Castello, San Lio 6015; tel. 041 5229038 (a lovely bacaro with first-class pea risotto and irresistible 'baicoli'

Do Mon, San Polo, Calle dei do Mon 429; tel. 041 5225401 (one of the oldest and best bacari near the Rialto market; try the piquant 'lagenprosecco cartizze' and choose from some 90 tasty accompaniments such as steamed artichoke tips and dried cod tramezzini)

Do Spade, San Polo, Sottoportego delle Do Spade 860; tel. 041 5210574 (this very old bar "of the Two Swords" also lies near the Rialto market; in 1741 Casanova is said to have enjoyed an unforgettable night of passion with a beautiful local girl in the room of the same name; try the stuffed pigs' trotters, smoked neck fillet of beef or the piquant tramezzini)

Flore, San Marco, Calle delle Botteghe 3461; tel. 041 5235310 (wide selection of cicheti, including spicy meat dumplings and fried fish)

expensive jewellery, and of course the renowned antique shops and the delicatessens which offer specialities from all over Italy. The main shopping areas are the Mercerie (see entry) between St Mark's Square, the Accademia and Rialto Bridge. Here there is a large selection of souvenirs of all types, but shoppers soon notice that Venetian prices are comparatively high.

Casellati, San Marco, Calle Larga XXII Marzo, tel. 041 5230966 (largest antique dealer in Venice)

Frezzati, San Marco, Calle Larga XXI Marzo 2070, tel. 041 5227789 (Venetian paintings of the 14th–19th c.)

Francesco Saverio Mirate, San Marco, Calle della Verona 1904, tel. 041 5227600 (beautiful picture frames and vases)

Grafica Antica, San Marco, Calle Larga XXII Marzo 2089, tel. 041 5227199 (old engravings and historical views of Venice)

Scarpa, San Marco, Calle Larga XXII Marzo 2089, tel. 041 5227199 (old Italian masters)

Luisa Semanzato and Patrizia Walcher, San Marco, Mercerie San Zulian 732, tel. 041 5231412 (old engravings, majolica and porcelain)

Veneziartigiana, San Marco, Calle Larga San Marco 412/413, tel. 041 5235032 (various dealers exhibit traditional masks, old glassware and antique jewellery in a former pharmacy)

Antiques

Arsenale Punto Libri, Santa Croce, Calle dei Vinanti 29, tel. 041 5229495 (good selection of books about art and architecture; near the university)

Bertoni, San Marco, Calle della Mandola 3637b, tel. 041 5229583 (second-hand editions)

Fantoni Libri d'Arte, San Marco, Salizida San Luca 4121, tel. 041 5220700 (art books, catalogues and magazines)

Goldoni, San Marco, Calle dei Fabbri 4742, tel. 041 5222384 (large selection of Venetian literature)

Sansovino, San Marco, Bacino Orseole 4, tel. 041 5222623 (books about Venice and a good antiquarian book department)

Santi Giovanni e Paolo, Castello, Campo Santi Givanni e Paolo 6358, tel. 041 5229659 (foreign language literature)

Toletta, Dorsoduro, Sacca della Toletta 1214, tel. 041 5232034 (worthwhile special offers)

Books

See below, Masks and costumes

Bac Art Studio, San Marco, Campo San Maurizio 2663, tel. 041 5228171 (beautiful books about the carnival)

Carnival

Coluccio, San Marco, Calle dei Fabbri 925, tel. 041 5225878 (Venetian specialities and Tuscan bread)

Delicatessen

Laura Biagiotti, San Marco, Calle Larga XXII Marzo, tel. 041 5203401 (extravagant and ornate dresses)

Borsato, San Marco, Calle Vallaresso 1318, tel. 041 5225525 (exquisite haute couture)

Camiceria San Marco, San Marco, Calle Vallaresso 1340, tel. 041 5221432 (first-class made-to-measure shirts)

Paola Carraro, Dorsoduro 869, tel. 041 5206070 (hand-knitted items with Picasso and Matisse patterns)

La Coupole, San Marco, Frezzeria 1674, tel. 041 5206063; San Marco, Calle Larga XXII Marzo 2366, tel. 041 5224243 (unusual dresses from Rena Lange, Kenzo and Valentino)

Elite, San Marco, Calle Larga San Marco 284, tel. 041 5230145 (classical fashion for her and him)

Elys,e, San Marco, Calle Goldoni 4485, tel. 041 5236948 (stylish fashion from Giorgio Armani)

Fashions

Shopping and Souvenirs

Elys,e Due, San Marco, Frezzeria 1693, tel. 041 5333020 (fashion from Armani, Cerrutti and Versace)

Gianfranco Ferre, San Marco, Calle Large San Marco 287, tel. 041 5225147 (up-to-date fashion)

Fiorella Show from Fiorella Mancini, San Marco, Campo San Stefano 2806, tel. 041 5209228 (unusual fashion; curiosities: hermaphroditic Doge figures as dummies)

Giuliana Longo, San Marco, Calle del Lovo 4813, tel. 041 5226454 (subtle hat creations)

Maricla, San Marco, Calle Larga XXII Marzo 2401, tel. 041 5232202 (underwear to dream of)

Valentino, San Marco, Salizada San MoisS 1473, tel. 041 5205733 elegant fashion from a leading designer)

Versace, San Marco, Calle Large XXII Marzo 2359, tel. 041 5232162 (stylish and sporty clothes)

Volpe, Rialto, Sant' Aponal 1228, tel. 041 5238041 (Dolce & Gabbana, Moschino jeans and Le Garage shirts)

ZetaSport, San Marco, Calle dei Fabbri 4668, tel. 041 5220718 (sporting clothes from Fila, Ellesse and Sergio Tacchini)

Fortuny design

Venezia Studium, San Marco, Calle XXII Marzo 2403, tel. 041 5229281 (pliss, dresses and Fortuny lamps)

V. Trois, Tessuti Artistici Fortuny, San Marco, Campo San Maurizio 2666, tel. 041 5552905 (Fortuny materials)

Glass

Barovier & Toso, Murano, Fondamenta dei Vetrai 28, tel. 041 739049 (traditional and modern articles from the workshops of the famous glass-blowing families)

Cenedese, Piazza di San Marco 139, tel. 041 5229399 (traditional and modern Murano glass)

Ferro & Lazzarini, Murano, Fondamenta Navagero 75, tel. 041 739299 (lamps and chandeliers)

I Lirici, Piazza di San Marco 114, tel. 041 5227223 (creative Murano design)

Angelo Mantin, San Marco, Calle Fiubera 953, tel. 041 5238107 (Venetian glass pearls)

Mazzega, Murano, Fondamenta Da Mula 147, tel. 041 736888 (superb glass craft – antique and modern)

Murrina, Murano, Fondamenta Cavour 17, tel. 041 739255 (expensive chandeliers and lamps)

Salviati, San Marco, Piazza di San Marco 78, tel. 041 5224257 (traditional design and magnificent chandeliers)

Paolo Scarpa, San Marco, Mercerie San Salvador 4850, tel. 041 5286881 (beautiful Murano glass pearls)

Venini, San Marco, Piazzetta Leoncini 314, tel. 041 5224045 (unusual Murano vases from Carlo Scarpa, Tapio Wirkkala, etc.)

Gondola oars

The traditional Venetian rowlocks "forcole" are sold by, among others:

Carli S.d. Brandolisio, Castello, Calle Rotta 4725, tel. 041 5224155

Spaziolegno, Castello, Fondamenta del Tintor 3865, tel. 041 5225699

Jewellery

Chimento, San Marco, Campo San MoisS 1460, tel. 041 5236010 (top address next to famous restaurant Bauer-Grünwald

Nardi, Piazza di San Marco 69, tel. 041 5225733 (exquisite high fashion jewellery)

Salvadori, San Marco, Mercerie San Salvador 5022, tel. 041 5230609 (exclusive jewellery since 1857)

Lace

Jesurum, San Marco, Ponte Canonica 4310, tel. 041 5206177 (embodiment of high-class lace since 1870)

Kerer, Castello, Calle Canonica 4328a, tel. 041 5235485 (renowned lace shop)

Maria Mazzaron, Castello, Fondamenta dell'Osmarin 4970, tel. 041 5221392 (finest Burano lace)

Merletto Antico, Burano, Via Galuppi 215, tel. 041 730052 (exquisite Burano lace; small museum)

La Bauta, San Marco, Mercerie San Zulian 729, tel. 041 5223838 (Prada, Granello and Henry Beguelin, etc.)

Bottega Veneta, San Marco, Calle Vallaresso 1338, tel. 041 5228489 (plaited leather dreams)

Casella, San Marco 5048, tel. 041 5228848 (fashionable shoes)

Fendi, San Marco, Salizida San Moisé 1474, tel. 041 5205733 (Italy's top make)

Bruno Magli, San Marco, Frezzeria 1582, tel. 041 5223472 (bags and shoes – first-class classical design)

Rolando Segalin, San Marco, Calle dei Fuseri 4365, tel. 041 5222115 (since 1932 the best made-to-measure shoes)

Fratelli Rosetti, San Marco, Calle San Moisè 1477, tel. 041 5220819 (modish, elegant shoes)

Leather and shoes

Charta, San Marco, Calle dei Fabbri 831, tel. 041 5229801 (various beautiful papers and original ink pots)

Legatoria Piazzesi, San Marco, Campiello della Feltrina 2511, tel. 041 5221202 (imaginative paper prints and a doll's theatre)

Paolo Olbi, San Marco, Calle della Mandola 3653, tel. 041 5285025 (artistic stationery)

Marbled paper

The largest market in Venice with numerous fruit, vegetable, fish and souvenir stalls is held daily, except Sundays, from 7am to 1pm near the Rialto Bridge (see entry). Fruit, vegetables, fish and reasonably priced household goods are also on sale on weekdays from 7am onwards in

Markets

Colourful fruit and vegetable markets are part of the townscape of Venice

205

the Via Garibaldi in Castello. Smaller markets with vegetable, fish and flower stalls are also held in the morning in Cannaregio near the Ponte delle Gulie, in Dorsoduro on the Campo Santa Margherita and in San Marco on the Campo Santa Maria Formosa. Fruit and vegetables are sold at the canal bank, directly from the boat, on the Campo San Barnaba.

Masks and costumes

Il Ballo del Doge, San Marco 1823, tel. 041 5226859 (expensive masks, marionettes and magnificent Rococo costumes)

Cartapesta & Co., Castello, Barbaria delle Tole 6656, tel. 041 5223110 (classical masks and tasteful picture frames)

Laboratiorio Artigano Maschere, Castello, Barbaria delle Tole 6657, tel. 041 5223110 (masks made according to old engravings)

La Mano (5 studios with first-class handicrafts): Castello, Calle Longa Santa Maria Formosa 5175; Cannaregio, Rio Terrà dei Biri 5415; Castello, Barbaria delle Tole 6468; San Polo, Ruga Rialto 1032; San Marco, Calle Fiubera 818)

Mondonova, Dorsoduro, Rio Terrà Canal 3063, tel. 041 52847344 (individual creations)

La Venexiana, Castello, Ponte Canonica 4322, tel. 041 23 35 58 (magnificent theatre and carnival masks)

Metalware

Renato Burelli, Dorsoduro, Calle Lunga San Barnaba 2729, tel. 041 5224309 (brass fittings and colours)

Valese, San Marco, Calle Fiubera 793, tel. 041 5227282 (gondola ironmongery and old door knockers)

Textiles

Mario Bevilacqua, San Marco, Fondamenta Canonica 337b, tel. 041 5287581 (brocades, tapestries and the finest cloths)

Colour Casa, San Polo 1990, tel. 041 5236071 (beautiful textiles)

Frette, Calle XXII Marzo 2070, tel. 041 5224914 (marvellous bed linen)

Rubelli, San Marco, Campo San Gallo 1089, tel. 041 5236110 (beautiful designer textiles)

Wooden articles

From panels through furniture to books, all made of wood; such things can be found at:

Livio de Marchi, San Marco, San Samuele 3157a, tel. 041 5285694

Sightseeing Programme

City tours

Many organisers and the tourist information office offer city tours. The latter also organises individual tours with an English-speaking guide (see Information).

See page 52, Sightseeing

Sightseeing by Vaporetto

Every visit to Venice should include at least one city tour by vaporetto (water bus).

Lines 1, 82

Lines 1 and 82 travel in both directions on the Grand Canal (see A to Z, Canal Grande) between the Piazzo San Marco and the railway station. There is sufficient time en route to admire the magnificent façades of the Patrician palaces and churches and possibly to take a break at one stop.

Line 52

Line 52 takes you round the centre of the city in about two hours. It starts at the Riva degli Schiavoni next to the Doges' Palace. From there it travels through the Arsenale to Fondamenta Nuove where a visit to the cemetery island of San Michele, past the islands of Murano, Burano and Torcello, can be included. The return journey circles around Cannaregio with the Madonna dell'Orto Basilica, and then through the Canale di Cannaregio to the north end of the Grand Canal leaving it at the Piazzale

Children's delight: feeding the pigeons on St Mark's Square

Roma to head through the western harbours to La Giudecca island reaching St Mark's Square again opposite San Giorgio Maggiore.

See Public Transport

See entry

Sport

To relax after an exhausting city stroll and cultural programme, drive to the wide beaches of the Lido which is covered with sunshades in summer. There, between the swimming pools and private beaches of the hotels is free access to the sea. Enthusiasts can water-ski and sail. It is also possible to ride and play tennis or golf (golf course in Aberoni, Lido, tel. 041 731015). Amateur pilots can land on the small San Nicolò airfield.

Club Venezia, Lido, Via Malamocco, Loc. Bassanello, tel. 041 770801

Eurotel, Lido, Lungomare Marconi, tel. 041 5268797

In 1997 a new bathing area was created near Pellestrina island where 50 million cubic yards of fine white sand have been used to protect Venice and the lagoon against sea erosion.

Telephone

In Italy the telephone service is not the responsibility of the Post Office

Gondola excursions

Boat excursions

Lido

Sport centre

Pellestrina

Telephone offices

but of the State Telephone Company SIP (Società Italiana L'Esercizio Telecomunicazioni). Long-distance calls can be made for cash payments in the telephone offices.

Public telephones

Direct telephone calls to other countries in the EU can only be made in public call boxes which have the orange telephone receiver symbol. Public call boxes take 100, 200 and 500 lire coins and some old ones take telephone tokens (gettoni, value: 200 lire). Most public call boxes are adapted to take magnetic telephone cards (carta telefonica). These are available for 5000, 10,000 and 15,000 lire in bars, newspaper kiosks or at tobacconists.

International dialling codes to Venice

From the United Kingdom 00 39
From the United States 011 39. From Canada 011 39
Since 1998 the local dialling code for Venice 041 is a fixed part of the number which must be dialled when making local calls.
    When making an international call the initial zero of the local dialling code should be omitted.

International dialling codes from Venice

To the United Kingdom 00 44. To the United States 001. To Canada 001.

Mobile telephones

The use of mobile phones is permitted. However, it is only possible on the D 1 and D 2 networks. With a dual band telephone calls can be made on the E network. The telephone companies Telecom Italia Mobile (access number: 2 22 01) and Omnitel Pronto Italia (access number: 2 22 10) have the most connections.

Theatres

Teatro La Fenice
    San Marco, Campo San Fantin 1965
    See A to Z
Teatro Goldoni
    San Marco, Calle Goldoni 4650, tel./fax 041 5205422
    Especially Goldoni comedies
Teatro A L'Avogaria
    Dorsoduro, Campo San Sebastiano 1617, tel. 041 5206130, fax 041 5209270
Experimental theatre and performances in dialect

Tickets can be bought in travel agencies, tourist information offices (see entry) and theatre booking offices. The brochure "Un Ospite di Venezia" lists details of the booking offices.

Time

Italy is on Central European time (one hour ahead of Greenwich Mean Time; six hours ahead of New York time). Summer time (two hours ahead of GMT; seven hours ahead of New York time) is in force from the end of March until the end of October.

Tipping (mancia)

Tipping is usual and should be a recognition of special services. Unrequested services need not be rewarded. It is recommended that you negotiate the price with the porter before he moves your luggage as it can be rather high.

Traffic Regulations

Italy's general traffic regulations correspond to the international stan- Motorways
dards. Tolls are charged on Italian motorways. Payment is made in cash,
by credit card or with a Viacard which can be purchased from automobile clubs, at the border crossings, at the most important motorway
entries, at tobacconists and petrol stations.

Vehicles may be driven with side lights on well-lit roads, but dipped Lighting
head-lights must be used in tunnels.
During the journey all passengers over 14 years of age must wear seat-
belts. Children's safety seats are specified by law for children up to 4
years old.

The maximum speed in built-up areas is 50kph and outside these areas Maximum speed
90kph
On motorways: cars up to 1100 cc 110kph; cars over 1100 cc 130kph.
Motorcycles under 149 cc are forbidden on motorways. Motorcycles up
to 349 cc: 110kph. Motorcycles over 350 cc: 130kph. A car with trailer:
100kph on motorways; on ordinary roads: 80kph

Motorcycles above 350 cc may only driven by people of 21+ years of Motorcycles
age. Motorcycles under 150 cc are forbidden on motorways. Motorcycle
trailers are prohibited.

A white or yellow square, standing on its corner with a red or black and Right of way
white edge, indicates that traffic on the main road carrying this sign has
right of way. Otherwise "right before left" applies, even on round-
abouts. On narrower mountain roads the vehicle driving up has right of
way. Trams and trains always have right of way.

The Italian customs authorities must be informed of write-offs otherwise Write-offs
import duty must be paid for the damaged vehicle under certain cir-
cumstance.

See entry Emergencies

Travel Documents

Since January 1st 1993 EU citizens no longer need a passport. However, Passports
since it remains a requirement to have a passport in airports and harbours
and random checks are made, visitors are strongly advised to carry these
documents. Children under 16 must have their own passport or be entered
on that of their parents. It is advisable to photocopy travel documents
since this facilitates the replacement of the originals in the event of loss.

You must carry your driving licence and registration documents. The Driving licences,
international green insurance card is strongly recommended. Vehicles etc.
must carry the oval national identification sticker unless it has been
replaced by the Euro sticker.

Dogs and cats entering Italy require a veterinary health certificate (valid Pets
for 30 days from the date of issue) and a rabies immunisation certificate
issued at least 20 days earlier and not older than 11 months. Larger dogs
must wear a muzzle and must be kept on the lead.

When to go

Venice has visitors all year round. During the main tourist season in summer there are a great many visitors, often making it difficult to find accommodation and seats in restaurants. For this reason, and also bearing the weather in mind, it is better to plan a visit between April and June or September and October; both times of the year when average air temperatures are above 15°C and average water temperatures are at least 17°C. Winter tourism has grown considerably in recent years because of the special atmosphere and thanks to the revival of the February Carnival when the city is transformed into something resembling a gigantic masked ball. However, it should be noted that the weather can be quite cold at this time of year. The average temperature from December to February is about 6°C. It is important to book a hotel in good time all year round.

Young People's Information

Rolling Venice

This passport to Venice for young people between 14 and 29 is valid all through the year and offers a rebate on charges for public transport, museums, exhibitions, theatres, cinemas and sport, as well as reduced bed and board in associated guest houses. Information: Assessorato alla Gioventó, San Marco 1529, tel. 041 5346268, fax 041 5342293; Information offices in the Santa Lucia railway station and the new Procurator's offices on St Mark's Square.

Youth hostels
(Albergho della
Gioventù)

Venezia, Fondamenta Zitelle 86, La Giudecca, tel. 041 5238211, fax 041 5235689, e-mail vehostel@tin.it
Open: 7.30am–9am, 2pm–11.30pm (closed: Jan. 16th–Feb. 1st).

Index

Airport 172
Ala Napolenica 138
Arsenale 58
Art History 31

Basilica di San Marco 59
Biennale Pavilions 110
Burano 69

Ca' d'Oro with the Galleria
   Franchetti 89
Ca' da Mosto 84
Ca' del Duca 76
Ca' Foscari 78
Ca' Grande 74
Ca' Pesaro with Galleria
   d'Arte Moderna 90
Ca' Rezzonico with
   Museo del Settecento
   Veneziano 91
Cafés 172
Camp Sites 173
Campanile 139
Campo San Vidal 160
Campo Sant'Angelo 161
Canal Grande 71
Capitaneria del Porto 72
Casina delle Rose 74
Chemists 173
Chiesa degli Scalzi 89
Chioggia 92
Churches 174
Collezione Peggy
   Guggenheim 93
Conversions 174
Culture 31
Currency 174
Customs Regulations 175

Death in Venice – The
   Lagoon City in film 45
Deposito del Megio 87
Disabled Access 175
Dogana da Mar 72
Doges 21

Early printing 41
Economy 13
Electricity 175
Embassies and
   Consulates 176
Emergencies 176
Events 176
Excursions 178

Famous People 26
Fondaco dei Tedeschi 94

Fondaco dei Turchi
   with Museo di Storia
   Naturale 95
Food and Drink 179

Galeria d'Arte Moderna 90
Galeria Franchetti 89
Gallerie dell'Accademia 95
Galleries 183
Gesuiti 105
Getting to Venice 183
Ghetto 105
Giardini Pubblici 110
Giardini Reali 71

History 184
Hotels 184

I Frari 150
I Gesuiti 105
Il Ghetto 105
Information 188
Islands in the Lagoon 113

La Giudecca 111
La Grazia 114
Language 188
Lazzaretto Nuovo 114
Lazzaretto Vecchio 115
Le Vignole 115
Libreria Vecchia di San
   Marco 115
Lido 115
Loggetta 139
Lost Property offices 191

Madonna dell'Orto 116
Medical Assistance 191
Mercerie 117
Monumento di
   Colleoni 118
Murano 118
Museo Archeologico 138
Museo Civico Correr 138
Museo d'Arte Vetrario 118
Museo d'Arte
   Orientale 90
Museo del
   Risorgimento 139
Museo del Settecento
   Veneziano 91
Museo dell'Estuario 168
Museo di Storia
   Naturale 95
Museo Fortuny 134
Museums 193
Music 193

Nightlife 194

Opening times 195

Palazzi Barbaro 75
Palazzi Contarini degli
   Scrigni 76
Palazzi Donà 82
Palazzi Mocenigo 76, 79
Palazzi Tron 82
Palazzo Balbi 78
Palazzo Barbarigo 75
Palazzo Barbarigo 86
Palazzo Barbaro 74
Palazzo Barzizza 83
Palazzo Belloni
   Battagia 87
Palazzo Bembo 83
Palazzo Bernardo 82
Palazzo Businello 83
Palazzo Cavalli
   Franchetti 75
Palazzo Civran 84
Palazzo Contarini dal
   Zaffo 75
Palazzo Contarini del
   Bovolo 119
Palazzo Contarini delle
   Figure 79
Palazzo Contarini Fasan 73
Palazzo Corner 74
Palazzo Corner Contarini 88
Palazzo Corner Contarini
   degli Cavalli 83
Palazzo Corner della
   Regina 86
Palazzo Corner Gheltoff 79
Palazzo Corner Loredan 83
Palazzo Corner Spinelli 82
Palazz0 Dandulo 83
Palazz0 Dario 74
Palazzo degli Dieci Savi 83
Palazzo dei Camerlenghi 83
Palazzo Dolfin Manin 83
Palazzo Ducale 119
Palazzo Falier 76
Palazzo Farsetti 83
Palazzo Flangini 89
Palazzo Flangini Fini 73
Palazzo Genovese 73
Palazzo Giustinian
   Grimani 79
Palazzo Giustinian 78
Palazzo Giustinian Lolin 76
Palazzo Giustinian
   Morosini 72
Palazzo Grassi 77

Index

Palazzo Griffi 88
Palazzo Grimani 83
Palazzo Gussoni
    Grimani 86
Palazzo Labia 88
Palazzo Loredan
    dell'Ambasciatore 77
Palazzo Malipiero and San
    Samuele 77
Palazzo Manolesso
    Ferro 73
Palazzo Marcello 88
Palazzo Michiel delle
    Colonne 85
Palazzo Mocenigo
    Gambara 76, 79
Palazzo Morosini
    Gatterburg 161
Palazzo Papadopoli
    Coccina 82
Palazzo Pesaro 85
Palazzo Pesaro Degli Orfei
    with the Museo
    Fortuny 134
Palazzo Pisani 161
Palazzo Pisani Moretta 79
Palazzo Querini-
    Stampalia 134
Palazzo Sagredo 85
Palazzo Stern 77
Palazzo Treves Bonfili 72
Palazzo Valmarana 85
Palazzo Vendramin
    Calergi 87
Palazzo Venier dei Leoni 93
Palazzo Zenobio 162
Palazzo Zulian 86
Pescheria 84
Piazza San Marco 135
Piazzetta 141
Ponte di Rialto 141
Ponte Scalzi 89
Postal Services 195
Printing 41
Procuratie 136
Public Holidays 195
Public Transport 195

Quotations 48

Restaurants 198
Rialto Markets 84

San Bartolomeo 142
San Francesco del
    Deserto 115
San Francesco della
    Vigna 143
San Giacomo dell'Orio 143
San Giobbe 143
San Giorgio Maggiore 144
San Giovanni
    Crisostomo 145
San Giovanni in
    Bragora 145
San Gregorio 73
San Lazzaro degli
    Armeni 115
San Marco 59
San Marcuola 88
San Michele 115
San Moisè 146
San Nicolò 146
San Nicolò da
    Tolentino 146
San Pietro di Castello 146
San Polo · San Paolo 147
San Salvatore 147
San Sebastiano 147
San Silvestro 148
San Simeone Piccolo 89
San Staè 86
San Trovaso · Santi
    Gervasio e Protasio 148
San Vidal 161
San Zaccaria 148
San Zanipolo 156
Sant' Angelo Raffaele 148
Sant' Erasmo 115
Sant' Eustachio 86
Santa Fosca 167
Santa Geremia 88
Santa Maria Assunta 105
Santa Maria dei
    Miracoli 154
Santa Maria del
    Carmine 162
Santa Maria del Rosario ·
    Chiesa dei Gesuati 154

Santa Maria dell' Orto 116
Santa Maria della
    Fava 149
Santa Maria della
    Salute 154
Santa Maria Formosa 149
Santa Maria Gloriosa dei
    Frari · I Frari 150
Santa Maria Zobenigo ·
    Santa Maria del Giglio
    155
Santi Apostoli 156
Santi Giovanni e Paolo ·
    San Zanipolo 156
Santo Stefano 159
Scuola di San Giorgio degli
    Schiavoni 164
Scuola Grande dei
    Carmini 162
Scuola Grande di San
    Marco 159
Scuola Grande di San
    Rocco 162
Seminario Patriarcale 72
Shopping and
    Souvenirs 201
Sightseeing 52
Sightseeing programme 206
Souvenirs 201
Sport 207
Squero di San Trovaso 148

Teatro La Fenice 164
Telephone 207
The Venetian City State
    under the Doges 21
Theatres 208
Time 208
Tipping 208
Torcello 166
Torre dell'Orologio 137
Traffic Regulations 209
Transport 14
Travel Documents 209

When to go 209

Young People's
    Information 210

Principal Sights at a Glance

★★

Basilica di San Marco
Burano
Canal Grande
Ca' d'Oro
  with Galleria Franchetti
Ca' Rezzonico
  with Museo del
  Settecento Venziano
Collezione Peggy Gugenheim
Gallerie dell' Accademia

★★

Mercerie
Murano
Palazzo Ducale
Piazza San Marco
Piazzetta
Santa Maria Gloriosa dei Frari
Santa Maria della Salute
Santi Giovanni e Paolo/
  San Zanipolo
Scuola Grande di San Rocco

★

Campanile
Ca' Pesaro
  with Galleria d'Arte Moderna
  and Museo d'Arte Orientale
Casa Goldoni
Chioggia
Fondaco dei Turchi
  with Museo di
  Storia Naturale
I Gesuiti
Il Ghetto
La Giudecca
  Il Redentore
Islands in the Laguna
Libreria Vecchia
Lido
Madonna dell'Orto
Monumento di Colleoni
Palazzo Contarini del Bovolo
Palazzo Mocenigo
Palazzo Pesaro degli Orfei
  with Museo Fortuny
Palazzo Querini Stampalia
Patrician Palaces
  on the Canal Grande

★

Procuratie
  Cafés
  Museo Archeologico
Museo Civico Correr
Ponte di Rialto
  and Rialto Market
San Francesco della Vigna
San Giobbe
San Giorgio Maggiore
San Nicolò da Tolentino
San Salvatore
San Sebastiano
San Staè
San Zaccaria
Santa Maria Formosa
Santa Maria dei Miracoli
Santa Maria del Rosario
Sant' Angelo Raffaele
Scuola Grande dei Carmini
Scuola di San Giorgio
  degli Schiavoni
Scuola di San Trovaso
Teatro La Fenice
Torcello
Veneto-Villas

Imprint

117 photographs, 13 maps and plans, 1 large city map

German text: Madeleine Reincke, Evamarie Blattner, Helga Cabos, Rupert Koppold, Michael Machatschek, Reinhard Strüber

General direction: Madeleine Reincke, Baedeker Redaktion

Cartography: Gert Oberländer, Christoph Gallus

Editorial work English edition: g-and-w PUBLISHING

English translation: Babel Translations, Norwich (GB)

Source of illustrations: see picture credits

Front cover: Powerstock/Zefa
Back cover: AA Photo Library (D. Mitidieri)

6th English edition 2000

© Baedeker Ostfildern
Original German edition 2000

© 2000 Automobile Association Developments Limited
English language edition worldwide

Published by AA Publishing (a trading name of Automobile Association Developments Limited, whose registered office is Norfolk House, Priestley Road, Basingstoke, Hampshire RG24 9NY. Registered number 1878835).

Distributed in the United States and Canada by:
Fodor's Travel Publications, Inc.
201 East 50th Street
New York, NY 10022

A CIP catalogue record of this book is available from the British Library.

Typeset by Fakenham Photosetting Ltd, Fakenham, Norfolk, UK

Licensed user:
Mairs Geographischer Verlag GmbH & Co., Ostfildern

Printed in Italy by G. Canale & C. S.p.A., Turin

ISBN 0 7495 2087 6

Notes

Notes

Notes

Baedeker's

VENICE

Hints for using the Guide

Following the tradition established by Karl Baedeker in 1846, buildings and sights of particular interest are distinguished by one ★ or two ★★ stars.

To make it easier to locate the various places listed in the Sights from A to Z section of the guide, their coordinates on the large map included with the guide are shown in red at the head of each entry.

Coloured strips down the outside edge of the right-hand pages are an aid to finding the different sections of the guide. Blue indicates the introductory material, red the descriptions of sights, and yellow the practical information at the end of the book.

Only a selection of hotels and restaurants can be given: no reflection is implied, therefore, on establishments not included.

In a time of rapid change it is difficult to ensure that all the information given is entirely accurate and up to date, and the possibility of error can never be entirely eliminated. Although the publishers can accept no responsibility for inaccuracies and omissions, they are always grateful for corrections and suggestions for improvement.